INDURAIN

For N., who knows why: 31.10.2002

By the same author:

The End of the Road
Reckless
The Eagle of Toledo

INDURAIN

ALASDAIR FOTHERINGHAM

EBURY
PRESS

1 3 5 7 9 10 8 6 4 2

Ebury Press, an imprint of Ebury Publishing
20 Vauxhall Bridge Road
London SW1V 2SA

Ebury Press is part of the Penguin Random House group of companies
whose addresses can be found at global.penguinrandomhouse.com

Penguin
Random House
UK

First published by Ebury Press in 2017

www.penguin.co.uk

A CIP catalogue record for this book is available from the British Library

ISBN 9781785032059

Typeset in India by Integra Software Services Pvt. Ltd, Pondicherry

Printed and bound in Great Britain by Clays Ltd, St Ives PLC

MIX
Paper from
responsible sources
FSC
www.fsc.org FSC® C018179
Penguin Random House is committed to a sustainable
future for our business, our readers and our planet.
This book is made from Forest Stewardship Council®
certified paper.

Contents

Prologue: How Could it Come to This?   1

Chapter 1: Back to the Roots   5
Chapter 2: The Little Priests   26
Chapter 3: Le Tour de la CEE   47
Chapter 4: Invisible Robocop   72
Chapter 5: 1990: The One That Got Away   89
Chapter 6: Neither Monk Nor Martian   110
Chapter 7: 1992: Indurain Is Spain   140
Chapter 8 1993–94: A Strip of Sandpaper   177
Chapter 9: Le Tour du Record   201
Chapter 10: 1995–96: The House of Cards   222
Chapter 11: Exceptionally Normal   260
Afterword: A Face in the Crowd   285

Palmares   295
Acknowledgements   305
Bibliography   307
Index   311

Prologue: How Could It Come to This?

Back in the day, there used to be an urban legend amongst cycling fans that whoever led the Vuelta a España at the summit of the Lagos de Covadonga climb, deep in the mountains of Asturias, would be declared the outright winner when the race ended in Madrid. But on 20 September 1996, even before stage thirteen of the Vuelta had begun to climb the nineteen-kilometre ascent to Covadonga, it felt as if cycling had lost one of its most crucial battles.

The event that cast an enormous pall over what was in theory the Queen stage of the 1996 Vuelta – and in fact was to cast a shadow over the entire race – unfolded on the difficult ascent of the Fito, the first major climb of the day. A single attack by Tony Rominger, one of the 1990s' most talented Grand Tour racers, began to split the peloton into pieces. In what was essentially a skirmish before the big battle on the slopes of Covadonga itself, the flurry of controlling moves and accelerations that Rominger's attack produced had a single, devastating consequence: Miguel Indurain, five times winner of the Tour de France and arguably

Spain's greatest ever athlete, was dropped. He was not sweating unduly or swaying over the road as the single line of riders in the peloton drew away from him further up the climb. Indurain had simply run out of energy and rather than go so deep to try to keep up that he then cracked afterwards, he was taking the coldly logical path: eking out whatever scant strength he had left to minimise the damage and limit the gaps.

This, then, was no death-or-glory defeat. Utterly characteristic of his dislike of any kind of histrionic behaviour on or off the bike, Indurain was quietly laying down his arms. Racing in such an economical style was a simple recognition of a simple fact: despite not being ill or injured, his physical condition was such he had lost all chance of winning the Vuelta, and there was absolutely nothing he could do about it. As the other top favourites put minutes into Indurain in a matter of a few kilometres, it was a curiously dignified last act of the drama and controversy surrounding Indurain's long-awaited participation, after so much Tour success, in the Vuelta a España.

Yet there was no getting away from the fact that Indurain, one of cycling's most brilliantly calculating racers, had become the victim of a gross misinterpretation of his strength. Someone, be it the rider or the team, had made a serious error. In sporting terms, in this race, there was no possible solution.

Indurain's getting dropped from the front group of roughly forty riders occurred exactly as the television coverage of the Vuelta briefly switched channels from the minority TVE2 over to a couple of minutes of live coverage and updates in Spain's prime time early afternoon news on TVE. It was as if fate had decided these crucial moments of Indurain's career should not be confined to viewing by Spain's diehard cycling fans: this was something everybody should witness.

Indurain, who received messages of encouragement from ONCE's *directeur sportif* Manolo Saiz as he drove past, then had a word with his own Banesto team car as it pulled alongside. The contents of the discussion quickly became clear when he gestured to Marino Alonso – the only Banesto rider to have supported him in all five of his Tour victories and now hovering just ahead of him, waiting for instructions – that he should make his own way to the finish, rather than support his team leader.

As Indurain rode over the top of the climb around five minutes down on Rominger and the rest of the main GC contenders, riders who had earlier been dropped began passing him again on the twisting, wooded descent. Spain's Herminio Díaz Zabala, an ONCE *domestique* and former Reynolds team-mate, was one of the last to do so, clapping a hand on Indurain's shoulder in sympathy before moving on. It was another recognition that the Indurain–ONCE battle in the Vuelta, it seemed, was over.

This was no rapid surrender, though. Indurain's lengthy solo ride, lasting nearly half an hour before he finally pulled up, became an extended opportunity for fans and the cycling community to contemplate the Tour de France's greatest star going through a sorry, drawn-out and public exit from his country's biggest bike race. If Indurain was physically in good enough shape to stay with the favourites for most of the first two weeks of the race, how on earth had he found himself in this predicament and where was he going from here? How, to put it bluntly, had it all come to this?

For a few moments, the TV cameras lost sight of Indurain when he was caught by the 'grupetto' – the sixty or so non-contenders and sprinters who, with no option of fighting for the win, had dropped off the pace completely by the foot of the Fito. Two months earlier he had been battling for a sixth Tour de France; two days earlier, he had been the strongest opponent of the all-conquering ONCE in the Vuelta. Now, though, he was just making up the numbers.

And suddenly, as Indurain stopped on the roadside, waited for a gap in the race traffic, then pedalled across a hotel forecourt and out of the race itself, he was not even doing that any more.

CHAPTER 1
Back to the Roots

Turning the clock back en route to Villava is not so hard. Just like when I first went to scout out the home village of Miguel Indurain twenty-four years ago, it still takes fifteen minutes for the local bus to crawl there in rush hour traffic from Pamplona, the capital of Navarre. And there is still very little of interest to look at on the way.

The view out of the bus window as the broad avenue out of Pamplona narrows into an A-road or *carretera nacional* remains largely unchanged: one weather-beaten, well-appointed high-rise block of flats after another passes by, their ground floors an interminable succession of single-room hairdressers, cafés and bakers, some announcing their services in crenellated Basque lettering. Look upwards and brighter colours of clothing on washing lines are briefly visible between the crumbling granite slabs of the balconies. There is an occasional glimpse of the few pieces of wasteland, too, and rough pasture between city and dormitory town upon which the local constructors have yet to encroach. Then the driver calls out that this is the closest stop to Villava's centre, the bus's glass doors hiss and glide back and you are there.

Just one square kilometre in size geographically, Villava is one of the smallest and – because of its location so close to Pamplona – most densely populated *pueblos* in Navarre. By the 1990s, whatever building space was available for those working in nearby Pamplona was already heavily exploited, and where the constructors could not build sideways, they built vertically. As the scaffolding and iron beam cages of embryonic blocks of flats rose steadily skywards, Villava's population, some 3,000 in the 1950s, climbed to nearly four times that number in official record books, and probably higher in reality.

With age, the high red-brick tower blocks are all a shade battered-looking, and the same goes for the well-appointed paved squares, flanked with colonnades and archways to keep the inhabitants out of the region's incessant winter rain. What is surprising, perhaps, is that Miguel Indurain's first cycling club remains and looks exactly as it has done since 1994. Its offices-cum-storerooms are situated behind a large glass door on the right-hand side of a two-storey structure that houses the local *frontón,* the large hall with a court for Basque handball. The building is utterly functional, without any adornments. The lower half of the outer wall is white cement, the upper segment corrugated iron painted light green. Above the glass door is written its name in thick green letters: *Club Ciclista Villavés.*

The interior of the club's downstairs room, perhaps eight metres square at most, is almost unchanged, too. Metal shelves packed with boxes of cycling equipment are jammed against the walls, along with photos of professional riders who cut their teeth in the CC Villavés. There is Miguel Indurain, of course, but also his brother Prudencio and Xavier Zandio, the former Banesto and Illes Balears rider grimacing as he comes within a whisker of winning a Tour de France stage in 2005. There is another of former club member

Koldo Gil, briefly a minor star in Spanish cycling in the 2000s with Liberty Seguros. In another corner is a row of bike frames, with and without wheels, leaning together and hanging on walls. One of them, a green model without a particular brand name, belonged to Indurain in his teens, but – as if symbolic of the club's attitude towards all its young riders as a whole, whether they are lacking in talent or a future Tour winner – whilst clean and in good nick, it doesn't get any place of honour or plaque.

With a yell of 'Come up!', there, leaning on the railings of the stairs to his office above is Pepe Barruso, the heftily built, loud-voiced heart of the club, as he has been virtually since its inception in the mid-1970s. It was Barruso who, ironically enough, might have deterred a less determined Indurain from cycling altogether. In early September 1975 Barruso refused (rightly, let it be said) to allow the tall, gangly eleven-year-old with a shock of thick dark hair, accompanied by his father, take part in his first race, organised by the CC Villavés, because he did not have a racing licence. At the following week's race, though, Indurain was back, his newly acquired licence in hand. After that, Miguel was in for good, remaining with the club for the next seven years. He only left when he had to, aged eighteen, the point where the CC Villavés, which did not cater for riders any older, would send its most promising riders up a level, to one of the top amateur clubs in the area.

Back in 1975, the Club Ciclista Villavés was, like Indurain, taking its first faltering steps in the cycling world. Formed just a few months before Indurain's father knocked on the clubhouse door, the race Indurain had wanted to take part in, the I Circuito Miqueo, was actually the first event ever to be organised by the club.

Barruso, who worked as a welder building poultry barns and who has lived in Villava almost all his life, had dreamed up the idea of the CC Villavés one weekend afternoon of 1974 as he came home from the *frontón* – where the cycling club is located now – with two other local friends, José Ignacio Urdaníz and Juan Antonio Almárcegui.

To say the organisation was initially top-heavy with management is no exaggeration. Whilst José Ángel Andueza was a fourth early key supporter and the club's first president, the club contained a single junior fourteen-year-old local rider, Juancho Arizcuren. The aim of its founders, in 1974, was purely to be sure he got a licence and thereby give the previously team-less Arizcuren a chance of racing. 'We didn't have any members,' Almárcegui would later explain, 'and we had a lot of problems finding them.'

There was a dearth of competitors too. 'The first race we organised,' Barruso recalls, 'there were more race officials standing around than there were riders in it.' Members and rivals weren't the only thing the CC Villavés was lacking, either: with no official colours for the club, Arizcuren would race as a team of one, kitted out for races in a T-shirt with red, yellow and white stripes. He would get to events on his father's Vespa scooter, his bike slung over the back. The first prize, in those times, was often food, such a rack of pig's ribs. After a successful race, he must have made quite a sight riding home.

The first CC Villavés 'team car' was simply Barruso's own family vehicle, the ubiquitous Seat 600 – nicknamed *el ombligo* (the belly button) in Spain because everybody had one – costing 29,000 pesetas (€200). It was not until 2 September 1975 that the club was officially registered with the Navarre Federation, becoming one of six amateur clubs in the region at the time, and opting for dark red and green as the club's colours for all the riders' kit. Money was tight, too, with an annual budget of just 100,000 pesetas (roughly equivalent to €700 today), and up until 1978, the entire organisation's financial support came in the form of contributions of 100 pesetas (€0.70) from individual backers. 'Even when we got sponsors, at first we couldn't afford new jerseys with the new names,' Barruso recalls. 'We'd get one of the mothers [of a rider] to unstitch the lettering on the old ones and then sew on the new logo.' Local support was limited, too, to the point where to fill all the club's posts the Federation forms demanded, the four founders made use of the names of relatives and friends.

Having given Arizcuren a club all of his own – and he repaid the CC Villavés by staying with them right through to turning amateur – the club's longer-term *raison d'être*, Barruso told the *Diario de Navarra* newspaper in the mid-1990s, was to show the kids of Villava the benefits of sport as a healthy hobby. 'We never wanted to train champions, like Miguel, we wanted to help young people grow up the right way. It's a very dangerous society for them, back when we were young there were only three bars in Villava, now there are twenty. What we're doing is social work.'

But if their goals were clear enough, in the first few years the CC Villavés headquarters itself was permanently in transit. The first residence was a spare room lent to them by a local political party, the Carlists. (In one of the earliest photos of the club line-up with no fewer than five Indurain cousins, stuck on the wall behind them is almost certainly a Carlist poster, complete with silhouettes of figures with the party's characteristic Basque berets.) Next to provide a temporary home was a Church association and when that agreement ended, the CC Villavés then occupied a room behind a bar – the *Jaizki*, where years later Miguel Indurain's fanclub would be based. An agreement with an aunt of Indurain's, to use a basement in a building she owned on Villava's main street, looked like offering some kind of stability.

But that deal fell through when the room was found to lack any furniture, although the aunt was good enough to give them back half of the rent already paid.

In the late 1970s, the CC Villavés took over a small backroom in the former knacker's yard, best known in the *pueblo* as the improvised operating room for visiting vets to vaccinate local dogs. By this point, thankfully, rather than continue their nomadic existence, Villava town hall stepped in and provided the CC Villavés with a twenty-year lease on the same room in the knacker's yard building – later to become the town's *frontón*. That is where the club remains today, although the inside received a major overhaul in late 1994. 'I'll never forget the moment the town hall clerk told me that whatever happened, there'd be something for us every year in the annual budget,' Barruso remembers.

A quick look at the club's roster of riders shows that the Indurains were a key part of the CC Villavés from the outset. Of the seven riders registered in 1975, three – Miguel and his cousins Luis and Javier – were Indurains. 'It was very much a family thing, my cousins with my parents and uncles and all the rest of us, we'd all go and race or watch the race, have a good time together', recalls Prudencio Indurain, who joined the club in 1976. 'My father liked cycling, took us along, and it was a way for us to spend our Sundays.' The bike was not just for leisure, though. 'As farmers, my parents worked outside on the land a lot, it's not like now when your parents take you everywhere by car, you'd ride your bike to a lot of different places.' A fourth in the photo of the young Indurain tribe of cousins in CC Villaves kit is José Luis Jaimerena, who, slightly older than Miguel, would go on to be a team-mate of his in the amateur category and then co-direct the professional Reynolds team. Indurain would also cross paths with others who would then return to his life later on, such as Javier Luquin, his key rival in 1981, his last as a *juvenil*. Luquin later became a team-mate and friend in Banesto. Pedro López, meanwhile, a rider who beat him in the gymkhana events in the *infantil* category, later became a Banesto mechanic, and was present, watching from the team car, on the last day Indurain ever raced in a Grand Tour, at the 1996 Vuelta.

As a project, no matter its widely varying location and no matter the money available, the CC Villavés clearly worked well. Riders from as far away as Elizondo, Jaimerena's town, which was, prior to modern-day tunnels and bypasses, a good ninety-minute drive away on difficult roads, travelled down to join. Barruso's friendly, undemanding style also proved a draw.

'Barruso was like a father to us. It didn't matter if you were good, bad or indifferent as a racer,' recalls Prudencio. 'And he's still the same now. He wasn't someone to get you to win races, the important thing was to get people to do sport and that they enjoyed it. There'd be a nice *bocadillo* and glass of Coca-Cola afterwards and that was it, that's the fundamental thing. He never shouted at us, he never told us about tactics. It was just a question of going out and racing.'

'We'd go to races nearby in Alsasua, Tafalla, Estella, towns round and about. The cars weren't as good then, and we'd load them down, no air conditioning. Everybody would pile into the 600 and off we'd go. It was a good time of life. Me and Miguel were never in the same category, we didn't train together or anything. Four years age difference at that time of life is a world apart. It was only when we were amateurs that we'd train more together and then as pros, every day.'

'In that era, Pepe was more like a big brother to us all, there was no pressure,' Jaimerena recalls. 'They would take us to races, help us out, let us race almost for free. My parents didn't even have a car at that time, so I'd get a bus down there and then they would drive me all the way home from Pamplona up to here in Elizondo. I don't know how many kids he had in his own family, but if there were two races on a Saturday and a Sunday, we'd all sleep over in his flat, too. At first there weren't too many of us in my category, maybe twenty-five or thirty kids in all of Navarre.

'My feeling towards people like that is one of gratitude, people spending their own free time, all weekend after working all week to drive you around, set up the races, organise it all, and doing it for year after year. And thanks to those people, riders of all kinds have a chance. If you've got a family, it'll be hard to sacrifice your time for them. I can't help wondering who's going to do that kind of work when they finally quit.'

It was not only their time Villava's 'founding four' initially had to spend in abundance. It was their money, too – for petrol, for food, for equipment – and property, particularly cars, which the club worked its way through at a tidy pace. Once Barruso's Seat 600 'died', next to be sacrificed on the club's long hauls to races was a yellow Renault 5 belonging to Urdaniz and loaned for free to the club. That was followed by a Renault 8 of Almárecegui's and then a Renault 12 TS, bought again by Barruso. Barruso recounts in the club's official history that 'after a few months, I changed the R12's motor from petrol to diesel, thinking I'd save some money, and the only thing I achieved was to lower its maximum speed to 80 km/h. Driving the way back to Villava from the mechanic's I was so upset with myself at what I'd done I barely made it.'

By 1984, the club finally acquired its first own vehicle, but Miguel Indurain, who had left two years earlier, has vivid memories of the Seat 600, saying, 'it was quite something to travel in. The engine would overheat a lot because there were five of us in the car, plus all our bikes and equipment. There were times we'd have to stop on the side of the road to let it cool down.'

As the number of races organised by the CC Villavés slowly increased, starting with just two in 1975, then five in 1976, seven in 1977 and nine from 1978 onwards, so did the number of riders. From seven in 1975, the club had nineteen (including four Indurains) in 1976. Names of figures that would be key to Indurain's career in the future, like Juan Fernández, a director of the rival Clas-Cajastur team in the mid-1990s, and Marino Lejarreta, the future leader of the rival ONCE squad, started to appear in the list of top three finishers in the races run by the club.

In the mid-1970s, the creation of the local SuperSer team in Pamplona, briefly containing Spain's greatest Tour de France racer of the time, Luis Ocaña, acted as a beacon for cycling interest. So too, did the Tour de France's brief visit to Navarre in 1977 (although only in the northernmost area, en route to Vitoria), and the arrival of the Vuelta a España in Pamplona and Villava in 1979. According to contemporary reports, using the Pamplona avenue closest to Villava as a finish proved controversial: the lack of barriers and organisation in the midst of massive crowds helped caused the *commissaires'* cars and following vehicles to snarl up the whole area. One top rider, former Giro d'Italia winner Michel Pollentier of Belgium, went flying into a rear window, and suffered severe concussion. Stage winner Sean Kelly had injuries to his head and ear and needed around half a dozen stitches, runner-up Noël Dejonckheere had a badly bruised shoulder, and a middle-ranking Italian sprinter, Daniele Tinchella, fractured his hand.

Pollentier, blood dripping copiously from his face, claimed, 'We're risking our lives here every day' and several riders protested about the lack of police to control the crowds. Tinchella continued to shout 'criminals' at the public even as he was being loaded onto a stretcher and Kelly, in his autobiography *Hunger*, recalls, 'It was like the running of the bulls ... after the finish the lead car was stopped 30 or 40 metres ahead, I squeezed the brakes like they were a pair of nutcrackers but there was no time to stop.'

The next day's start in Villava was also chaotic, and a TV car and team car had a total of six tyres slashed. But on the plus side, such visits by the Vuelta gave the local youth like Indurain an opportunity to see the real professional racing scene, right on their doorstep. It could hardly fail to make an impression.

As for that September morning in 1975 when Indurain Senior and Miguel came knocking on his door, Barruso says he never received a direct explanation from either father or son, as to why Indurain had decided to opt for cycling. There was, according to Prudencio Indurain, no tradition whatsoever of cycling in any category in the Indurain family history, so that can hardly have been a reason. Not that Barruso ever saw the need for one.

'They saw we organised races and the boy would have liked the idea of racing. That's often the way. A lot of them come through that door the first time because they've got a friend who's already racing and the dad turns up.' It later turned out that what Indurain liked the most was the chance to see other villages in different races, or the soft drink and sandwich the club gave to its young competitors after each event. 'We still do,' reflects Barruso. 'A Coca-Cola or Fanta and a *bocadillo* of chorizo or ham or *mortadela*. The minute the race had finished we'd shoot off for the sandwich,' Miguel says in the official club history, 'I remember it always went down very well. That period of my life was the best time as a rider, because you don't feel the obligation to win.'

Once Indurain was part of the club, he was there to stay. For one thing, Indurain's family, who had agricultural smallholdings on both his mother and his father's side, had no need to leave the area. By contrast, both of Spain's two previous Tour de France winners at the time Miguel was growing up, Federico Martín Bahamontes and Luis Ocaña, had had far more tumultuous childhoods: Bahamontes fleeing the bombardments and the death threats to his father in Toledo in the Civil War to work as a road-mender aged twelve; Ocaña and his family becoming economic emigrants in France in the 1950s after years of impoverished existence in eastern Spain.

Indurain's parents farm was, in fact, the last to survive inside Villava, but one which was set to endure. 'This is good land and there were no bad harvests,' points out Prudencio Indurain, 'why would we want to go?' The farm was not huge though, and only had one regular farmhand: 'Of course we'd help, that's what it's all about in the country. It was very hard work, the planting, harvesting and so on, but we liked it … '

The reason for Indurain's love of the outdoor life is clear: he was born into it, grew up in it, and knew little else. 'It certainly wasn't like the town kids here who have to go down to the square to find some open space,' observes Barruso. 'They could go out and play on all that land their father owned whenever they wanted.'

Apart from owning the farm together with his brother, Miguel Indurain senior also rented out their tractors and services to other farmers. Indurain's grandfather, Toribio, had bought land on a nearby hillside for a vineyard and parts of it were sold off for urban development. As one of four original landowners in Villava, they would have enjoyed a healthy profit. Thus the family, according to Prudencio, never reached a point where leaving Villava and the farm was ever considered an economic necessity, and if further proof were needed of that financial stability, according to Barruso, Miguel, like his brother and three sisters, were partly educated at private, fee-paying schools.

The family's strongly held Catholic faith was almost certainly another major pillar of that inner stability. Navarre is one of the most deeply religious areas of Spain – the nickname for Indurain's future team, Reynolds, was *el equipo de los curas* (the priests' team) – and the Indurain family were practising Roman Catholics. Father Jesús María Zubiri, the now-deceased parish priest who lived just a few hundred yards away from the Indurains and who was a regular visitor, once told the *Diario de Navarra* newspaper, 'Since the times of Toribio, the first Indurain I met, the Indurain family have always been very religious … They have passed those beliefs on from one generation to the next.' He also proudly noted that Indurain took his First Communion 'just two weeks before he got his first racing licence.'

Not that the Indurains used their financial well-being as a way of keeping themselves apart from the rest of the town, either. 'They had money but they have never had any airs or graces. They were – and are – the most down-to-earth, humble people you can meet,' Barruso says. To underline his point, he uses an example from the area he knows best: races. Parents who are overly convinced their children are a cut above will take them to the event but then 'keep them sitting in their own car, rather than come over to mine for the director's meeting of all the riders, right up until the start. And the same goes after the race, when they'll get their kid straight into their own car, rather than attend the debriefing.' Indurain's father 'would never do that and neither does Indurain when he takes his own son to races now.' Miguel Indurain would later recall that his mother 'would complain a little when we turned up with our race clothes dirty, but when it came down to it, they would never ask us to quit cycling.'

Despite making money from selling land, farming remained, for many decades, the central element of the Indurains' lives – both parents and sons. Indeed, there were apocryphal stories that Indurain abandoned the Tour on two occasions in order to help his father with the harvest. Indurain cannot, therefore, be portrayed as the clichéd working-class hero who wanted to escape a world of agricultural hardship to make his fortune by riding his bike: rather, the two areas – Indurain's love of things rural and his love of cycling – were strongly connected. In 1991, shortly before winning his first Tour, Indurain spent his free time repairing agricultural implements for his father. 'He would be a good farmer and he drives a tractor better than anyone I know,' his father once proudly said. For Indurain, the 'fruits' of his cycling life were like the harvests at the culmination of a farming season: the tangible confirmation of a job well done.

Even the way Indurain acquired his first racing bike was because of his love of the rural life. When he was around eleven, he cycled to where his father was working with his lunchtime sandwich, and had a drive on his tractor whilst he was eating it. But whilst he was doing so, two individuals walking across the fields decided to steal his bike. To make up for his disappointment, Indurain's father opted to buy Miguel a second-hand racer, a GAC. 'Just figure what we would have missed out on had he continued with the old one,' his father used to joke. With a racer for the young lad, knocking on the door of the CC Villavés presumably seemed like a natural next step.

Although all three of Miguel's three male cousins – Javier, Daniel and Luis – joined the CC Villavés, it was Miguel and his brother who lasted there the longest. 'Miguel would get a new bike and then when he outgrew it, he'd pass it on to me,' Pruden, tall and heftily built like Miguel, once recalled. It was not at all rare, either, for each brother to win a race in the same village on the same day but different categories: Miguel in the under-fifteen *infantiles* category; Pruden in the under-eleven *benjamines*.

Such tenacious loyalty to the CC Villavés makes it easy to trace the line of Indurain's progress as a young rider and his developing strengths and weaknesses, in the club records. For example there are the details of the the twenty-eight defeats he suffered one season at the hands of one particular rival, Joaquín Marcos in the *infantiles* category. Rather than quit, Indurain clearly rationalised the situation – his rival was one year older than him and therefore was naturally stronger – and kept plugging away. Eventually, it was Marcos who was regularly, relentlessly defeated by Indurain.

It should be pointed out that Indurain had plenty of other options in Navarre at the time had he wanted to leave the CC Villavés. In 1975 there were just 181 registered riders of all ages up to eighteen in the whole of Navarre. But by 1979, following a big upturn in local interest, there were 569: by 1981, 862; and by 1983, 1,332. As Barruso recalls, there were so many clubs and under-18 riders in the area for that the region was divided into five separate areas by the local federation, to ensure that races were not over-booked with starters. (Now, with Navarran amateur clubs down to half their number, there are just two).

But Indurain never moved on. It seems fair to say that with Indurain, such loyalty – be it to a team, to a club, to his village or to his family – is one of the keys to understanding his entire career. Once something or someone had received his approval, it was to be very rare that Indurain would change his mind, or let himself be persuaded to change it.

Slowly but surely, Indurain's loyalty and persistence started to hone his talent and reap him rich rewards. After four races in which he did not win – his bike wheels were a smaller radius than his rivals' which may well have been a factor – in 1976 there was no stopping him. 'As I recall,' Barruso says, 'he ran second in his first race [in 1976], in the village of Luquin, and then he made up for that the following one, in Elvetea, where he won.' That season, Indurain won the staggering total of fifteen races, one more than his closest rival, Pablo Bacaicoa, making him the outright champion of Navarre in his category. All this was achieved despite, as Indurain once said, 'barely training. My longest training ride at the time would be heading over to my mother's town, Alzórriz, around 25 kilometres away. If it got to 27 kilometres I was absolutely exhausted.' Another favourite excursion at the time was up to Pamplona to buy sweets at a stall near the bullring: a 12-kilometre round trip.

Whilst Indurain's talent for bike racing shone through very early, so too did his reticence about showing his emotions in public – another facet of his personality that would endure until he retired. Barruso remembers that Indurain was not one for celebrating, to the point where he once said, 'I never remember him making a single gesture of victory until he won on Luz Ardiden [in the 1990 Tour].' Indurain's dislike of what he considered showy behaviour could be explained by Father Zubiri's comments that 'He was – and has always been – a very normal person, but shy, he didn't want to stand out. When I went to visit his house I'd see him studying or playing, but always trying to do so without being noticed.'

'You'd be in the team car and of course you wouldn't be able to see what was going on,' Barruso recalls. 'So afterwards I'd come up to him and say, "Hey, Miguel, how did you get on?" And he'd say in a very quiet voice, "first". Others, they'd be boasting about it at the tops of their voices, but not Miguel.'

'That's how he's always been,' confirms Pruden. 'He'd be happy inside and what he feels – well that's for him. I know him very well, I'm his brother, I don't need him to talk to me to know what he wants. He's never been a big talker, but he talks a lot when he's not in public. He's not shy, he's just like that.'

Indurain could have done a lot of celebrating had he set his mind to it. 'He was unbeatable in circuit races. A lot of the time, he'd win alone. He was very, very clever as a racer,' says Barruso. Nor did he need much advice. 'I can recall going to Zaragoza with him and we had to sign him onto the list of starters. The race was about to begin so I left him with somebody's parent whilst I went off to do that. By the time I got back he was already three minutes clear of the field ... There was one other rider of his age in the club [Marcos] who would always be trying to get ahead by not working in the break, then winning at the sprints. But in the end, Indurain would get the better of him.' A very high level of ambition, though, according to Pruden has always been a key part of his personality, even if 'there's never been much euphoria. But he's a winner, he doesn't let you win even at billiards [a Spanish saying for those who are ultra-competitive]. That winner's instinct, that's in him.'

This habit of winning without overly celebrating – as the Spanish say *la misa va po dentro*, the church service takes place inside the building – meant that Indurain gave the impression that success was something that came naturally, rather than anything special. That slightly mechanical edge towards beating others in races was something his rivals would find intimidating, and which throughout his career gave Indurain a psychological advantage.

Contributing to that 'superhuman' factor was Indurain's gift for avoiding crashes and accidents. 'During all his time with us, he might have broken his arm once, but that'd be about it,' Barruso says. 'I never saw him fall, apart from once in a race near Irún where the entire team, all six of them, went down – and I wasn't there anyway.' His ability to handle stressful situations also shone through early on. During another race as a teenager, two rivals began throwing *bidones* at each other, one of which struck Miguel a glancing blow, and which could have hit him full on. Indurain was frightened, but whilst the case ended up going to court, he did not protest: it was not his concern.

'Indurain had a great gift, which was his interior calm,' observes Manolo Saiz, director of the ONCE team that acted as Indurain's greatest rivals inside Spain throughout his career. 'But to my way of thinking, one of his best qualities as a racer was his father's attitude towards life, which Miguel applied to cycling. The idea, the real countryman's idea, that you have to sow in order to reap, but that things take their natural time. People try and separate sport from life, give it different values, but you can't. Those values that you learn from your environment are the ones you apply to sport.'

Aged fifteen, Indurain moved up to the cadets' category, where as Barruso states 'he won fewer races, but that was due to team tactics. At that level, there were just four or five squads in a lot of races, so it was rare to get enough collaboration between them for breaks to be pulled back. His climbing, though, gradually got better.'

Indurain, therefore, was denied many opportunities of unleashing his fast finish from the bunch, the strongest card in his suit. Back when he was very young, on flat finishes with a curve to the right more than those with a curve to the left, Indurain was all but unstoppable. As a cadet, though, he still won eight races, in a single season three of them against riders in the amateur category, another level higher, and his progress was only briefly broken as an unwanted result of a trip to Ponferrada to race the National Championships in 1981. A bad case of sunstroke in a team time trial was followed by a rare crash when Indurain was caught up in a mass pile-up in the bunch on a downhill and suffered a broken wrist. Even though he was still suffering from his wrist injury, in a race immediately afterwards in Sanguesa Indurain still managed to blow the field apart on one climb, the Leyre, to soften up the opposition for his team-mates. He only stopped pedalling, Barruso later said, when he was beyond a state of normal exhaustion – the kind of selfless performance that gained Indurain numerous friends in his club.

Persistent, talented and generous towards his team-mates: there seemed to be no end to Indurain's gifts on the bike. But Barruso adds another two – Indurain, even as a youth, was remarkably thorough, and above all he knew how to suffer. 'It was good that he was a fantastic bike handler, he had won a load of gymkhanas, maybe thirty a year,' Barruso says. 'What made a bigger difference was his endurance, because others in the club were equally good at the technical side of it. I remember when one of the other amateurs got signed by Reynolds. After a year they kicked him out. He'd get to the 100-kilometre mark [in races] and then he'd crack.' Not, it seemed, Miguel.

On top of that, 'He was always very methodical. It didn't matter if it was a big family meal, one of those that always go on and on, if it got to half past three and half past three was time to go training, he'd be up from the table and off out to ride.' The question is almost inevitable – did Barruso see the young Miguel Indurain as a Tour winner? He says, in all honesty, he did not: 'a World Champion maybe, but he reminded me more of a [Francesco] Moser or a [Sean] Kelly.'

'His condition was supernatural, it'd make your hair stand on end to see how good he was,' adds Juan Carlos González Salvador, who, together with his brother Eduardo, would cross paths with Miguel at races from a very young age. 'I first met him when I was a junior, eighteen or so and I was racing in a nearby region, Alava, in the Basque Country at the time and winning a lot, but there weren't many events there so we'd go to Navarre. Miguel was top dog in

Navarre and I was pretty much the same in Alava, so although we got on very well, there was a lot of rivalry between us. '

Juan Carlos González Salvador recognises that Indurain's natural talent on a bike left his rivals demoralised even before a race started. 'It did my head in, though, because he worked a lot on his parents' farm. As the elder brother of the family he had a lot of jobs to do and barely had time to train. I was absolutely obsessed with racing, I lived for it, and it would cost me heaven and earth to beat him. I almost had to cheat to do it. I could beat him in a sprint. Just. But if you went on a break with him, it was absolute torture. Even though he hardly trained, he was that good.'

Juan Carlos González Salvador agrees that Indurain's racing philosophy owed much to his agricultural roots: 'His attitude was, "I'm a decent, hard-working type, but I know that if I'm going to get a return for that work, it's like planting a kilo of potatoes, I have to put the work in, care for them and make sure they come through well – and I won't get it through talking."' As the rider who perhaps knew Indurain the best in his first five years as a professional, Dominique Arnaud, puts it, 'He had the wisdom of a countryman, he'd know how to stand back, look around, reflect and then act, like all rural people. The word in French is *sagesse*. Taking the time not to react too quickly. That kind of calm, that always being *tranquilo*, that comes from the country.'

Perhaps given his consistency throughout his career, it's no surprise that Indurain's thoroughness, calmness, bike handling skills and innate brilliance at racing – as well as not crowing about his superiority – were all facets that he showed from a very young age. But as an amateur Indurain showed no sign of one of the chinks in his armour as a professional: a dislike of racing in the cold and wet. That, however, was more circumstantial, according to Barruso: 'When he raced with us, the races were short ones, just fifty or sixty kilometres, not like the professionals which are six hours on a bike. I've seen him win races in Pamplona when it was snowing and he was only wearing a hairnet helmet [as was the custom at the time]. It was more of a problem when it was hot, he used to suffer from allergies' – a problem that was to dog him throughout his career.

Father Zubiri also described the young Indurain as 'cold'. But this was not, it appears, in a negative sense, rather that 'he finds it hard to exteriorise his feelings'. That did not mean that Indurain could not empathise with others in his squad or, indeed, in general. As Barruso once said, 'If it was a race where he had to work for another team-mate, he'd do that without complaining. He always collaborated, he was polite, everybody liked him. He was basically a guy who didn't cause problems. And if he was quiet in professionals, as an amateur, he was even quieter.'

Juan Carlos González Salvador believes Indurain's quietness is hereditary. 'His father was very similar, very friendly and somebody you'd get to like very quickly, but it wasn't because of how he talked. Miguel's the same, he thinks "What's the point of talking if I'm not going to say anything?" But when Miguel finally does say something, you know it's worth writing down.' Yet that reticence also meant that in crucial areas of his career, Indurain left it up to others to understand what he wanted. In the eight years Indurain spent at the Club Villavés from 1975 through to the end of 1982, Barruso says Indurain 'never once said that he wanted to be a professional. Whilst he would go on racing in different places, it was us who talked to José Miguel Echavarri [the manager of Indurain's longstanding professional team Reynolds] about when Miguel was going to turn amateur.'

The reason why Barruso went to see Echavarri that autumn after the village festival had ended was that October was an unofficial deadline for signing the top crop of young riders turning amateur the following season. 'He told me he'd already seen Miguel, he knew what he was worth … But the Reynolds management hadn't said anything to Miguel. And October went by, November and December and after four months, he called me to say Miguel was in.'

At this point Barruso says it was not clear that Indurain was going to be heading towards Reynolds: 'There were other teams interested in him, particularly the local Racesa squad. It took such a long time for Reynolds to call, he was beginning to get nervous and he was very close to signing for them.' It is intriguing to think what direction Indurain would have taken had he ended up with another squad, rather than what turned out to be his lifelong team. As it was, once he had started with Reynolds, Indurain's career path quickly became close to being set in stone.

CHAPTER 2
The Little Priests

In 2005, the sports section of the newspaper *El Diario Vasco* published a report on the Hostal Manolo, a small, family-run hotel in a quiet, paved square in the Basque village of Zegama. The article described a gathering there of a group of around a dozen men, all in their late thirties or forties. Amongst them were Prudencio and Miguel Indurain.

The reason for their meeting up was to celebrate the thirtieth anniversary of the birth of the Reynolds amateur team. For years, Hostal Manolo was the unofficial headquarters of the squad. Run by a team *soigneur*, Manolo Arrizkoreta, the amateur riders from outside the Basque Country and Navarre lived in the *hostal* during the season for up to a month at a time, whilst the others would join them there for races.

Between races, their bikes were stored in the garages next door. At the end of the day, Arrizkoreta would give them a massage, then they would head down to the the hotel restaurant, run by his wife María Luisa Echarte. Here, they ate their meals every evening, before heading upstairs to the *hostal*'s simple bedrooms. An hour's drive from Pamplona and the Reynolds *service course* and conveniently close to the Basque sierras of Azkorri, there were training rides aplenty, and in a village with just over 1,200 inhabitants, few distractions. Having Zegama as a base was yet another indication of how closely linked Navarran cycling is to its Basque equivalent, still considered the powerhouse and heartland of Spain's cycling culture.

The Hostal Manolo continued to be the amateur team's base until it disbanded in 2000. But if the sponsor had changed by then to Banesto, the memories lived on. When María Luisa Echarte died in September 2001, the Spanish riders on the professional team, many of whom had lived for long spells in the Hostal Manolo, dedicated all their wins on that year's Vuelta to her. 'The team bosses were delighted with the place,' *El País* reported on her death. 'The riders were kept on a leash but simultaneously they felt like they were at home.'

Both Arrizkoreta and María Luisa were keenly aware of the strengths and weaknesses of the characters in their charge. If there were riders who felt like sneaking out for a few evening drinks, María Luisa would keep a disapproving eye on them throughout the supper beforehand. If she knew that someone had a habit of coming into the kitchen for a furtive midnight feast, 'then she would hide the biscuit jar.'

At the same time, Jaimerena – by then the *directeur sportif* for the amateur team – 'would send her the evening menu of what we could have, and he specifically banned us from having any of her homemade cake,' José Luis Rubiera, a Banesto amateur and later a pro with Kelme and US Postal told *El País*. She did not take kindly to having her food criticised, either: 'If somebody complained that their the steak wasn't well done enough,' Carlos Sastre, the future Tour de France winner, said to the newspaper, 'she'd get a hunk of fresh meat and take it outside, cut it up with an axe and chuck the raw steak on the rider's plate.'

In 2005, when the earliest generations of riders met up again for a commemorative reunion, Indurain was by far the most famous of those present. On the bar walls – the hotel had closed down when María Luisa Echarte learned she had cancer – Indurain's yellow and pink jerseys from the Tour de France and Giro d'Italia were in pride of place. But amongst those dozen who gathered in 2005 were other well-known Spanish riders like Juan Carlos González Salvador, a Spanish national champion in the 1990s, Iñaki Gastón, one of Sean Kelly's greatest lieutenants, and all-rounder Vicente Ridaura. Indurain towered above them all in terms of *palmares*, but these riders were still winners of solid, middle-ranking races, many of which are now long defunct: the Volta a Galicia for Ridaura; stages of the Vuelta a Aragón for González Salvador; or the hill-climb to the Basque sanctuary of Arantzazu for Gastón.

Go to Zegama today and although Hostal Manolo, a sturdy three-storey building with its shutters firmly down looks to have closed down, over the last couple of decades there have been few other changes, as is the case with Villava. From where the village lies at the head of a valley dotted with pinewoods, there is still just one main road leading south out of Zegama and one main road leading north over a winding, six-kilometre-long pass set amidst snowcapped mountains.

Streams and rivers form a patchwork of waterways across the village centre – where the tallest building is a sizeable church – with its two small bars and one tiny guesthouse. Inside one bar, there are handwritten notes in a hybrid of Spanish and Basque offering sand-wiches of *chorizak* and *lomeak* and on a door nearby an invitation to join an upcoming protest against the installation of some telephone antennae has been tacked up on the frame. A large Basque *ikurriña* flag flaps in the breeze outside the town hall. But as for posters of

Indurain or a signpost outside the village proudly announcing his team's connections with Zegama? If present, they are well hidden.

Equally, apart from the Indurains and Jaimerena, it is hard to find former Reynolds amateurs who still live locally: in 2005 Gastón worked in the chemicals industry in the Basque Country; Ridaura was a fireman in Requena in Valencia, five hours south; others were in León, a four-hour drive to the west. A few, like Marino Alonso, had proved impossible for the organisers to find. Those that did turn up gave Manolo Arizkorreta a plaque, as a token of their appreciation. Although as *El Diario Vasco* sagely observed, 'if Miguel Indurain had been the team's only rider, the whole squad's existence from beginning to end would have been amply justified.'

Miguel Indurain's career as an amateur with the Reynolds squad was spellbindingly brief and jaw-droppingly successful. In less than two years, Indurain managed to become Spain's youngest ever amateur national champion at eighteen, win the Navarran regional championships, take part in the Los Angeles Olympic Games, race several semi-professional events and sign his first contract with his lifelong professional team. On a personal level, there were key developments too. Indurain began working with one of the two directors who was to shape his career: Eusebio Unzué, responsible at the time for the Reynolds amateur squad. The two were not just connected through racing: Unzué's family were local agricultural seed merchants, and had the Indurains as customers. 'But we didn't get a discount,' Miguel Indurain once pointed out with a wry grin.

The first key point in Indurain's fast-tracking into the professional world was actually a non-event. He was excluded from Spain's then obligatory year-long military service programme because there was a surplus in required numbers. This meant that unlike one of his key rivals as a junior, Joaquín Marcos, Indurain did not face the risk of a twelve-month break in his progress. Some riders doing the *mili* were allowed to continue training as a special concession from their commanding officers, but others, like Marcos, were not. As he later recollected, the long spell away from racing indirectly wrecked his potential career as a pro.

Indurain, by contrast, was heading in the opposite direction: cycling was his only real option after his academic education slowly fizzled out. His primary and secondary school teachers, interviewed at length by the local media during the years when Indurain attained star status in Spain, tended to describe him as an unexceptional student who never gave them any problems. 'He was no better and no worse than others,' Jesús Guembe Iriarte, his English teacher at a religious secondary school in Pamplona, told the *Diario de Navarra*. 'He had no problem getting on with everybody, but he didn't stand out that much. He was out of the school pretty quickly at the end of each day, onto the bus for Villava, with his cousin Daniel and brother Prudencio.' Guembe Iriarte recalled 'numerous conversations' with Indurain about cycling, particularly concerning Eddy Merckx and Bernard Hinault, and that he 'always brought some wonderfully large sandwiches.' Along with his *bocadillos* Indurain's height also meant he stood out physically – his school nickname was 'Torpedo'. But academically, as Indurain always said later, he never shone.

Part of the problem was the school. Indurain failed to adapt well to the Pamplona college he was sent to for his secondary education, and he began failing four or five subjects, out of ten, each year. 'My parents wanted me to study and go on to do a degree, and I didn't want to at all,' he later commented. Aged fourteen, Indurain was switched to a secondary school-cum-technical college in Beriain, just south of Pamplona, where he did four years of vocational studies in mechanical engineering and tool design – the latter with the long-term aim of helping his father out on the farm. The idea of university was quietly dropped.

Indurain stuck at the school in Beriain for four years, but then, having just turned nineteen, he quit studying for good. Whether or not the decision was to do with cycling, Indurain's studies had already cost him participation in one major event – the Vuelta a Navarra in 1983, his home race and one of the most important in Spain – because Unzué felt he had not done enough basic training due to his swotting too hard. On top of that, Unzué observed, the Vuelta a Navarra coincided with his exams. The next year, by the time Indurain had quit studying for good, he already had a contract with the professional team.

When Indurain signed with the Reynolds amateur squad in the spring of 1983, the team had come a long way from its starting point in 1970 as a threadbare, tiny junior team from the little-known town of Irurzun in north-western Navarre. Since 1980, Reynolds had had both an amateur and professional squad, the latter soon to contain figures as well known as Ángel Arroyo and Pedro Delgado. Reynolds themselves would go on, first with Arroyo, then with Julián Gorospe, another promising Basque rider, Delgado and Indurain, to become Spain's most successful team of all time, and – with the team still running – it has now become cycling's longest-running squad in the post-War era. Movistar, Reynolds' latest mutation, has now been ranked the world's number one team for the last three years.

Whilst Indurain's best-known director in his professional career was José Miguel Echavarri, Echavarri's key partner in Reynolds was Unzué, Indurain's director in the amateur squad. Inside or outside Spain, it would be hard to find two directors of a cycling team who have had such an enduring, united or productive relationship as the two Navarrans. Their partnership lasted through to 2007 when Echavarri retired and Unzué, a few years younger, has continued at the head of the Movistar squad. As Unzué once put it, he and Echavarri were 'the accelerator and the brake pedals in the same team car.'

'Right from the start, what enabled Unzué and Echavarri to work so well together was how seriously they both took bike racing,' David García, the author of the official history of the squad, *Nuestro Ciclismo, por un Equipo* [Our Cycling, Thanks to a team], told me in an interview for the British magazine *ProCycling*. 'Spain at the time was crawling with squads that either never paid their riders, or paid them badly, and which were simply interested in riders winning and burning them out in the process. Reynolds was never like that. Unzué and Echavarri always believed that the image of a team, its stability, was as important as the results it obtained. And that was one of the secrets of their longevity.'

'They had a classic relationship of good cop, bad cop with their riders,' recalls Eduardo González Salvador, who was an amateur alongside Indurain in Reynolds in 1983, having joined the squad the year before. 'Echavarri had a gift for talking to people that captivated them. He was like a father figure, but ...' he grins, 'dealing with Eusebio was like dealing with your mother-in-law! Maybe in private they were equally good or bad as people, but José Miguel, to talk to, was delightful. It was like he'd just dropped out of heaven – in fact the other teams' nickname for the two was "the little priests" ... You felt like you'd been shown the grace of God.' As directors, they complemented each other well, 'because Eusebio was much more aggressive and José Miguel much more conservative. They were good at forming alliances, particularly with [Spanish director] Javier Mínguez.' Much later, Mínguez was to fuse his professional team, Amaya, with Echavarri's and Unzué's.

Partly thanks to their hugely successful track record with riders like Delgado and Indurain, partly thanks to their longevity and partly because of their team's immense influence, Unzué and Echavarri have long been senior figures in the Spanish cycling establishment. Since the inception of Reynolds, few top Spanish riders of recent times failed to come under their sphere of influence at some point. Joseba Beloki, three times a Tour podium finisher, is one, and double Tour winner Alberto Contador is another, but even 2008 Tour champion Carlos Sastre, who never raced for Banesto's professional team and who signed for arch-rivals ONCE was part of Banesto's amateur team.

Unzué and Echavarri's unbroken association with Reynolds makes it unusually easy to trace back the team's fragile, low-budget roots in Irurzun. The squad began in 1970, as a team of fewer than a dozen riders in their early teens backed by two local restaurant owners and brothers, José and Jesús Legarra. José was initially the only director, and Unzué, after two years of racing in the squad in 1972 and 1973, quickly opted to move into the team's management, aged eighteen.

In 1974, making what was a clear break with his own past, Unzué sold his racing bike, used the money to buy a car (a second-hand Seat 124), and started directing his former team-mates in what was then called the 'Irurzungo-Alay' squad. From then on, as Unzué would later say, 'For many, many years, the team was more like an adventure than aiming at a particular goal.' His idols of the time, 'Merckx, Ocaña and Fuente, were the ones I followed. What impressed me the most was the spirit of self-sacrifice they had, the amount they would push themselves to triumph in the sport.'

The creation of SuperSer, Navarre's first major professional team, in the mid-1970s, spurred Unzué on to expand the team as quickly as possible. 'Navarre has always had very strong links to cycling, and Miguel was the crowning moment of that,' Unzué observes, 'but the links go a long way back. Two of the brothers who created SuperSer, electrical appliance chainstores, for example, were themselves riders, as well having Ocaña in their line-up, even if he was in decline by then. Their team was part of that culture.' And so too was – and is – Unzué's.

At the same time Navarre's cycling links with the Basque Country are stronger than with the rest of Spain – which partly explains why so many foreign journalists would later write that Indurain was himself Basque. Navarre and the Basque Country, although considered by some local nationalist political parties to be part of a greater whole, are separate entities. But with Basque and Navarran races forming part of the same league, there comes a point in the past where their cycling roots, at least, are one and the same.

After Reynolds, a multinational aluminium manufacturer with a plant in Irurzun, stepped in as main sponsor, Unzué's eight charges learned that the team's budget had tripled to 100,000 pesetas [€600] for 1975 and they would soon be wearing newly designed team-kit – inspired by a near-mythical pro team Brooklyn. With a lot more money and Unzué and José Legarra at the helm, the team flourished. As its riders grew older and worked their way into the higher categories of non-professional racing, the team also moved its operating field upwards alongside them, from junior to amateur at the end of 1975. All the way, Reynolds matched their progression with increased financial backing.

By spring 1976, Reynolds was a middle-ranking amateur club made up almost exclusively of Navarran-born riders, and at management level the team retained an equally strong local flavour. When José Legarra quit to do his military service, his brother Jesús took over again. Unzué, meanwhile, had added another string to his bow, as the trainer for the Navarran regional amateur team.

Another major step forward came early in 1978, when José Miguel Echavarri joined the team's management: the partnership with Unzué that was to last through Indurain's entire career was forged. A former pro with Jacques Anquetil's BIC squad, Echavarri had been working after his 1971 retirement in his parents' hotel-cum-restaurant, whilst retaining his contacts with the cycling world. As a result, he took a small Spanish national squad to Uruguay as his first ever directing job, and when he returned, he brought a top local rider, Hector Rondán, for the Reynolds squad. Rondán paid for the flight over from Latin America and Echavarri put him up in his parents' hotel. 'I was just a youngster at the time, I was 24 or so and me and José Miguel started to have discussions,' Unzué says about how Echavarri began to form a greater part of the team. 'It was the typical situation where you start to want to see if you can make a dream turn into something more real.'

'He wasn't a friend at the time but José Miguel was always very passionate about the project and could see how we'd been growing as a team. And with the support of the people from the club from Irurzun, we started to see how he could work with it, and direct, too. At the same time, the director of the INASA company [Juan García Barberena], the factory which produced the Reynolds aluminium in Irurzun, was very enthusiastic about it all.'

Rondán's performances instantly placed the Reynolds squad on another level. The South American won races of the calibre of the top-ranked Vuelta a Valladolid, seeing off another top squad, Moliner, containing no less a figure than Pedro Delgado and run by one of Spain's best known sports directors, Javier Mínguez. In total Rondán took 21 races in two years, hugely boosting the amateur team's status. He later earned a footnote in cycling's history books when he became the first ever rider from Uruguay to take part in the Vuelta a España.

Echavarri's arrival all but coincided with both Unzué's return to the squad after his spell as Navarran team coach, and with the announcement that Reynolds, having got as high as they could in the world of amateurs, would start a professional squad in 1980. The bulk of the pro team, in keeping with the duo's liking for building on foundations they had created themselves, was to be taken from the amateur ranks. A deal with Pinarello, signed in 1979 after Echavarri and his wife had driven over to Italy in search of top-range bikes – 'although you'll have to pay 50 per cent of the sale price,' he warned his riders – was shelved for two seasons, but then reinstated in 1982 until 2013, in what proved to be one of the longest-standing agreements between bike manufacturers and teams in the history of the sport.

Echavarri had sealed the deal with Reynolds thanks in part to his acquaintance with Barberena, previously the town hall clerk in Abarzuza, where Echavarri's family lived. The squad's initial budget was small, just 15 million pesetas. 'If I gave them any less,' Barberena once joked, 'they'd end up hitchhiking to races.' For all that, much was made in the local press of how Reynolds were the successors, chronologically speaking if not in size, to Navarra's biggest ever pro team, SuperSer, which had folded in dramatic style in 1976.

To begin with, Reynolds were a long way off from SuperSer's star-studded line-up, massive team bus and top-of-the-range equipment. However, they had equally strong local roots and quickly showed they were no fly-by-night operation. Reynolds was the first ever team in Spain to ensure their riders were registered employees with the Spanish social security system – even if their application was initially turned down and it took three years of court battles for Unzué and Echavarri to get their riders recognised as workers.

Starting their first training camp on 25 December – 'we'll let them have New Year with the family' – was another sign of the project's seriousness, as was contracting a team trainer, José Luis Pascua Piqueras and a team doctor, the first in a Spanish team, a couple of years later. Echavarri's decision to exploit the side of the team's *maillots* and put extra publicity on them, making them the first team in cycling history to do so, was another sign of their willingness to break a few moulds. From 1982, they got the SuperSer bus back, with none other than Jesús Legarra – the former amateur director – at the wheel.

In 1980, though, all that was to come. 'Reynolds was a tiny team,' recollects Dominique Arnaud, one of the Reynolds riders that year and again from 1986. 'Just twelve riders, ten neos and two pros, Ángel López del Alamo and Anastacio Graciano, who didn't have that big a motor but he was a veteran, very good at his job and who really helped shape my career. We were the smallest team in Spain, but Echavarri got us into some of the biggest races right from the start. We began with a training camp in Mallorca and from there on we went to the Vuelta a Valencia, Tirreno-Adriatico, Milano–Sanremo.'

'It was small but it was never *bordelique* [chaotic]. They did as well as they could with very limited means. But they were scared of doing the Tour, they had too much respect for it. Finally when they went in 1983, they had a huge inferiority complex. But little by little, they improved. At the end of the day, like everybody else, they had two legs and a bike.'

'It was something that happened a lot in that era,' Pedro Delgado, who joined the team in 1983, observes. 'If you look at the number of Spanish professional teams, it goes from two or three in 1980 up to seven, eight, or nine by 1983 or 1984. Most of them were amateur squads with a long history in that sector, like

Reynolds, who suddenly got given a bit of extra money and hit the big time, in that they found themselves in a position to race the Vuelta a España. The problem was that with this sudden proliferation of teams cycling got a lot more expensive too, and some of these new professional teams found that they couldn't afford their riders' wages so had to fold and disappear.'

What made Reynolds stand out from the rest of the multiple professional rookies' squads, though, was not just that economically Unzué and Echavarri made the team as secure as possible. In addition, rather than fold when the professional Reynolds team began, the amateur team was maintained and even improved as a result. 'When the professional team began, we were all part of the same overall structure, we had the same equipment,' Jaimerena, who raced with Indurain for one year in the Reynolds amateur squad in 1984 before taking over from Unzué as director in 1986, recalls. 'Only the jersey was slightly different.'

'In terms of infrastructure, the two squads, professional and amateur, were very united,' Eduardo González Salvador adds. 'I can remember going to the professional training camp in Font Romeu [in the Pyrenees] that January, for example, and spending a week there with them. Training camps weren't that normal at that time, and we'd mix skiing on some days with training on our bikes on others.' His brother Juan Carlos, also in the same team for three years, puts it very simply. 'We felt like we were professionals, racing in the amateur leagues.'

Staff also alternated between the two squads, and the amateurs usually went to races with a support level which was close to that of the professionals – two *soigneurs*, two mechanics and a director. Riders were, unusually, paid a wage. Indurain received 10,000 pesetas (60 euros) a month, which he used to do up his room in his parents' home, already plastered with posters of Bernard Hinault, whilst Eduardo González Salvador remembers earning roughly 15,000 pesetas a month ('Eusebio was always a tough negotiator, and he only paid me half of what I'd earned in Baqué, my previous team, because I was no longer national champion.')

It reached the point, at times, when the entire Spanish amateur national line-up for a major race would be made up of Reynolds riders. Eduardo González Salvador has one photo of the 'baby Giro', as the amateur version of the Giro d'Italia is called, where the whole Spanish squad, management included, was from Reynolds. The only thing indicating they were racing for Spain was the red-and-yellow national kit. 'It was a boom time in general for the sport. We'd race in Italy, in France on the other side of the border close to Navarre. Basically we were able to fight for the win in almost any part of the country,' adds Jaimerena.

'The Reynolds amateur squad was really well organised,' adds Eduardo González Salvador. 'Eusebio always made sure everybody knew which job they had to do, too, and the team was well disciplined. Eusebio could read races extremely well, even if he did put his foot in it from time to time.' Indeed, José Legarra, the first amateur team director in the early 1970s, recalls Unzué, then a seventeen-year-old amateur, taking the almost unheard-of step of dropping back to the support car during a race to give his boss his reading of how he thought it would play out.

The consequence for Indurain of signing for such a well-structured, solidly organised team with such strong roots in his home region was that his progression into the world of amateur racing was both painless and almost instantly beneficial. That he needed far bigger targets than he could find in junior racing was obvious. But at the same time there were none of the external issues that could well have arisen had Indurain been forced to leave home in order to pursue his career. With Reynolds he had the best of both worlds.

Indurain was, says Eduardo González Salvador, 'a little bit spoiled in comparison to the rest of us. It was logical: he was from Navarre, the team was from Navarre and Unzué had "discovered" him. Unzué has always had a soft spot for local riders, too, whether it's Indurain or somebody else.' This regional favouritism was hardly surprising – it was said at the time that in a top Basque team, Baqué, Julián Gorospe, as the local star, was given an easier time than the rest. But Indurain himself was no prima donna. Eduardo González Salvador does not recollect him ever demanding special treatment: 'He had a few kilos he needed to lose and when you were an amateur, they'd always tell you you could lose some weight. Indurain was another one who got told that. He was one more face in the crowd.' Echavarri told *Cycle Sport* in 1995 that he was 'impressed by his stature and build. I knew he'd been winning a lot of races in the area – everybody in Navarre did – but I was really taken by the fact that here was a Spaniard who was more like a Belgian or Dutch *rouleur'* – a solidly built racer whose strengths are best exploited on flatter stages and short, punchy climbs – 'than your classic climber.'

Whilst Reynolds' professional team were finding their feet in the early 1980s, the amateur squad was already one of Spain's top four outfits of the time together with Orbea, which also had a professional team, and CajaMadrid. There was also a fast-growing Basque team, Baqué, who had forced their way into the hierarchy of better established amateur teams in 1981 when, headed by Julián Gorospe, its riders took all three top spots in Spain's biggest one-day race, the Memorial Valenciaga.

Reynolds, though, had one key advantage when it came to the squad's longer-term development. Whilst various teams were fighting for different riders in the better-established Basque Country cycling world, Reynolds, as the only top-level home side could benefit the most from Navarre's rapidly growing new racing scene. Unsurprisingly, the strength of the squad and its crop of top local riders netted Reynolds the highest number of victories in Spain for any amateur team in 1983. Yet Unzué is insistent that Indurain stood out, even amongst a very talented squad, as exceptional. He even says, 'What impressed me the most about Indurain was not so much what he did later, but as an amateur.'

'He was a great observer, always almost in silence, because he's never been a great communicator, but no matter how obscure the corner of the world we might be in, he'd remember what it was like. That hugely intelligent approach to things – that's how he grew up, that's how he was and that's how he is now ... Everybody could see how good he was from the day he won his first Tour, but in fact he was doing brilliantly from the moment he turned amateur. In that era, that a rider who was 1.86 metres tall and who weighed in at nearly 90 kilos could become what he became was all but inconceivable.' One of the more scurrilous rumours about Indurain as an amateur is that whenever the race hit a hill, the cry would go up in the peloton: 'Here comes Miguel'. But not because he was on the attack; rather it would be a warning that a hefty lump of Navarre-born bike rider was struggling on the ascent.

'When you saw the strength he had, the details,' Unzué says, 'that made you think he was able to do anything. You could see that something indefinable, but something very great, was there. It was clear from the start that he was a great time triallist, but his physique made that something to be expected. I remember the way he raced in the Vuelta a Toledo on one stage, the way he handled the echelons in a Tour de l'Avenir [Tour of the CEE – as was]. You had to be there to appreciate it. At the same time, he was a rider that only improved slowly on the physical front. Until he toughened up, his bones, his chassis, if you like – the wrists, the knees – were not able to handle the power his motor was able to produce. So it took time. But he was always brilliant at reading a race. When a break came down to three or four guys, I'd tell him "Hey, keep an eye on that rider" and he'd answer, "No it's that one we've got to watch." And you'd say to yourself, "Fuck, he's right, how on earth did he know that?"'

At the same time, Indurain's loyalty to his family and to his roots never faltered: 'I remember taking him home to his house in Villava when he was eighteen, we'd drop him off and normally he would take hold of his grandfather's jacket, put it on, go through to the living room and just stay there. Anybody else, Pruden or whoever, would go off after the race to look for his friends. Not Miguel. He'd stay put, there in the living room with that jacket on.'

As teenagers, the two brothers were beginning to ride together regularly. 'We'd go out for long, long training rides … up to ten hours. All the way to the Pyrenees, it's only two hours away from here,' recalls Pruden. 'There were no pulsometers, no mobiles, no trainers, nothing like that at all, it was all on feelings, feelings, feelings. Sometimes you'd go out with the idea of doing two hours and do six, and sometimes you'd gone out to do six hours training and you'd do two. It was another era. We'd just go out, ride our bikes and then we'd come back.'

'We weren't going slowly: in fact, we'd barely talk, we'd be going so fast. But there'd just be the two of us. We'd both take a good long while sorting out the bikes, cleaning them up, getting them ready. We were both very meticulous.' Whilst cycling books and magazines did not abound on the shelves, he confirms that the two of them were both 'Bernard Hinault fans. Sometimes we'd go off to see the Tour, with our parents and cousins, sometimes on the Tourmalet.'

But even if there was less and less time for family outings when they turned professional, their unplanned training rides continued, with just the two of them riding their bikes through Navarre right the way through Indurain's career. They would always start the next year's training, Prudencio recalls, too, on exactly the same day – 1 December, come rain or shine.

Indurain's first big breakthrough and indeed his first 1983 win for Reynolds came when he captured the Navarran amateur championship in late May. As Barruso recalls, 'He was driven to the race by his dad in the same Seat 1,500 we'd used to get to Barcelona.' But if Indurain's mode of transport to the championships was an unintentional nod to his recent past, his victory was a clear sign of what to expect in the future. At the end of the championships, Indurain outsprinted three former breakaways, including the arch-rival of his teenage years, Javier Luquin. 'He beat me in the last metre. I thought I was going to win and he came past me like he was riding a motorbike,' Luquin later told the *Diario de Navarra*. 'Whenever he wanted to, he'd beat us. It wasn't a surprise that he stood out so much later on. After that, you could see it coming.'

Indurain expressed the hope that he would then be able to take a stage win or two in the upcoming Vuelta a Navarra. As the biggest local race on the calendar, no event mattered more to the amateur squad: as Eduardo González Salvador put it, 'For Eusebio, the Vuelta a Navarra was like the Tour de France.' However, Unzué's decision was to exclude Indurain because of his academic commitments. If Indurain was disappointed, he showed he knew how to bounce back at the Spanish Nationals.

Riding so well in the blazing heat in inland Alicante was an indication of Indurain's future ability to handle extremely high temperatures. But what truly stood out was his ability to read a race well, even given his relative inexperience in a category, as a first year, where many riders would spend up to three or four seasons. There was no stopping Indurain from getting on the right wheel, following Orbea's Jokin Múgica as the Basque broke away, then beating him comfortably in the final sprint. 'The youngest ever amateur national champion there's been,' recalls Unzué proudly. 'Spectacular. Something I'll never forget. We were seeing things about Miguel in that first year that made it very clear that he was going to be a really big name.'

'It was a really hard race, a tough little circuit in the mountains of Alicante,' Eduardo González Salvador, who raced that day, recalls. 'It was the first big warning to everybody about what he could do, particularly because of the way he'd won. Before that he'd just been some big young kid from Navarre, who was a bit hesitant, a bit scared, because he'd just come up from the previous category.'

'They spelled his name wrong in at least one national daily, *Indurian* not *Indurain*,' observes Pepe Barruso, who still recollects – and appreciates – the phone call he received from Unzué to 'tell me Indurain had won it.' The race radio commentator, too, gave out the incorrect name for the winner, as one Fernando Pacheco, which underlined the surprising nature of Indurain's victory.

The results in the second half of the season were patchier, with an unremarkable performance at the World Championships complemented by a stage win in the Vuelta a Toledo in August – organised by none other than Federico Martín Bahamontes, Spain's first ever Tour de France winner – and an outright victory in another top event, the Vuelta a Salamanca in September. But that unevenness was only logical, given that Indurain was finding his feet in the category, albeit in some races much more quickly than in others.

Yet there were already strong indications that Indurain's directors did not believe it would be long before he shifted up the final, definitive rung in rider categories and turned pro. In January 1984, as Eduardo Gonzàlez Salvador had done in 1983, Indurain attended the Reynolds professional team pre-season training camp before linking up with the Spanish national amateur team for their equivalent camp, with a focus on the Olympics.

The Vuelta a Navarra was, understandably, the centre of the amateur team's summer again, and on this occasion, there was no question about Indurain's selection. Apart from taking two stages himself and the King of the Mountains prize, Indurain's teammate, the late Alvaro Fernández, took the overall, with Indurain in second. Stages in the Vuelta a Toledo, the Vuelta a Vizcaya and victories in a string of one-day races made it clear that it was only a matter of time before Indurain turned professional: the only question was when.

'He was always a good racer, won a lot of stuff, but being a pro wasn't something we'd really expected,' recalls Prudencio Indurain. 'He never really said "I want to be a pro", partly because in that time in Navarre there were only a very few pros round here. So it wasn't an objective, and nor was standing out as an amateur. We just wanted to have fun on the bike.' Their lack of long-term planning was such that they had not, Pruden says, 'heard much about the pro team, just the amateur team that signed him. That was where we started to have a relationship with Reynolds.'

Abroad, Indurain was not so successful, with an unremarkable performance in the Peace Race that May. Indurain's participation in the 1984 Olympic Games did not work out so well, either. In a whistle-stop six-day trip to the far side of the USA, the four-rider Spanish amateur squad arrived far too late to adapt to the time differences. The photos of the riders in Los Angeles show them all looking bleary-eyed and Indurain abandoned the road race. 'We only got to see the word Hollywood on a signboard in the distance, a long way away,' Indurain later recalled. Only one Spanish rider, the future national coach and Vuelta a España course designer Paco Antequera, managed to complete the course, in 13th place. Indurain and the other two riders abandoned with two laps left to go: 'I would have finished an hour down. It wasn't worth it,' Indurain later explained.

If Indurain's Olympic participation was not a particularly satisfactory way of bringing down the curtain on his amateur career, Reynolds remained more than keen to bring Indurain into their professional team, even before the end of the season. But before he switched, Indurain did have one last opportunity to pay unintentional homage to one key component of his amateur squad. Just a few days before he took part in his first professional race, the Tour of the CEE/de l'Avenir, Indurain took part in the amateur event in Zegama during the village's annual festivities for its patron saint, St. Bartholomew, placing second. Twenty-one years later, Indurain would be back again, with his former team-mates from the amateur squad, remembering Zegama's key place in their past.

CHAPTER 3
Le Tour de la CEE

After turning professional for Reynolds in September 1984, the first two and a half years of Miguel Indurain's career are bookended by his success in one race: the Tour de l'Avenir, at that time briefly renamed as the Tour de la CEE. For whilst 1984 saw Indurain take his first professional win in the ten-day stage race, 1986 saw him win it outright. The Tour de l'Avenir was Indurain's first major international victory, the one which confirmed his amateur success could be matched at professional level, and which Indurain later recalled as his favourite race win too – even more than the Tour de France.

Then as now, on paper the Tour de l'Avenir has – as its longer-standing name suggests – a specific role: to act as a show-case for promising top-level amateurs and young, up-and-coming professionals. It is currently open to riders aged 19 to 22 and raced in national teams in France. But in its 55-year-old history, the criteria for participation and its geographical location have fluctuated wildly.

Originally designed by organisers *L'Équipe* as a mini-Tour de France, up until 1967 it was initially run on an identical route over the second half of each actual Tour stage but two hours ahead of the main event. Then, having moved to a September slot in 1968, the race still used many of the Tour's usual climbs. But for six years, from 1986 to 1991, the l'Avenir changed its name to the Tour de la CEE and massively broadened out its geographical limits to become an EEC-wide event. Parallelling, perhaps intentionally, the well-established amateur-only Peace Race in the Eastern Bloc nations, stages were held across Western Europe from Portugal and Belgium to Austria and Italy. All of this makes Indurain's progression, from a single stage win in 1984 to two in 1985 and then the overall in 1986 – his last Tour de l'Avenir but the first under these new, much tougher, geographical conditions – even more impressive.

From 1981, too, the amateurs-only regulation disappeared and for the next three decades, trade teams could take part and the age restriction was briefly dropped as well. The consequences for Indurain were mixed: on the plus side all of his three participations were with Reynolds; on the downside, he was fighting against a dauntingly varied mixture of national and trade teams and riders, ranging from hugely experienced East European pros to greenhorns like himself.

It's true, even now, that only five Tour de France winners – Indurain, Felice Gimondi, Laurent Fignon, Joop Zoetemelk and Greg LeMond – have won the Tour de l'Avenir. But that one of them, Fignon, won it in 1988 four years after taking the Tour de France for a second time, suggests just how difficult the l'Avenir was. Indeed the host of major names that makes up its stage winners and final podiums is an indication both of its toughness – only one rider, Russian Serguei Soukhouroutchenkov, has won it twice – and its usefulness as a reference point for future greatness in the sport. This was perhaps never so true as in the 1980s, when during its short-lived spell as the Tour de la CEE, the young guns of Indurain's era were taking on a much more challenging range of opposition over more varied terrain than ever before.

When Indurain joined the Reynolds professional squad at the end of the 1984 season, his success in the Tour de la CEE parallelled a new, and very recent, upsurge in Spanish cycling across the board, much of it to do with his team. As Pedro Delgado puts it, ever since the decline of Luis Ocaña began in 1974, 'Spanish cycling, on an international level, didn't exist.' By the early 1980s, things had reached such a low point that, 'In modern-day terms, us going to the Tour de France would be the same as if a really small Portuguese team suddenly found itself in the WorldTour. There were years when nobody wanted to go to the Tour. Since the era of Ocaña, everybody had ended up abandoning.'

Dominique Arnaud, who turned pro in 1980 with Reynolds and was later to be one of the most important figures in the team, recalls that 'In my first years as a pro, when the Spanish teams came to France, they were very scared. For example,' he says, citing the case of one middle-ranking Spanish rider of the era, 'Jesús Blanco Villar was a very good racer in Spain but in France, it didn't work out for him. I didn't see why that had to happen.'

Echavarri, however, was determined that this inferiority complex about racing the Tour had to end. 'If we hadn't gone, then nobody would have done,' says Delgado. 'It was Echavarri who went to find [Tour boss Félix Lévitan] and said, "Hey, there should be a Spanish team in your Tour."'

Echavarri and Unzué struck paydirt beyond their wildest dreams on their first ever Tour. In fact, Reynolds suddenly went from being the token Spanish squad to being the team that, to judge by results at least, had come closest to challenging winner Laurent Fignon. There had been a kind of precedent: in the 1983 Vuelta, Julián

Gorospe had offered a spirited, if ultimately futile, resistance against five-time Tour winner Bernard Hinault. But for Reynolds to do so well in the Tour de France represented a considerable raising of the bar. The team returned to Spain with a first and second for Arroyo and Delgado in the time trial at the Puy de Dôme, four further runners-up spots on stages, and last but by no means least, a Tour de France podium finish in second place for Arroyo. In the process, Reynolds confirmed that the ten-year Spanish drought on Tour success was at a definitive end.

As Delgado sees it, all that held Reynolds back in that year's Tour was their almost complete lack of experience. 'I always said the problem we had with our first ever Tour de France, in 1983, was that we went there to see what happened and to finish the race. As the race progressed we should have adapted. Instead, it was "Oof, look what we've done, it can't get any better than this." We were running scared.'

'The whole team was learning, the same as us. And we'd gone from being nobody to being real protagonists on the Tour.' As a way of indicating how Reynolds were walking a tightrope between disaster and success, Delgado points out that 'On the same day that I turned in a really strong ride in the Pyrenees, three of our riders abandoned.'

The most outstanding example of how Reynolds were doing it all by trial and error, though, was surely their purchase of hospital patients' food in a mushy, baby-food-like format, which Reynolds bought for their riders to eat on the Tour with the theory that it'd be more easily digestible: 'The team bus had a fridge, but it only had space for two bottles of water, not for all those bottles. It was very hot, the food spent over a month in the bus but not in the fridge ...' Riders consequently fell severely ill with food poisoning and as Delgado jokingly puts it, 'it was pretty weird that none of us died!'

'My riders had talent and were able to take on riders at an international level,' Echavarri claimed. 'It wasn't as straightforward as all that, France was not an important market for Reynolds, but they felt the sporting interest of the Tour should take precedence over everything. Those that claimed to understand cycling laughed at us and said our presence was an insult to the Tour. Those who did not wish to recognise Arroyo's talent were forced to do so on the Puy de Dôme and when he stood on the podium in Paris.'

Delgado points to one hugely beneficial long-lasting effect for Reynolds of racing the Tour in such an adventurous way: 'Riding on instinct and with zero experience brought us together as a squad. It really united us. The other teams at that time were always very envious of how well we got on in Reynolds.' That close-knit feel to Reynolds was something Indurain would particularly appreciate. 'You go to Italy and the *soigneurs* switch teams every year, but Reynolds commanded a huge degree of loyalty from its staff,' says one rival Spanish director. 'They were always something of an old-fashioned squad, but if there was one thing I could have taken from Reynolds, it was that.'

Delgado and Arroyo's Tour success created the start of a huge spike in media interest in cycling which – after later events caused this interest to increase radically – reached the point where television stations like Antena 3 would organise Vuelta 'launches' across Spain to show the public just how many vehicles and journalists they were taking to the race. (When one reporter from a rival media outlet, Cadena Ser, was informed that Antena 3 had their own helicopter to film the event, the journalist responded, 'Huh, so what? We've got a plane!')

But what was really vital for Indurain's objectives in the years to come was that thanks to Arroyo and Delgado, the Tour had begun to feature once more on Spain's sporting radar. It no longer felt as if the Tour was an area where the Spaniards would automatically lose.

In 1982, Reynolds had already hit the jackpot on a national level, taking the Vuelta al País Vasco with José Luis Laguía. The team also won the Vuelta a España thanks to Ángel Arroyo (later to be stripped of his title because of a positive dope test) as well as five stages and the King of the Mountains prize. 'Teams like Zor and Teka were better, on a man-to-man level,' Eduardo González Salvador says, 'but then each year Reynolds was getting a bigger slice of the cake.'

But behind the scenes, as Delgado says, Reynolds were still far from organised. 'The team logistics?' he says rhetorically, as if such a concept was inconceivable. 'I knew what I was going to race, but there were riders who would get called up on the last day, and told to go and get their bike and suitcase to go to, I don't know, somewhere like Murcia. There was even a theory, which I didn't believe, that they [the management] operated like that so that nobody had any idea where or when they were going to race, they'd be kept on their toes and stay race-fit the whole time.' It was only when Delgado raced for PDM in Holland that he discovered, to his surprise, that there were teams 'where everybody, not just the leaders, knew at least a couple of weeks before what was happening.'

In Spain, team operations were far more hand-to-mouth – although in a way, that only makes their achievements all the more impressive. 'José Miguel was more of the man for the logistics,' Eduardo González Salvador confirms. 'There was an accountant, probably. Either way, that was it.' Possibly one of the few differences was that Reynolds had a French assistant, Francis Lafargue, who came on board in 1983, which reflected how seriously the team took the challenge of making it to the Tour de France. 'José

Miguel spoke French more or less, I spoke a bit, maybe one other rider spoke a couple of words,' says Delgado 'but you needed somebody French in case there was a problem or when you needed to delegate. If you're a director you can't be everywhere – dealing with team meetings, bikes, going to the supermarket to buy food, looking after riders. Francis was like our guide in France.'

Apart from Lafargue, whilst the team had the standard 'two *soigneurs*, two mechanics, a director for the races,' the signs that it was well-off, such as being one of just two Spanish squads at the time with a team bus, were there, too. The wages were also very good. 'In 1984, I earned 90,000 pesetas a month,' says Eduardo González Salvador, 'which was quite a bit of money, and 150,000 pesetas in the second year, which was really big money, and almost more than what riders in that position would be earning now. They were, I think, the only team in Spain that would sign their amateurs up on two-year contracts. They had a really good reputation in the peloton.'

'It was a very small-scale team, but despite that they were organised,' Manu Arrieta, the team *soigneur* from 1982 to 2003, adds. 'This is why they got better and better riders signing for them. As for the staff, we were treated very well.' Reynolds was a hugely popular squad, too: 'We'd get to the hotels in the Vuelta in 1984 and there would be so many people wanting to greet us, we couldn't get through the doors,' says Eduardo González Salvador. 'They'd rip my race number off my back! Now you go to a hotel and there is barely anybody at all. The level of expectation was much higher. Things had a much greater impact in terms of the media.' In Pamplona too, Reynolds was treated 'as the home side', a kind of national team for Navarre in everything but name. 'But they were very popular in the Basque Country too, because they had so many Basque riders.'

'Echavarri was the linchpin. At the time, it was all very like talking to a priest, very mystical,' Delgado recalls. 'Javier Mínguez was the big name director of the era in Spain, and he was always yelling and shouting at the riders, "Ride for your mother, for your country, for your *cojones* [balls!]" José Miguel was the opposite end of the spectrum. He'd be contemplative, gently admonishing, he'd say gently, "You've made a mistake there." He'd never give you a bollocking.' Not that Echavarri could be taken for a ride himself: 'He wasn't a director who let you get away with things, he was very intelligent. You could con him once, but never twice or three times. José Miguel knew everything that was going on. He was really on top of things.'

In an interview I did for *Cycle Sport* magazine in the 1990s, Josu Garai, then a top cycling journalist with the sports daily *MARCA*, told me 'Echavarri is always two stages ahead of everybody. Always.' Echavarri always made a point of getting up early to read all the sports press, he said, 'so that by the time other people start dragging themselves out of bed, he's already read the news and is planning his next move ... he adores taking apart [team] rivals, not just their form but their psychology as well. It's a kind of hobby for him to find out exactly what they're like.'

At the same time, Echavarri's dislike of bellowing orders at his riders and his treating them more like his equals helped create an unusually close-knit team. As José Luis Laguía pointed out in an interview with *Diario de Navarra*, 'in its earliest format, Reynolds was barely professional. What was most important was our friendship with José Miguel Echavarri. We'd have our base for the professional squad in his *hostal* in Campanas and that was my second home. There were times when he'd give me the post-race massage himself because all the *soigneurs* had left already. [But] Miguel wasn't there at the time when cycling had that kind of romantic edge to it, rather he came to the team when it was more modern. Riders like myself, Delgado, Arroyo and Gorospe kept the Reynolds name in the thick of the action whilst that wasn't yet his responsibility.'

Reynolds, though, did not have an unlimited budget and were unable to stop Delgado and Arroyo quitting at the end of the 1984 season. With Gorospe seemingly so inconsistent he was labelled with the somewhat sarcastic term of an *eterna promesa* [always promising much but fulfilling little] by the Spanish press – Echavarri and Unzué had started to look for new riders with potential. Signing Indurain, given the brilliance of his one and a half years as an amateur, combined with his Navarran roots and his clear chances of progressing, made all the sense in the world – to the point where they did not even wait until the following season to bring him into the professional squad.

'He was very young, but I was advised to let him turn pro,' Unzué would later say. 'He had won everything that could be won as an amateur.' By September, Indurain had signed for what he later recollected 'as probably a little less than one million pesetas a year. But the money wasn't the most important factor for me, I value other things more.'

Whilst Arrieta's first recollections of Indurain, from a staff point of view, are 'somebody really quiet and serious, not the type to tell jokes,' Laguía's earliest memories of Indurain are of a gentle giant, as he told the *Diario de Navarra*, 'A rider who physically was very striking and who was able to perform really well on the bike. I remember when he attacked, his rivals would claim they hadn't seen him go past them because nobody wanted to have to chase him down.'

'When I was one of the team's veterans, his father asked me if Miguel would be good in the future. I told him Miguel was an outstanding apprentice, someone off the scale. I remember in the physiognomy tests he did in the laboratories of the Clínica Universitaria hospital in Navarre, he broke the machine because of his strength. I had to wait for another two days for it to be repaired before I could be tested on it.'

As a bike handler Indurain could not be faulted, either. His seeming invulnerability when it came to falls and crashes would later become legendary, although one team-mate from his early days, who requested anonymity, does recollect a race where – something unheard of in later years – Indurain actually crashed twice: 'In a Vuelta a Murcia, he managed to come off twice in one day. The first time, he rode off the road and although he didn't fall, he had to put his foot down on the ground. The second time he rode into the back of a commissaire's car. And he was extremely unhappy with me, because he said it was my fault, for not letting him sleep because I was larking about in the hotel room!'

Laguía had one criticism of the early Indurain: a lack of the driving ambition that did not really begin to appear until the 1990 Tour. But as he points out, it was up to the Reynolds directors to foster that ambition – and up to the team to make Indurain aware of just how far he could go. Indurain's qualities, for the team, were partly his excellent time trialling on flatter courses and his strong sprint in small breaks. Indeed, his talent for stage racing did not – as it would do later – overshadow his one-day racing ability and Echavarri predicted him a great future in the Classics, not multi-day events. There was no doubt that Reynolds had a major gap to fill there: things even got so bad in 1986 that the team was not selected either for Milano–Sanremo, the opening Monument of the year, or for the key warm-up race run by the same organisers, Tirreno-Adriatico, or for any of the Ardennes Classics, because of their lack of one-day racers.

It was possible that Indurain might well just fill that gap. After all, aged just twenty, he had scored his first professional win in the Tour de l'Avenir/CEE, in a time trial against a future team-mate in four of his five Tour wins, France's Jean-François Bernard. Indurain had also been a lynchpin in an utterly unexpected team time trial victory for Reynolds in the same event, which saw his team-mate Carlos Hernández take the overall lead. (Hernández later crashed out, with Charly Mottet taking the final win.) But where Unzué recalls he was most impressed was how a rider who was so heavily built had handled some of the biggest climbs in Europe. I realised, then and there, that with patience we had a great rider in our ranks.'

Much has been made of the wisdom of Unzué and Echavarri's decision to give Indurain a chance to participate in a Grand Tour at the first possible moment – aged just twenty, in the Vuelta a España in April 1985. (The Vuelta changed to its current late-summer slot in 1996.) Indurain seized his opportunity with both hands, heading the overall classification of the Vuelta for four days in the first week, a feat that made him the youngest rider ever to lead the race. Yet giving Indurain a spot in the Vuelta was no calculated gamble on the management's part. Rather, as Eduardo González Salvador recalls, Indurain was only able to take part because González Salvador had fallen sick with bronchitis at Tirreno-Adriatico and Reynolds needed a replacement.

Not everybody was convinced that Indurain would naturally rise to the occasion. According to Eduardo González Salvador, Vicente Belda, later to earn a reputation as a top director and 'discoverer' of riders with the Spanish team Kelme, 'was still racing and he chewed my head off ... saying "How is it possible that you are not going to the Vuelta when you can climb so much better than that great lump of a rider?" Miguel was very heavy at the time, and all we knew was that he was a brilliant time triallist. There was clearly a lot of polishing to do.'

The latest reminder of Indurain's talent for time trialling had come in the opening stage race of the season, the 1985 Ruta del Sol. Second in the opening prologue, second in the final time trial, and third in a long breakaway through the sierras of Córdoba gave Indurain the runner-up spot overall behind Germany's Rolf Golz, auguring well for such an inexperienced young racer. So, too, did his performance in the Tour du Midi-Pyrénées, where Indurain placed second in the opening prologue, just one second slower than double Tour de France champion Laurent Fignon.

That time trialling capacity was all Indurain needed to pole-vault himself into a top position overall in the Vuelta a España. In a short, flat prologue on broad, well-surfaced avenues in the northern city of Valladolid, Indurain punched well above his weight with a second place behind Holland's Bert Oosterbosch, one of the top prologue specialists of the era. Indurain's time on a technical course with two segments of *pavé* and many corners was also three seconds faster than Julián Gorospe, the Reynolds leader for the Vuelta a España. 'It is a second place that tastes of victory, given that he is new to the category,' observed *El Mundo Deportivo*.

(Indurain was not the only newcomer in the Vuelta a España that year, which was witness to the only time a Soviet amateur team somehow wangled its way into the line-up of a Grand Tour – and fulfilled all the clichés about dour, cagey East Europeans in the process. Interviewed before the race, the Soviets' director refused to reveal who their best sprinters and climbers were, saying, 'that's a secret'.)

On stage two, at 266 kilometres the longest of the course, the peloton were witness to what, with hindsight, proved to be a historic moment: Indurain, despite being injured in a crash the previous day, moved to the top of the overall classification of a Grand Tour for the first time. On this occasion it was more a process of elimination than shining in his own right. Race leader Oosterbosch could not handle even the smallest climbs, in this case three third category ascents, and, as the Colombians upped the pace dramatically in a bid to shake up the overall classification, and then Reynolds took over, the Dutchman lost over twenty minutes by the finish in Ourense.

With Oosterbosch out of the running, Indurain, despite his injuries, moved into the lead. To make a good day for Reynolds an even better one, Gorospe moved up to second and José Luis Laguía took over in his talisman classification, the King of the Mountains. The only thing missing for Reynolds was a victory in the day's bunch sprint, which went to Sean Kelly after Laguía was foiled in a late attack on a short climb into Ourense city centre.

Echavarri argued afterwards that Oosterbosch had opted to throw in the towel more quickly than others who knew they would have had a real chance of retaining the yellow. But Indurain was more upbeat. Apart from saying that his crash had caused him to suffer more than usual, particularly when combined with 'far more kilometres than I am used to,' Indurain described himself as deeply satisfied, if aware that he would not be able to hold the jersey into the mountains. He had suffered badly on the final climb into the Galician city and thought he, too, would be dropped. As it was, he made it into the lead.

Indurain held onto the jersey for three more days as the race wound its way through the *mesetas* of northern Spain and through Galicia towards the first real challenge of the Vuelta: stage six's ascent to the dauntingly steep Lagos de Covadonga climb. As Indurain had predicted, he was unable to stay with the out-and-out climbers, but for a neo-pro, holding onto the lead for such a lengthy spell was already a considerable achievement.

What the 1985 Vuelta showed the cycling world and Indurain in the long term was both a clear sign that he had the talent to make it to the very top of the leader board, and also that his climbing was by no means strong enough to keep him there. After Covadonga, where he dropped to 56th overall, Indurain hoped to return to the top spots overall in a time trial in Alcalá de Henares the final week, even though he warned that as a young pro 'the ideal distance for me is 30 kilometres and that one is 42 kilometres long.' (Much later in his career, Indurain was at his strongest at more than double the distance). However, Indurain did not manage to make any impact in the Alcalá de Henares time trial, although he achieved a respectable eleventh place overall. As he had predicted, the distance was too great for him to handle.

Two trademark tendencies regarding both his race programme and the media were noticeable in Indurain's first major brush with the limelight. First of all, when asked if he was going to take part in some top time trials such as the Trofeo Baracchi or the GP Nations, Indurain's answer was that the team, not he, would decide his race programme: in other words, he was letting somebody else make the decisions. Secondly, there was Indurain's use of the first person plural, rather than the singular, to answer questions, something much commented on by the Spanish press as unusual at the time. In a pre-PR era, what would now be taken as a way of deflecting responsibility and giving emphasis to the 'team spirit' was quite possibly simply Indurain's strategy to avoid standing out too much.

Indurain completed the Vuelta a España, his first Grand Tour, albeit in 82nd place. Reynolds were impressed enough with a new facet of Indurain, his ability to handle three-week races well, to select him for the Tour when a gap arose in the initial line-up. As first reserve, Indurain was once more a late call-up, on this occasion because of Gorospe suffering from tendinitis. However, his experience there, racing just four days before abandoning, strongly suggested that throwing a neo-professional into a Grand Tour twice in the same year was once too often.

Whilst Echavarri and Unzué had planned for Indurain to quit on stage eight, illness left him out for the count from the word go. Finishing 100th in the prologue, 172nd on stage one then second last, 177th and nine minutes down on stage two, after a dismal performance in the team time trial, an ill Indurain was forced to quit on stage four after barely an hour's racing. 'I've got a fever of 38.5 degrees and I've got some kind of bronchitis. It's a pity because in the team time trial the course suited me perfectly and I couldn't take a turn on the front in the early part, only at the end,' Indurain reflected.

It would be a mistake to think that Indurain's presence – or absence – went unnoticed. The pre-race edition of the influential French magazine *Vélo* had even argued that Indurain could win the opening prologue in Plumelec. 'Reynolds loses Indurain on the eve of the Roubaix stage' was how one Spanish newspaper opened its report of that day's racing. Either way, after a major high in the Vuelta a España and the relative disappointment of the Tour de France Indurain finally regained some traction in the Tour de l'Avenir, where he repeated his previous year's victory in the time trial, pushing Jean-François Bernard once again into second place, and then took his first road win, too, in a two-up break from Albi to Revel. Together with his lead in the Vuelta, his brace of stages in the race boded very well: 'He's shown we'll have to keep him in mind,' commented Echavarri.

There was another reason for Indurain to look at more distant frontiers for his career: Reynolds' increasingly international line-up.

The 1985–1986 off-season saw Reynolds lose another of their star riders, Eduardo Chozas, but sign a large number of non-Spanish pros, most of them French. Milano–Sanremo winner Marc Gomez was one and won two stages of the 1986 Vuelta – which Reynolds almost did not race after falling out with organisers Unipublic over payments for hotels – as well as leading the race for four days. Another was Stéphane Guay, who rewarded Reynolds' faith in him with victory in the first stage of his first ever professional race, the Vuelta a Andalucía, whilst Franck Pineau, now a director with the Française des Jeux team, was signed as a *stagiaire* in August. Most importantly for Indurain, one of his key future *domestiques*, Dominique Arnaud, returned to Reynolds as road captain after a five-year absence with French teams.

Arnaud says that the team had developed noticeably in his absence, but more in terms of results than infrastructure or finance. 'Reynolds still had a medium-sized budget in 1986, smaller than PDM and La Vie Claire. There was nothing fancy, but we still had everything we needed. Reynolds made me an offer so they could have a more structured squad in the Grand Tours, something I knew about from two perspectives. I'd been with one French team, La Vie Claire, where everything was built around one leader, but also with Wolber, which was much less well-organised.'

Once the Mallorca training camps were completed, Arnaud's relationship with Indurain deepened both personally and professionally, with the Frenchman, as Reynolds' newly incorporated *capitaine de route*, developing Indurain's capabilities as a team worker. 'I taught him a lot of what he knew, he was one of the best *domestiques* I've ever had,' Arnaud recalls. 'Quick to learn, and he'd do whatever he was told.' Indeed, there was even one point where Arnaud says Indurain's strength was such that it all but backfired on him – in his team-mates' eyes at least: 'The first time I came across

Miguel directly was in Mallorca, in the Reynolds training camps, and we'd be doing series work in the training rides. And nobody wanted to train with Miguel because he was so strong naturally, we knew he'd show us up!'

Even before that, whilst he was with Hinault at La Vie Claire, Arnaud knew of, and was wary of, Indurain's strength. 'La Vie Claire once did the Tour des Midi-Pyrénées, as the Route du Sud is now called. And I remember this great big hulk of a rider who went off on a break on one of the early stages, and we didn't see him again. We chased and chased and chased and finally we brought him back, right at the finish. It took us all day to get him. That was Miguel.'

Once the relationship grew closer, Arnaud was impressed for another reason: Indurain's unflappability. 'I met him as a professional and he was twenty-one and he was pretty quiet then, that was just his nature. He was always very calm, even if he did his job *a bloque* [full on]. The word that sums him up for me is that of *tranquilo*. If there were really big problems – *tranquilo*. If they could be solved – *tranquilo*. And if they couldn't – the same. Perpetually.'

Indurain's first overall stage race success came very early in 1986 in an event where time trialling, rather than climbing, was a key factor, and where once again his habit of building strong early-season form was an advantage. In that year's Vuelta a Murcia, a five-day stage race in March in south-east Spain, the most serious climb was a steady, but unchallenging, three-kilometre grind up the Cresta del Gallo. Indurain, in the lead since winning the prologue time trial, was more than able to see off his main challenger, Pello Ruiz Cabestany, and lay the foundations for his first professional stage race win by a handful of seconds.

What arguably represented a greater danger was that the entire event could have disintegrated on the last day. The last stage should have consisted of 30 laps of a city centre circuit followed by a single ascent of the Cresta del Gallo climb. But that plan was jettisoned when the riders began a go-slow protest over safety following a bad crash the day before involving Indurain's team-mate, Marc Gomez.

On the first lap two more crashes saw the peloton grind to a complete, brief halt and not even the temptation of a 20,000-peseta *prime* on each second lap could induce them to move at anything more than a snail's pace. After 20 laps (ten of the original 30 were cut out in order to avoid too much of a delay) when the peloton moved off towards the Cresta del Gallo, race organiser Alfonso Guzman reportedly used the PA system on the winner's podium to inform the public who was to blame. 'They are doing this because I paid them a million pesetas in advance, next year I will have no professionals in the race' and, 'This is an insult to the people of Murcia' were apparently some of the kinder phrases he used. 'If anybody from the peloton had actually heard him, then the race would have been over straight away,' claimed one local newspaper report. As it was, they didn't – and Indurain's first stage race win in Spain was in the bag.

That Spaniards made up nine out of ten of the top places overall and the tenth, Roland Leclerc, also rode for a Spanish team, Orbea, is one indication that Murcia was not a major competition. But even so, for a second-year professional, this represented yet another step in the right direction.

Indurain's strong run of early time trialling success meant he was a firm favourite for the opening stage of the Vuelta a España in April, which started with a 5.5 kilometre prologue on Palma de Mallorca seafront. In the event, Indurain ran third, and his pre-race hopes that the jersey would then fall his way like in 1985 – 'I can hold it all the way to Asturias,' he had predicted – were dashed when team-mate Marc Gomez seized the lead with a long break on stage one. After that, Indurain's duties were that of team worker, although a sixth place in the final time trial on the last day of the race in Jerez de la Frontera was another solid indication that he might have the physique for handling a three-week stage race.

Without any illness to trouble him in the Tour de France, Indurain was more than capable of handling Echavarri's plan that he race up to eleven stages, the race's half-way point, before making a planned abandon. As well as finishing just ten seconds off the pace in the opening prologue – a considerable improvement compared to the sixty-one lost to Bernard Hinault in 1985 – Indurain also made it into two breakaways in three days. Neither of the moves would have any long-term impact on the overall, and in neither case did Indurain realistically have any chance of winning. But for a second-year professional, this was not the point. Rather Indurain's interest was in testing his limits on the hilly and flat terrain of the first week. His battles in the mountains would come later.

In the first test of strength on stage five, Indurain was involved in a two-rider counter-attack behind eventual stage winner Johan Van der Velde. Given that Indurain was shadowed by Eddy Planckaert, a ferociously talented Classics rider, he had little chance of success, and duly finished fourth.

As the Tour crossed Normandy, Indurain's attack in a twelve-rider break on stage seven to Saint-Hilaire-du-Harcouët was a much more serious effort. 'I started the move on a series of little climbs, then a big group led by [stage winner] Ludo Peeters made it across, but to tell the truth I didn't mind, it was easier to get to the finish,' he said afterwards. 'Looking ahead I don't know if it'll be easier or harder to go for the win because I don't know my level yet. What I do know is that Echavarri has given me the green light to go for flat stages in this first week.' Indurain also had carte blanche to race hard in the first week's time trial, a 61-kilometre effort, and finished an equally promising thirteenth.

These performances were all encouraging signs of growth, rather than concrete proof. However, Indurain provided the confirmation of his progress in the Tour of the CEE, which despite all the changes, remained a real showcase race for the up-and-coming generation and a hugely prestigious one: what other event, for example, at this level would have European Commission President Jacques Delors as the guest of honour at its first stage? 'We're here to show a united Europe,' Delors claimed, as the riders prepared to rattle across five kilometres of heavily cobbled streets in central Oporto.

Indurain, as was almost to be expected given his track record throughout the season, won the prologue, although his margin, of over eleven seconds, on the second-placed rider was strikingly large – given that the next twenty riders were all timed within a ten-second band. It was a hugely promising start, but events two days later showed just how difficult controlling a 138-rider peloton with teams of six would be.

On stage two across the flatlands of western Spain, America's Roy Knickman, already a multiple junior US national champion and a team-mate of Bernard Hinault's in La Vie Claire, charged off the front. For all he was shadowed by Indurain's team-mate Enrique Carrera and a large bandage beneath his right knee revealed he was injured, Knickman built up a lead of nearly twelve minutes. By the time he roared past the archways of Salamanca's central avenue, the American was still eight minutes ahead. Overall, Indurain slumped to fifth, with a 7–40 disadvantage. It was a time gap in Knickman's favour that looked more than definitive.

Although Indurain battled hard to get on equal terms – he placed second in one bunch sprint stage, in Vitoria, and led in a chase group behind some breakaways at Valladolid – Knickman initially proved more than his match. For all their prowess in the team time trial of 1985, Reynolds, whilst third in the 26.5 kilometre race against the clock in Valladolid on stage four, only regained twenty-two seconds on La Vie Claire. This minimal advantage was then knocked back by Knickman in Pamplona, when he snatched twenty seconds back on Indurain, in a day of wind and echelons – on home soil, to boot.

Albeit wihout gapping the peloton, a second place in a sprint at Pau in France showed Indurain was far from throwing in the towel, though, and on a stage finishing at Luz Ardiden, the tide began to turn in his favour. On a day of tremendously poor weather and featuring three major Pyrenean climbs, Knickman started to struggle. The American dropped back even before the race had reached the Aubisque and Col du Soulor. On the final ascent of the day, Indurain made one of his grinding, low-gear attacks, first passing Norwegian rival Janus Kuum but in turn getting overtaken by another breakaway challenger, Spain's Laudelino Cubino. Behind, Knickman was receiving some timely support from fellow-American Guido Winterberg, but suffering from a severe stomach upset, was barely able to hold his wheel. Finally, Knickman lost nearly two minutes to Indurain, whose fourth place allowed the Spaniard to soar up the overall rankings to second.

Knickman's advantage of 5–25 on his Spanish rival should have been sufficient, had he recovered. Instead, Indurain delivered a near knock-out blow in the race's only long individual time trial, held at Carpentras on a day of baking heat. The Spaniard had no need for the aero-helmet Knickman used, or even the encouragement yelled at him by Unzué from the following car: on a rolling

27.4 kilometre course, Indurain had two minutes' advantage on the American by the mid-way time check. By the finish, Indurain's advantage for the stage win over his nearest rival Esnault was up to twenty-three seconds, and Knickman, although still in yellow, was now out of the top twenty on the stage. Plainly, he remained in trouble, whilst Indurain, now wearing the green of points competition leader, was at a little more than three minutes overall.

The next stage was a brutally hilly affair over the Mévouillon and L'Espreaux on relentlessly rough roads. Knickman was dropped as soon as the first climb. Waving a team-mate ahead and constantly staring at his handlebars, within an hour's racing he was six minutes back. As Reynolds upped the pace on the front of the pack, after a second hour the gap had yawned to twenty minutes. Taking off his jersey and sweating heavily, the American got into his director's car, defeated. By default but also thanks to his tenacity, all Indurain had to do was complete the stage to take over in yellow.

With a three-minute deficit for Indurain behind Knickmann suddenly switching to a 1–05 advantage over Esnault at the top of the GC classification, the Navarran was nonetheless anything but boastful of his first stage race lead outside Spain. He refused to raise his arms when he donned the jersey and only waved once at the crowd, out of respect for his vanquished American rival.

Nor, despite there only being three stages remaining, was Indurain anywhere near home and dry. On a treacherously short 110-kilometre stage from Gap to Briançon over the Izoard, Indurain began to struggle on the Alpine climb and was dropped by his closest GC pursuer, Esnault. Driving along behind, Indurain managed to limit the gap over the summit and turned in a majestic descent, tackling the downhill curves with an ability that few others of his age could match at the time. When he caught the Frenchman, he shot past as if to show him who was boss. The Spaniard lost six seconds on the final ascent to Briançon's citadel, but with only one very short straightforward Alpine stage remaining before the final descent into Turin, outright victory was looking increasingly probable.

Unzué later argued that on that stage, the Izoard represented the first major mountain challenge of Indurain's career where he had to defend a lead in a top international event on the climbs. The conclusions he came to were, to say the least, vital for Indurain's future. 'We talked to the Colombians,' Unzué once recounted, 'and asked them if Abelardo Rondón would lend Indurain a hand by pacing him on the climb and Indurain was able to limit the gaps on his top rivals. That was the day that I realised that at some point in the future, he would be able to battle for a Tour de France. We already knew he had it in him to do OK on the very hilly stages, but the Izoard – that was another league altogether. Getting through that without having a fully honed body, without lowering his weight, that was really important. It was like laying the first of the foundations for everything that came later.'

The last, even shorter, mountain stage consisted of a single ascent to a climb that would figure large in Indurain's career – Sestriere in Italy. Indurain lost a further sixteen seconds to Esnault, but overall his time margin contained the bones of a minute. The final stage, a long grind out of the Alps and down long, steady descents towards Turin, held few real challenges. Four Reynolds riders controlled the peloton and for Indurain, all that remained was to make sure he stayed upright.

Finishing forty-seven seconds clear of Esnault, Indurain secured the first victory for Spain in twenty-one years – and a convincing one in terms of his future. Without Knickmann's illness, there might well have been a different result and overall winner in Turin. But regardlesss of such speculation, in the long term, the implications of such a solid, tenacious performance by Indurain were enormous. Despite the huge time losses of the first week, he had not become demoralised, but instead had chipped away at Knickman's advantage. That he won both the points competition and the 'combination' classification was indicative of Indurain's tremendous consistency in an event which, in terms of difficulty, rivals and endurance levels, was very much at the upper limit of what a young professional could be reasonably expected to achieve. Most important of all, though, was how he had managed to defend his lead in the mountains, in what would become a carbon copy of his success in the Tour in later years. In all those senses, Indurain's actual result – although it could not be bettered – was the least important element of the race.

The signs that Indurain was tipped for future greatness could hardly have been clearer as, grinning broadly, he tucked into a cake shaped like the European flag that night in Turin with his team-mates. 'It was where I said, for the first time, that Miguel could win a Tour before he won a Vuelta,' says Unzué. 'It was partly because of the Alpine climbs which suited his style better, plus as a young rider his knees used to suffer a lot in the cold and wet, which was typical April weather. Finally his hay fever meant that there'd be limits at that time of year to how fast he could go. That's why, for example, he could never do a good Vuelta al País Vasco, apart from it having those short, punchy hills which didn't suit him.'

'You could see it coming all the way from juniors, it wasn't a sudden explosion,' insists Juan Carlos González Salvador. 'There were hints all the way from when he was my lead out man in the amateurs and he used to go so hard in the bunch sprints I could barely follow him. It got to the point that we'd drop the entire field. I'd win, he'd be a second behind and the bunch would be at three.'

Given Unzué's comments about the Izoard, did Unzué and Echavarri know, at that point, that they had a future great in their ranks? Juan Carlos González Salvador is convinced they did. 'They were very Navarran about it all, very conservative, very much "let's keep him under wraps and make sure we don't ruin him, not take any risks". They would be beating around the bush a bit, approach it all from sideways on – Miguel or any subject. I remember when Eusebio came to sign me, he was so indirect about it all, I felt like telling him "Hey, it's me, for goodness sake, what do you need, my identity card?"'

In keeping with the strong influence of the Catholic religion in Navarre, González Salvador describes their ultra-softly-softly approach as 'very priest-like ... you felt like saying, for Pete's sake, Miguel's [going to be] the best rider Spain has ever known. Can't you see he's God?'

CHAPTER 4
Invisible Robocop

Miguel Indurain's time as a professional started with two-and-a-bit seasons of spectacularly promising success in the 1985 Vuelta a España and 1986 Tour de la CEE, as well as some more minor triumphs. In fact the Tour de la CEE was, together with a stage win for Julián Gorospe in the Tour and the Vuelta King of the Mountains prize for José Luis Laguía, one of the high points for Reynolds that year.

But for all this early promise, it wasn't until the spring of 1989 that Indurain's future as a contender, if not a winner, in top events became increasingly clear. In the years in between, it was as if Indurain's career went into a period of suspended animation. Above all there was a lack of clear direction, a sense that although Indurain was talented enough to go in various directions, he was not actually moving forwards in any of them.

Unzué had already discussed Indurain's potential for Grand Tours becoming clear on the Izoard in the Tour de la CEE. But what Indurain had achieved in the Vuelta prologue and flatter stages, not to mention his physique, hinted instead at a career as a *rouleur* or perhaps a top-level time triallist, particularly for shorter races against the clock where his technical ability could prove a great advantage. Then there was the option of developing him on the track in events like the Six Days of Madrid, which he raced in the winter of 1986, alongside Danny Clarke, one of the most experienced track racers of the era. José Miguel Echavarri would later recall that in 1984, even before Indurain had turned pro, he and Unzué, inspired by Francesco Moser's recent Hour Record bid, had discussed the idea of Indurain tackling the same challenge.

In late 1987 Echavarri and Indurain visited Italy to obtain advice from the controversial Professor Francesco Conconi – of whom more later – on weight loss, advice they finally did not follow to the letter because Indurain later said it was too harsh. This visit indicated that rather than bulking out, his team might want him to focus on stage racing. At the end of the 1986 season, Echavarri had already promised he would change Indurain's race programme. But in fact, with the Vuelta and Tour at its centre, barring making an unspectacular debut in Paris–Roubaix and the Ardennes Classics, 1987 remained remarkably similar to what had come before, but with fewer high points.

As for Reynolds as a team, after Unzué began to work full-time with the professional squad alongside Echavarri in 1986, it was the absence of top results in 1987 that really shaped the squad's future. Indurain took several minor victories, but Gorospe failed to win anything at all and flopped completely in the Vuelta a España after injuring his knee. Ángel Arroyo garnered a single stage win in the low-level Vuelta a Aragón in the entire year. It was partly for that reason that despite strong rumours that he had already reached a deal with Kelme, Reynolds re-signed Pedro Delgado, now Spain's top racer, during the Volta a Galicia that August.

'I had left Reynolds [at the end of 1984] because [they thought] Pedro Delgado was too expensive and because they'd got Julián Gorospe on their books, and so they told me "you're better off flying alone",' Delgado recollects. 'When they signed me back they pretty much gave me a blank cheque and told me to name my price.' Compared with the team Delgado had left three years earlier, 'It had changed a lot, but for the better. Tactically, the team's earlier limitations had disappeared. Reynolds was a team which was racing to win and they signed me out of desperation because they wanted to win big races and couldn't.'

Signing Delgado constituted a huge turnaround in Reynolds' fortune and, indirectly, provided the platform for Indurain's continuing progress without excessive pressure. Yet it had been touch and go whether the team would fold. According to Arnaud, in April 1987, Unzué and Echavarri had their doubts whether Reynolds would continue. Their co-sponsor for that year, Seur, went on to form their own team and with no guaranteed future backing mid-season, the two Reynolds directors started to put pressure on the riders in the Vuelta a España.

'The team was cracking,' Arnaud says, 'four riders abandoned and Gorospe had fallen and had a bad knee injury, we almost all had to wait for him and chase for fifty kilometres in Cerler. I got annoyed with José Miguel, for the first and last time ever, because there were just four of us to do all the work, of whom one wasn't going great, another [Arroyo] was too well placed on GC to have any room for manoeuvre, another [Julián Gorospe] who was in good shape but had half-broken his knee, and then there was me. Then the day after I got really cross, I went and won a stage.' The team had saved face, but it was clear that something had to be done to resolve Reynolds' future. Once Reynolds promised to continue sponsorship, Delgado, therefore, constituted the solution to many of the team's ills.

Indurain was on the team's books already, of course. But despite Gorospe's flopping and Indurain's triumphs in smaller races, the younger rider was yet to make a definitive jump towards leadership in a landmark event. As Delgado puts it, 'Miguel was still pretty green, even if it was common knowledge that he'd gone with Echavarri to see [Italian sports scientist Francesco] Conconi, something Echavarri had not done previously with any other rider.'

Echavarri thought Indurain was, possibly, destined for greatness. Yet what kind of greatness was anything but clear. 'What Conconi had told him,' Delgado says, 'was that Indurain was a one-day rider, made for the Classics. As for the Tours, Echavarri was taking him very gently: all this stuff of letting him race half a Tour de France then sending him home, that was absolutely unheard of at that time. It was usually more a case of "squeeze the cow's udder until she runs dry".'

Indurain's 'special treatment' did not, according to Delgado, produce any sense of jealousy in his team-mates: 'But what it did create was a heck of a lot of column inches in the newspapers, to the point where he was even known as "Robocop".' The thing was, Delgado explains, 'Nobody at the time went to specialist sports doctors' – as Indurain had, going to see Conconi at the end of 1987 – 'and in fact at the time there weren't any in Spain.'

'So José Miguel garnered a lot of publicity when he talked to the press about how "we're looking after Miguel", "what could a rider as special as this be really capable of doing" and so on. Even before Miguel really was somebody, he'd been "sold" to the media as somebody producing exceptional [physiological] data, somebody who had to get thinner, somebody with an amazing pulse rate or lung capacity, somebody who could do this, that and the other. All this in an era when this kind of stuff was rarely talked about. It all sounded like genetic gobbledegook, changing this chromosome or whatever, twenty-third-century jargon in a period when we were all thinking "Hmm, but isn't this the twentieth century?" He's still riding along like the rest of us, pedalling away, and he's still getting dropped from time to time, too ...'

The issue was that, as Delgado sees it, Reynolds knew they had a top rider on their books but what kind of top rider was yet to become clear: 'Miguel was still a *modesto* [a lower ranking rider] but the thing was nobody knew what he could do. José Miguel was always saying that he was going to be the first Spaniard to win a Milano–Sanremo'– something already achieved, in fact, by Catalonia's Miguel Poblet in the 1950s (twice), but still a huge target. 'So he later took him to Milano–Sanremo to see what he could do, motivate him for that and give him some very rigorous training plans so he'd be in good shape.' Again, this was a plan that never saw any real results.

For all Indurain was racking up multiple minor victories, the question marks were flourishing, and little else. A debut in the Ardennes Classics ended in an abandon in both Flèche Wallonne and Liège–Bastogne–Liège but for a still heftily built Indurain, hauling his fairly corpulent body over a series of punishing climbs was only marginally more to his liking. Echavarri was much given to saying in the years to come that Indurain 'had it in him to win Paris–Roubaix.' But there was no evidence that he felt it was important enough, in terms of publicity for Reynolds or later Banesto, for Indurain actually to try to do so.

Instead, Indurain went back to more familiar terrain in the Vuelta a España. On the plus side he turned in a memorable performance when the race wound its way up to the ski station of Cerler in the Pyrenees – his team-mates had to tell him to stop driving so hard – and on the downside, poor spring weather in Spain that year saw Indurain come down with flu two days before the start in Benidorm. In Asturias, as the race reached its half-way point, Indurain abandoned. 'I had built up for it the whole season, and it all went totally wrong,' Indurain later commented in his usual laconic, understated, style. 'I couldn't do much about it.' After previously catching pneumonia in the Vuelta 1985 and suffering the consequences throughout that summer, this was the latest confirmation that the Vuelta's weather conditions in April were not suited to him. But it was far from being the last.

After his Vuelta abandon Indurain was able to head for the Vuelta a los Valles Mineros, a small stage race in Asturias, where he snapped up three stages and the overall in the face of admittedly limited opposition. Even more pleasingly, Indurain took a victory in his home race, the one-day Trofeo Navarro, where he outpowered breakaway Iñaki Gastón. He was also able to claim victory in the fabled Subida a Txitxarro, a hill-climb criterium that rounded off the season for the Basque and Navarran pros.

In between came the Tour de France, which Indurain managed to complete for the first time. He finished in ninety-seventh place, with a sixth place in the final time trial the real high point. Completing the Tour is recognised as a rite of passage for any pro and as such Echavarri called Indurain back to the team car as the peloton was riding towards the Champs Elysées. The team director produced a paper napkin on which he had written 'On this day *Don* Miguel Indurain earned his licence as a professional racer.'

Had what until 1987 looked like a path of steady progress towards ever greater triumphs suddenly petered out completely, Indurain's team-mates had no doubt that he could have made it as a *domestique*. But throughout the season it was as if Indurain, one of the tallest riders in the peloton, had a lower profile than ever before – and not just in the Tour. Some might nickname him 'Robocop' but perhaps 'Invisible Robocop' might have been more accurate.

Arguably the most important moment of 1987 for Indurain was not completing his first Tour, but extending his contract with Reynolds for another three seasons. Interest ranged from PDM to Zor at home and Indurain refused the latter on the grounds that the 50 million pesetas he was offered by *directeur sportif* Javier Mínguez 'was an awful lot of money': 'I expected any answer but that one, and I didn't know what to say,' Mínguez said later. It was not only Mínguez who was stumped at Indurain's lack of financial ambition: according to Unzué, when his own team offered him a new contract, Indurain has been the only rider in their 36-year history who responded, 'Wouldn't that be too much?' One motive for sticking with Reynolds was arguably Indurain's intense sense of loyalty. There was also a chance to progress without as much pressure as he would have had as an outright leader – which he could have become, had Delgado not rejoined the Reynolds ranks.

What initially changed in 1988 was not so much Indurain, but his team. In less than seven months Reynolds went from its most disappointing season since its inception to winning the Tour de France with Pedro Delgado. After going from the boom years of 1982 and 1983 to being a near also-ran inside Spain for four more seasons, suddenly the pendulum of fortune swung back hard. Reynolds was now the leading squad nationally and one of the most significant ones abroad.

The difference was simple – Delgado. 'When I signed for Reynolds, Unzué and Echavarri asked me, what makes a great team? And I said, that's easy, a great leader,' Arnaud recalls. 'If you're racing a team time trial without a leader, then you'll do the best you can. If it makes the difference between your leader winning or losing the Tour, then it's all very different.'

Changes were everywhere. For the first time since its creation, rather than use the ski stations of the Pyrenees, the newly strengthened Reynolds headed south to Torremolinos for its first training camp of the year. But where media really perked up was when Reynolds announced that Delgado was heading for the Giro d'Italia, rather than the Vuelta. This was the start of an oft-repeated row between the Vuelta organisers and Reynolds, one which extended into the Indurain years, over which of Reynolds' leading riders would head the team in Spain's number one race. The strained atmosphere cannot have helped the riders focus on their goals.

To cap it all, the Giro did not work out at all well for Delgado. 'There was the legendary day over the Gavia and that was pretty much it,' he commented in his biography about a blizzard that caused a huge number of riders to abandon. 'I liked the race, but our lack of knowledge about it led us to make some important mistakes.' However, the team learned an important lesson for Indurain. Citing the case of a team-mate, Laguía, who discovered that he could actually improve his form thanks to the way the Giro was raced, Delgado argued, 'the first 150 kilometres of the Giro's stages were normally without many attacks, or none worth mentioning. Only the last 50 were flat out. You use up energy in the Giro, like in any Grand Tour, but it didn't punish you like in the Vuelta and on top of that, it left you in great shape for the Tour.' It was only by 1994 and 1995 that 'both the Giro's route in general and even the way they race it' had changed. The greater publicity value of having their leader race the Vuelta, as well as media and local organisers' pressure inside Spain, saw Delgado only return to the Giro once, in 1991. But for Indurain, in his first two Giros in 1992 and 1993, Delgado's analysis was to prove invaluable.

The media storm surrounding Delgado and Reynolds over his non-participation in the Vuelta can hardly have gone unnoticed by Indurain, either. Spain's best-known and most influential radio journalist of the era was José María García, who had been instrumental in the creation of Antena 3, Spain's first fully independent radio station in the post-Franco era. García was furious after Delgado, having announced he would not ride the Vuelta, was then hired as a special commentator for the race by arch-rivals Cadena Ser. García promptly announced he would not be namechecking Reynolds riders at any point during the Vuelta, simply referring to them as 'the team from Navarre'.

Javier Ares, one of Spain's top commentators and working for García at the time, recalled in *Nuestro Ciclismo, por un equipo* that 'It was an era when radio played a huge part in the Vuelta, not so much because cycling itself was important but because of the huge degree of competition between rival media at the time. García had quit Cadena Ser' – in 1981, although some sources say he was fired – 'to create Antena 3 radio and he saw cycling as the ideal scenario for expressing his fearlessness and ingenuity [as a commentator].'

As a result, radio stations from across Spain poured money into their Vuelta coverage, using everything from helicopters to motorbikes, mobile studios and a sizeable series of programmes, from live to behind-the-scenes to analysis that lasted well into the night. García himself had direct radio contact with each Spanish-speaking *directeur sportif* inside their team cars and what Ares calls a 'close collaboration' with Unipublic, the race organiser. Ares claims that García was so powerful he could help shape the outcome of the race itself, in particular when he used that radio contact to help determine the outcome of the controversial 1985 Vuelta, by 'preventing certain Spanish teams from chasing behind the [Pepe] Recio/Delgado breakaway.' Numerous factors are said, in fact, to have caused that infamous breakaway to work so well, and what degree of influence each had remains unclear to this day. The end result was so successful that Delgado won the race overall when he wrenched the lead from Robert Millar.

As Ares points out, in terms of gaining publicity for cycling the knock-on effect of García's influence was immense: his *Supergarcía* programme, which started at midnight each night, was by far the most popular of the era in Spain. At the same time, Delgado's huge charisma was clear, too, reaching a point where García's Antena 3 co-workers, fearing attacks from pro-Delgado fans, removed the publicity stickers from their race vehicles to avoid identification.

Most importantly this crisis situation, as well as García's ongoing interest in cycling, helped consolidate the Vuelta and by extension the Tour, as key events in the Spanish sporting calendar and for which the mass media of all kinds – print, radio and TV – was virtually obliged to provide blanket coverage. Indurain did not benefit directly at first, but it meant cycling had a fanbase and an impact on Spanish society during the Indurain era that it had not enjoyed since the Bahamontes–Loroño rivalry of the 1950s.

It was purely ironic, of course that even if *Perico* – as Delgado is nicknamed in Spain – was not present in the Vuelta, his non-participation garnered almost as much publicity as riding might have done. The symbolism in a picture taken of Delgado riding in the opposite direction to the Vuelta peloton when he and 180-plus riders accidentally crossed paths whilst he was out training became one of the standout photos of the entire race. As for Indurain, as in 1985 and 1987, he suffered badly, going down with tendinitis and a severe cold. He finally quit the Vuelta on the very last stage. With Arroyo and Gorospe also abandoning, and their best rider, William Palacio in twelfth place overall, the Vuelta had become a race for Reynolds to forget. For *Perico*, seventh in the Giro was hardly a result to remember, either.

The Tour was a very different story. With Stephen Roche, the defending champion, not taking part, Delgado was the de facto favourite. Despite losing a minute in the first week because of a crash, the Spaniard reached the mountains less than two minutes down on the race leader. Taking part in a strong attack by Lucho Herrera on the warm-up stage to the Alpine ski station of Morzine saw Delgado move up to sixth. The key stage though, was to prove to be on the road to Alpe d'Huez.

When Indurain was briefly dropped on the Madeleine climb as his team-mates Arroyo and Jesús Rodríguez Magro hammered away at the front, Delgado ordered the team to wait. Indurain's role – which having got back on, he then fulfilled to perfection – was to drive hard on the Madeleine's descent and on the flat towards the Glandon, the next ascent. Delgado's rivals were already on the back foot as a result of Reynolds' high-pressure approach and on the Glandon, race leader Steve Bauer, Lucho Herrera and Erik Breukink all began to suffer and Delgado went clear.

The race seemed all but sewn up in Delgado's favour, but a Colombian macro-alliance behind saw his advantage reduced to a minute by the foot of Alpe d'Huez. Nonetheless, third on the summit allowed him to take over as race leader, and a powerful display of uphill time trialling at Villards-de-Lans the following day both captured the Segovia-born rider the stage and strengthened his grip on the Tour. Reynolds had claimed their first ever *maillot jaune* and for Delgado, with just two tough days remaining in mountainous terrain in the Pyrenees, it appeared to be all over bar the shouting.

As Delgado recollects it, the news broke when he was in his hotel room in Bordeaux one evening, less than a week before the Tour ended and with the leader's jersey still snugly in his suitcase. Arnaud, his room-mate, repeated what the TV news had revealed

– that a rider in the Tour had tested positive. 'That'll be tough for whoever got caught,' Delgado remembers thinking.

It was indeed tough, particularly as the rider in question was Delgado himself. Just as it seemed that Reynolds had their first Tour victory in the bag, their team leader risked exclusion from the race and the Tour's director, Xavier Louy, reportedly asked Echavarri if he could remove Delgado from the race. Echavarri refused, but the pressure on Delgado and Reynolds could not have been greater. Reynolds had had a previous positive for a Grand Tour champion – Ángel Arroyo after winning the Vuelta a España in 1982 – but the news of Arroyo's test had leaked out in the quietest of ways. Arroyo, having no phone in his home, had learned he was the first ever Grand Tour winner to be stripped of a title when a journalist, acting on a tip-off, rang him in a supermarket telephone booth. This time, Delgado was under the full media spotlight, to the point where he was smuggled out of a team hotel using the garage to avoid the press waiting for him in the lobby.

Why Delgado was, finally, able to stay in the race – and win it – was because the product for which he'd tested positive, probenecid, was a masking agent that was banned by the IOC but not by cycling's governing body, the UCI. As a result of what some saw as a loophole, others (incuding the UCI) as an indication that the positive was not, in fact, a full-blown positive, Delgado was able to continue. After three days of serious tension, the UCI confirmed officially that he was in the clear. Reynolds' first Tour de France victory was, finally, in the bag.

What is striking is the degree of indirect support Delgado and Reynolds received from the Spanish sports establishment. It was perhaps to be expected that Spain's Luis Puig, the UCI president, should emphasise so strongly to the media that the UCI did not have probecenid on their 1988 banned list – although it was later added. But that Javier Gómez Navarro, Secretary of State for Sport, and Cecilia Rodríguez, head of Madrid's anti-doping laboratory, should travel specifically to the race 'to show solidarity' in the former's case and to defend a potentially maligned athlete in the latter's, underlines how significant and high-profile cycling had become for Spain. At times, Reynolds must have felt like the Spanish national cycling team by another name. As much as for the precedent of winning the Tour itself, this creation of much broader social parameters for cycling shows how Delgado acted as a pioneer across the board for Indurain – and the effect on Spanish society that a Tour de France win could have, inside and outside sport.

Within Reynolds, in any case, rather than the pressure breaking the team apart, Delgado's positive-that-wasn't created an internal cohesion that arguably proved to be the silver lining for Indurain's Tour years when the team found itself once again under the spotlight. Before each of the stages where Delgado's positive-that-wasn't continued to dominate the Tour, Arnaud would provide the key-note speeches. 'I come from a rugby background and I gave them briefings a bit like it was a rugby meet,' he recalls. '"Boys, we've got a team-mate in difficulties, and now, more than ever, we have to be by his side." I all but told them, "You don't want to do the work, you go home ... collectively," we did a last part of the Tour which was amazingly strong.'

Amongst those working so well was, of course, Indurain: 'By then, he was really strong, he was riding as if he could be, one day, the winner of the Tour. It got to the point where I'd tell him what to do, but run out of legs myself. And he'd go on plugging away at the front, knowing what his job was. Working for Pedro, when you've got Indurain's class, was an easy job.'

The 1988 Tour was also where Delgado first recognised Indurain as his possible successor – although the word 'possible' should be underlined after the Navarran had blown the field apart on the Tour's toughest day in the Pyrenees, on the Peyresourde ascent. 'Up until 1988 he'd shown that he could do well on the flat, shown that he could do well in time trials, but where he really surprised me that year was on the climbs,' Delgado says before qualifying that by saying, 'He still had a hell of a long way to progress.' Curiously enough – and vitally for his Tour success in the future – where Indurain was strongest was on the longer climbs. 'If it was just five kilometres long, then he needed to go at a higher speed up it, and he couldn't. But on the longer climbs, like the ones in the Pyrenees and Alps, 12, 15 or 20 kilometres long, he really had it nailed. Above all, what was impressive was that this was in the third week. Although to go from there to winning the Tour, it's a big leap.'

'There are lots of riders with an innate level of greatness in them. But you need a spark to set that greatness alight, to exploit it. It's like they've got the handbrake still on. In Spain, riders like Santi Blanco [in the 1990s] or Jesús Herrada [in the present] are presented to us as the "next big thing".' But as Delgado puts it – and he snaps his fingers for emphasis – 'There has to be a moment when that ...' *clack!* '... breaks through. They break the mould.' For Indurain that moment, Delgado says, did not come until 1990: 'the Tour he could have won, but didn't.' What 1988 showed, though, was that the raw materials for such a breakthrough moment were definitely there.

Encouragingly, almost as the season was drawing to a close, for the first time in two years Indurain finally began to regain a higher profile, with victory in Spain's second biggest race, the Volta a Catalunya. In his biggest triumph since 1986, Indurain beat one of the country's most talented climbers, Laudelino Cubino, albeit by a scant eight seconds. Cubino's prospects of victory in the Volta were somewhat limited by the route, with a 30-kilometre individual time trial, a team time trial, and few real incursions into the mountains. But for Indurain, Catalunya marked a turning point.

Nor was Catalunya an easy prey by any means. For many years considered more important than the Vuelta a España, Catalunya's status had been threatened when it was squeezed down from its usual eight stages to six in 1988 by the UCI. Undeterred, the Catalan club, UE Sants, which organised the Volta, responded by holding two days of split stages – which effectively brought the total of race days back up to eight. The list of contenders, too, was impressive, and included Greg LeMond, Delgado, Jean François Bernard, Sean Kelly and Erik Breukink.

Such a tricky route and a good line-up made for an unusually hard-fought event for so late in the season, and in exceptionally warm weather, the tension heightened right from the opening stage when Delgado, Bernard and Breukink were all eliminated from the running by a late crash. The key stage, though, proved to be the one really tough day through the Pyrenees, with even more favourites losing time on the lengthy Coll del Cantó. Indurain, though, maintained a steady pace on the difficult ascent and then on the more straightforward ascent to Super Espot, he closed the overall gap on race leader Laudelino Cubino to nineteen seconds. Cubino was unable to match Indurain when it came to time trialling, and after Indurain claimed the victory on the following day's time trial stage, the Navarran moved into the overall lead.

The margin was narrow, just eight seconds, but after two years of marking time, Catalunya at last confirmed that Indurain could now hold his own in major week-long stage races when Reynolds team leaders like Delgado were out of the running. Furthermore, he had proved that he could handle the longer mountain climbs, provided he could maintain his own pacing strategy, and even cope with hilly time trials like the one that decided the Volta.

There was also the question of handling pressure, time and again one of Indurain's strong points. 'The climb was tough enough to decrease the chances of all-rounders like Miguel [Indurain] and Pello [Ruiz Cabestany], whilst increasing that of Marino [Lejarreta], Pino and Cubino,' *El Mundo Deportivo*, Catalonia's leading sports daily, pointed out. 'But Indurain, seemingly oblivious to the heightened threats, simply added time trial bars and aerodynamic wheels to his usual bike set-up. He then gained time on the flat and descent, whilst holding off the climbers on the ascent.' Indurain's nerve also held on the time trial course's out-and-back format, with sections where, with no cones to mark out the middle of the road, it was perfectly possible to hit a rider coming in the opposite direction head-on. 'Up until now it has not been a great year for Indurain barring his work for Delgado in the Tour,' *El Mundo Deportivo* added, 'but just like that Bobby Darin song, "Come September", it's been another story this autumn.'

'It's true, I was starting to get worried, because over the last two years I hadn't made any progress,' Indurain said. 'I'd had a lot of problems in the Vuelta a España and that caused my form to drop off considerably. I know that I won't ever get to handle the mountains well, because I don't have the stature of the climbers. But I'm progressing in the hillier stages a lot, and I can be pleased with that. I've learned to suffer and that's what really makes a difference.' Nor was he ending the year feeling wholly satisfied, 'because whilst winning a race like Catalunya is always a boost to the morale, this hasn't been the season I wanted.' That would have to wait until 1989.

For Indurain, probably the two most important moments of his 'missing years' were Delgado's victory in the Tour and completing the Tour de France himself, for the first time, in 1987. Delgado's win ensured that Reynolds would continue to make the Tour their main focus of the year, rather than diversifying or encouraging their riders to look at other events and kept the public's attention on July and stage racing, too. Reynolds and Delgado therefore provided the right scenario, finally, for Indurain to concentrate on what he could achieve in the Tour de France. But equally important was his own confirmation that Grand Tours were for him – a moment that Arnaud, for one, believes arrived when Indurain reached the Champs Elysées finish line on the evening of 26 July 1987.

'It was one of the hardest Tours ever. I had to abandon on the 20th stage because I was burned out, it was so tough,' Arnaud says. 'That Miguel could complete the Tour that year says a heck of a lot about what he could do.' What Indurain had yet to do, though, was exploit that potential to the maximum, and see how much of the 'Invisible Robocop' label he could burn off in the process.

CHAPTER 5

1990: the One That Got Away

Bizarre as it sounds, the moment where Miguel Indurain's rise towards the summit of international stage racing began to accelerate hard seemed to be as much about runner-up spots as it was about overall wins.

In the spring of 1989, Indurain captured the overall of Paris–Nice, the greatest victory of his career to date – and Spain's first ever victory in the race, traditionally viewed as a showcase for the next generation to show their worth. Indurain certainly managed that, but curiously he did so without a single stage win, scooping second place in the Paris prologue, second on the race's first summit finish at Mont Faron, second twenty-four hours later at Saint-Tropez in a breakaway, and second, finally, on the Col d'Èze uphill time trial.

Yet this series of runner-up places actually underlined three of Indurain's greatest strengths as a stage racer: all-round consistency, a willingness to sacrifice minor success in order to strengthen his chances of overall victory and, equally importantly, no fireworks for their own sake. He was still only twenty-four, but Indurain's marked increase in all-round ability in such different terrains against rivals of the stature of former Tour winners Stephen Roche and

Laurent Fignon was impressive enough for one so young. But so, too, was his ability to keep his eye on the main prize rather than impetuously going for every win that was potentially on offer, and perhaps running out of energy in the process.

The crunch moment of the 1989 Paris–Nice came after the stage four finish on Mont Faron, a 5.5-kilometre ascent outside Marseilles where Indurain powered out of the pack and came within half a bike-length of taking the win from Bruno Cornillet. That explosive display of relentless climbing power, mowing down one rival after another as he closed on Cornillet, allowed Indurain to move up to third. However, on such a short climb, the gaps were small and Stephen Roche was just sixteen seconds behind at the summit. As a Tour winner and the winner of Paris–Nice in 1981, the Irishman – second overall behind Marc Madiot at that point – was once again catapulted into the role of odds-on favourite and as Roche himself put it, 'I believe I've got a very good chance of winning.'

Yet twenty-four hours later, Indurain had not only moved into the lead, but left Roche reeling. After Delgado had softened up the opposition with attacks on the Col de Vignon, Indurain charged away on the descent. Within no time at all, he had caught an earlier breakaway, Système U rider Gerard Rue. By the finish at Saint-Tropez, the duo had opened up a minute's gap. Rather than go for the win, in what was to become a classic Indurain tactic, the Spaniard gifted his rival the stage victory, whilst gaining a solid advantage over Roche and the rest.

This was effectively the first time outside Spain since the Tour de l'Avenir three years previously that Indurain was making his mark on one of cycling's top-level events, and thus represented another major breakthrough. It was also the first time that Delgado clearly opted to take a back seat and let his young 'successor' fight for the win of a top-level race. It would be all but impossible to imagine other giants of the sport, a young Hinault or a Merckx, say, being so calculating under such heady circumstances as Indurain proved to be on that crucial stage of Paris–Nice, letting Rue have his share of the glory without even disputing the stage victory. Apart from the evidence that shows his ability to look at the bigger picture, it is possible to see Indurain's good nature glinting through that decision, too. As he observed on another occasion, 'I race to win, but I don't race to humiliate anybody.' As for those who accused Indurain of 'lacking ambition', like the notorious firebrand Luis Ocaña, Spain's 1973 Tour winner, the Navarran simply paid them no attention whatsoever.

Physically, Indurain was also picking up his game. 'By 1988, Indurain was really strong, but overall 1989 and 1990 were the key years,' says Pedro Delgado. 'Also they were the years where Indurain lost a chunk of weight, too, dropped from 80 kilos to 75. At the same time, his climbing improved steadily.' This helped increase the odds, therefore, of Indurain moving up the cycling hierarchy at a greater pace, and Paris–Nice was a solid indication of that work in progress.

As Delgado observes in *Nuestro Ciclismo*, Indurain had a real head for sporting heights. 'He won coldly, with class, showing he knew how to handle being a leader at every single moment. Paris–Nice showed me for the first time that Miguel was stronger, as a racer, when he was in the lead. He was the complete opposite of all other riders, leading a race actually made him calmer, not the other way round.'

'Whenever it got really tough, you'd see Indurain up there, right at the head of affairs,' added an admiring Marc Madiot. (Analysing Rue's willingness to collaborate with Indurain, Madiot later claimed there might well have been an underlying desire by

Rue's sports director at Système U, Cyril Guimard, to settle an old score. Madiot was his former rider, and by getting Rue to work with Indurain, Guimard ensured that Madiot lost the lead. Whatever Rue's reasoning behind his collaboration, it was hardly Indurain's problem.)

On the Col d'Èze mountain time trial that concluded the race, Indurain turned in another unnervingly mature performance. Knowing that he had a 45-second advantage on Roche, rather than try to go for the stage win – and risk blowing completely – Indurain took it steadily, and had lost nineteen seconds to the Irishman by half-way up the climb. Yet by the summit, Roche had only gained another twelve seconds. Indurain was second again, but by limiting his losses and not panicking, his place as the first ever Spaniard to win Paris–Nice outright was guaranteed.

After recognising Paris–Nice as the most important victory of his career to date, Indurain pinpointed the Vuelta as the main target of his season, and, as after Catalunya the previous autumn, recognised that he had failed to progress for nearly eighteen months. Echavarri lauded Indurain to the rooftops, arguing, 'The best thing is he's got enormous potential and nobody knows, yet, what the upper limit to that potential is. I'm not going to predict anything for him, but my faith in him is total.'

Echavarri contradicted himself, though, when he subsequently likened Indurain to Francesco Moser, a 1970s and 1980s Italian Classics specialist who also won one exceptionally flat Giro d'Italia with extra-long time trials. Rather than Grand Tours, then – and in any case, with Delgado, Reynolds seemed amply covered in that quarter – Echavarri seemed to be thinking Indurain might perform at his best in the Classics. However, in the first big Monument that followed, Milano–Sanremo, Indurain was unable to shine when a mechanical incident left him out of the running.

But Echavarri's faith was to be quickly rewarded at the now defunct Critérium International, at the time one of the most prestigious two-day spring stage races. After forming part of a breakaway of seven on the Saturday's opening stage – where Madiot took the win, presumably without complaint – Indurain turned in a devastating time trial performance to take both the stage and the event overall.

No other rider under twenty-five in Spain at the time was capable of perfoming at this level and such was the fuss over his prowess in stage racing – then as now, valued far more highly in Spain than one-day racing – that Indurain's steady improvement in tough one-day Classics like la Flèche Wallonne, where he took seventh that spring, went all but unnoticed.

The Vuelta was a very different story, but in Indurain's case, for all the wrong reasons. Technically the leader with Pedro Delgado – after yet another massive media storm when it emerged that Delgado could be taking part in the Giro again, something he finally opted not to do – things could hardly have gone worse for Indurain. First, he turned in a poor performance in the crucial uphill time trial at Valdezcaray, which effectively relegated him to the role of *domestique de luxe*. After that a bad crash on the descent of the Fito climb in Asturias left him with a broken wrist, and although he could complete the stage, he subsequently abandoned the next day. Lying ninth overall at the time, as he told the *Diario de Navarra*, 'whilst seated, I could continue, the minute I tried to stand on the pedals, the pain was too much.' For the third year running, Indurain abandoned the Vuelta, further reinforcing his troubled track record at the Spanish Grand Tour.

'José Miguel had put Miguel in there as a leader because little by little that idea he'd had about Miguel being a Classics rider was fading,' recollects Delgado – although to judge by his comparison with Moser after Indurain's Paris–Nice win it still endured as far as that spring. 'He thought the Tour was too hard for Miguel, but he wanted to give him a test as a Grand Tour leader to see if it could last.'

'He'd had his big crack at the Classics in 1988 and it hadn't gone well at all, so he put him in the Vuelta in 1989 as co-leader. I wasn't that bothered, I'd won the Tour the previous year. So José Miguel told me to stay calm and not try to make any big moves because it was all on Miguel. The only problem was that I was going absolutely brilliantly right up until the moment when Miguel fell on the Fito and then after that, all the problems I could imagine turned up at once. But I got through.'

Ultimately, the Vuelta could not have gone better for Reynolds, with outright victory for Pedro Delgado, the first for the team – discounting Arroyo's in 1982 – in their home Grand Tour and the second for Delgado. For Echavarri and Unzué Delgado's victory represented a welcome addition to their team's credibility, too, given that the squad, despite its outstanding success, was on the point of losing its main sponsor.

The reason was essentially that Reynolds the team had outgrown itself, with its annual budget soaring from 15 million pesetas to 300 million by 1989. Supported only by the Spanish branch of the company, previous co-sponsorship with Seur had only lasted a year before Seur opted to form its own squad. However, the team's main backer in Reynolds, Juan García Barberena, was able to establish contact with Banesto – one of Spain's biggest banks – in early June. In what was a fast-moving operation that culminated fifteen days before the Tour, Banesto confirmed their interest in co-sponsorship of the team for the rest of 1989, providing an initial injection of 100 million pesetas into the team budget for that season, and taking over as main backer for a minimum of three further years.

Although the sponsor switch took place in record time, the solidity of the support from the bank could not be questioned, right up to the highest level. One of the driving forces behind Banesto's interest was Arturo Romani, the bank's vice-president, a keen cycling fan. Romani was responsible for persuading Mario Conde, the president of Banesto, to send the fax to Barberena that confirmed the takeover. When Conde's son, another cycling fan, found out that his father's bank would be supporting the country's number one cyclist and team, he was equally delighted: 'so you've signed *Perico*? Well, it was about time Banesto did something right, Dad.'

It was probably just as well that there was such a high level of support for *Perico* and the bank's new investment, given the events that were to befall Reynolds-Banesto at the start of the 1989 Tour. After the team had been officially re-launched and the riders had appeared in their new, rapidly redesigned Reynolds-Banesto kit as part of the Tour's team presentation in Luxembourg, a large number of bank executives stayed on to watch *Perico* and the rest of the team tackle the opening prologue.

Delgado's performance could not have been worse. Due to roll down the start ramp as defending champion at 5.16 p.m., because of some kind of misunderstanding, Delgado turned up over two minutes later. With Echavarri yelling himself hoarse at Delgado to start pedalling, the 1988 Tour winner raced away, completing the course just fourteen seconds slower than winner Erik Breukink. The 'only' problem was the two minutes and forty seconds that had to be added to his time because of the disastrous delay, and which sent Delgado plummeting right to the bottom of the overall classification.

Given that he had gone from winning the race outright in 1989 to an unmitigated disaster in the next Tour almost before he had turned a single pedal stroke in anger, Delgado was understandably a nervous wreck. In the following day's team time trial, the few Banesto executives who had opted to stay on would have witnessed a second debacle, this time collectively, as Delgado caved in mentally and was dropped on three successive occasions. 'We were going brilliantly, I think it was the best team time trial Reynolds had ever done. But then, at twenty kilometres from the finish, he cracked,' Arnaud recalls. Arnaud reveals that whilst the generally accepted history of the handover of power between Indurain and Delgado was that it took place in 1991, in fact, it could have occurred two years earlier, on the roads of Luxembourg. 'Delgado's head went because of the mistake he'd made the day before. We riders deliberated, for several minutes, whether we should leave Delgado behind and continue with Miguel, or wait for Pedro. And we opted for the second. The decision, though, was taken with Miguel's complete agreement, right in the middle of the race.'

'We knew that Miguel was strong, but Delgado was the defending Tour winner. And we waited. And after that it was all about *Perico, Perico* and *Perico*. Miguel went on working for another year, which he did very well.'

Reynolds finished the stage last. As a result Delgado was now seven and a half minutes down on Laurent Fignon, the leading French favourite after winning the Giro d'Italia. In terms of sporting disasters, Delgado's situation was truly memorable, but for little else. 'The prologue looked really bad, but where he lost the Tour that year was in the team time trial,' observes Arnaud.

However, in terms of comebacks, Delgado proved he had plenty to offer as well. Second place in the stage five time trial (Indurain placed a distant twelfth) behind LeMond – although there was an unwelcome near-repeat of Luxembourg when the Reynolds-Banesto team car was delayed in traffic waiting to cross a river and

Delgado had to reach the start on foot, his bike slung over his shoulder – allowed Delgado to regain over 100 places overall. Then on the race's first stage through the Pyrenees, Reynolds-Banesto – their collective morale boosted enormously by a fax sent from the bank's Arturo Romani, promising them his full support – opted to go on the rampage. But not just with Delgado, with Indurain as well.

Well before the final ascent to Cauterets, Indurain romped away from the main peloton on the descent of the Marie-Blanque, overtaking all those ahead of him in earlier breaks by the foot of the next climb, the Aubisque. He then soloed over three Pyrenean passes – far easier written than done – before tackling the final ascent alone to win at Cauterets. All this at the end of a 91-kilometre breakaway.

'I've never suffered so much, in my five years as a pro,' Indurain said about his first ever Grand Tour stage victory. 'If the climb had been three kilometres longer, I probably wouldn't have won. I paid a high price for doing the whole of the Aubisque alone.'

It only emerged much later that one of Indurain's least known skills – brilliant descending – had prevented anybody from getting across and ruining what was his only major solo break in a mountain stage of the Tour. 'Fede Echave tried to follow Miguel on the descent of the Marie-Blanque, and we told him not to bother, that there'd be no way he'd catch Miguel, but he tried anyway,' Delgado recalls. 'We next passed Fede on the descent, standing on a corner and trembling like a leaf.' (Delgado himself finished third on the stage: a position in the overall he would ultimately hold in Paris).

This mountain attack of Indurain's was not in any way an act of rebellion against the established hierarchy in Reynolds-Banesto. Although not preconceived prior to the stage, Indurain said he had directly followed Delgado's orders to attack on the Marie-Blanque's descent and the idea was 'probably that he would bridge across to me on the last climb.' On an ascent as comparatively gentle as Cauterets, though, Indurain recognised that 'probably the gap between the two of us was too big for that to happen.' That gap, though, was another sign that Indurain's strength in the mountains was far greater than even Echavarri had estimated after Paris–Nice.

With hindsight, Indurain's success in Cauterets is notable for its rarity. Together with Luz Ardiden in 1990, it was the first of only two summit finish wins he would ever take in his career in any Grand Tour, both preceding his overall reign in the Tour de France. Cauterets was also the first and only day that Indurain ever led in the Tour's King of the Mountains competition. These mountain stage victories have come to symbolise Indurain's continuing rise towards the summit of world cycling – rewind twelve months and as Delgado had soared towards outright victory, his role had been a much more anonymous one.

'There's always the doubt whether we should have gone on with Indurain at that point in the team time trial [in 1989], but – no,' says Arnaud. 'The race went the way it did. And in terms of Miguel's progress, it's always much easier to do that when you're racing in somebody's shadow. Why did LeMond win the Tour that year? He didn't have a strong team, but he didn't have the pressure either. In a sense, we were LeMond's best team after we'd messed it up in the prologue. Whenever there was a breakaway, who worked hardest to bring them back? Reynolds-Banesto. LeMond was very intelligent, he sat on Delgado's wheel for most of the race and finally, on the last day, he won the Tour.'

Nonetheless, something that spoke volumes for his potential role as designated successor was that Indurain's stage victories both at Cauterets and the following year at Luz Ardiden were the only ones for a Banesto rider in the Tour. The competition to succeed Delgado as Banesto's leader, at least inside the team, was diminishing. Neither Ángel Arroyo, who retired from racing mid-way through 1989, nor Gorospe, long seen as an alternative leader to Delgado but four years Indurain's senior, had similar roles or opportunities. Yet with *Perico* a Tour winner in 1988 and third overall in Paris despite his disastrous debut and still only twenty-nine, it was not yet clear how long it would be before Delgado allowed Indurain, Seventeenth both in the final stage and overall, to take over.

'Banesto, quite simply, got the wrong leader,' was how *L'Équipe* later analysed the team's collective performance in the 1990 Tour de France. The sight of Miguel Indurain sacrificing his own chances for Pedro Delgado in the Alps was not one that was easy to forget, particularly when Indurain subsequently produced the squad's one stage win in the high mountains – for the second year running. The issue still produces much debate, and when I visited Dominique Arnaud, he spent the first hour of the interview saying repeatedly, 'I know there's one question you're going to ask, everybody does it, all the journalists ask me the same.' Sure enough, the question is – did Banesto make an error of huge proportions, opting to have Delgado as sole leader in the Tour when it was so clear that Indurain was stronger than his leader? Although Indurain himself has never sought to create any controversy about Banesto's Tour hierarchy that year, his family were more outspoken. 'I always say Miguel won six Tours, not five,' his father once told me.

The controversy took a while to reach boiling point, given that although Indurain gained time on his leader in both the opening prologue and the time trial at the end of the first week at Épinal, this result could be explained by Indurain's natural ability against the clock combined with his being a year older and stronger. In the same way, whilst Indurain's excellent second in the 61-kilometre time trial in Épinal behind Raúl Alcalá was logical enough, it was Delgado's fourth place, a mere forty-four seconds slower than his team-mate despite such a long effort against the clock, that made it seem as if Echavarri and Unzué were right to designate him sole leader. That said, had Echavarri and Unzué looked at the previous Tour's long first week time trial results – in 1989 Delgado had finished second and Indurain twelfth – they might have perceived that in comparison, Delgado was actually more off the mark. Surely those results made the question of a leadership change more pressing, not less?

At the same time, Banesto – as of 1990 the team's sole sponsor – must have been afflicted by a sense of *déjà vu* given that just like in the Vuelta that April, an early break had gained far more time than anyone could have anticipated – and contained some potentially dangerous challengers. 'It wasn't a mistake on our part,' argues Arnaud, 'it was more that none of the teams, at that point, wanted to work.' Of the four riders who reached Futuroscope on stage one a massive ten minutes ahead of the bunch, Frans Maassen, the stage winner, was unlikely to cause much trouble, but Ronan Pensec had a sixth and seventh place overall in the Tour in his *palmares* – and was a team-mate of Greg LeMond's to boot. Canada's Steve Bauer, too, had finished fourth in the Tour one year. As for Claudio Chiappucci, at twenty-seven already the winner of the Giro's King of the Mountains jersey that spring and twelfth overall, the Italian was in the prime of his career and clearly on the rise. To cap it all, Banesto then lost between one and two minutes in the stage two team time trial to most of their main rivals. What did it matter if Delgado or Indurain led when after ten stages of racing and one massive individual time trial, both of them were over ten minutes down on race leader Ronan Pensec?

The answer to that was: a lot. and not just because whilst Maassen and Bauer quickly faded from the running as soon as the roads started to steepen in earnest, Pensec and Chiappucci managed to hold onto the main group of favourites in the first Alpine summit finish stage to St. Gervais/Mont Blanc. Rather, the problems for Indurain and Delgado arose as soon as the Tour began its assault on the race's first *Hors Catégorie* climbs – the Madeleine, Glandon and Alpe d'Huez – the pre-race favourites began to make serious inroads, for the first time in the race, into Chiappucci and Pensec's sizeable lead.

Spearheading the bounceback was Greg LeMond, defending champion and second behind Gianni Bugno – of whom much more later – on Alpe d'Huez. Erik Breukink, twice a podium finisher in the Giro, staked a claim on the final podium by clinching third on the 'Dutch mountain'. The one rider who had failed to garner big benefits was Delgado, eighth at forty seconds in what was, in theory, the terrain that favoured him the most, and after driving up most of the Alpe at the head of the favourites.

Banesto could draw scant comfort from the fact that the rider who had shown himself to be the strongest on a fair percentage of the climbs and the flat that day was Indurain. Their strategy with the Navarran had proved to be totally erroneous. His attack on the descent from the Madeleine had set the cat amongst the pigeons with the GC favourites. But, crucially, Delgado's failure to bridge across to him on the Glandon had made it clear that the 1988 Tour winner was not on his best day. When Delgado did finally reach his team-mate on the descent, he had both LeMond and Bugno tailing him. Instead of Banesto unleashing Indurain in his own right, they were effectively playing their rivals' game, and sacrificing Indurain in the process.

Indurain's subsequent spectacular drive up the valley road to the foot of Alpe d'Huez made it plain to see that he was in great shape, despite losing nearly twelve minutes afterwards as he paid for the massive effort he had made previously. But Delgado's failure to finish off the spadework, coupled with Indurain's earlier effort, made Banesto look like they had done nothing more than lay the foundations for the opposition – and opened up the question of whether it would have been better, as *L'Équipe* argued later, with Indurain as the Spanish team's top GC contender.

'If we had had Indurain as sole leader from the start of the Tour, people would have said we were nuts,' Echavarri later retorted. But Indurain could, others countered, have been a co-leader, or a plan B. Then when Delgado failed to live up to his 1988 and 1989 form, Indurain could have been let off the leash.

The argument continued to bounce back and forth on the next stage, an uphill time trial to Villard-de-Lans, where Delgado only lost thirty seconds to the winner, Breukink, despite needing a bike change. Yet Indurain's magnificent third place, following his monumental effort of the previous day, showed that the Navarran could hardly have been discounted from the GC either – were it not for those twelve minutes he had lost the previous day.

What raised an armchair debate to one of far greater intensity came on the stage to St. Étienne, where LeMond ambushed Delgado when he made it into a late breakaway. Indurain had made it into the same move as LeMond, but once again dropped back to prevent his leader from facing a complete disaster. Thanks to Indurain, Delgado only lost thirty seconds, but as Unzué observed on the line, it could have been a loss measured in minutes had not Indurain's chances been sacrificed.

The press, meanwhile, were having a field day slating Banesto's failure to recognise that Indurain should have been given co-leader status. 'If things go on like this and Delgado ends up winning the Tour, he'll have to gift Indurain a flat on the Mediterranean, or build him a monument outside the aqueduct in [Delgado's home town of] Segovia,' observed Javier de Dalmases acidly in *El Mundo Deportivo*. 'Indurain's no longer an errand boy, because that would be a waste of talent … Delgado can never be grateful enough for what Indurain has done for him,' said *MARCA*. Yet in reality, Banesto's decision to oblige Indurain to wait at St. Etienne was common sense, given that he had no chance of impacting overall by that point: the real damage to Indurain's chances had been done on the stage to Alpe d'Huez.

The evidence in the case for Indurain continued to pile up in the final two key stages, Luz Ardiden and the Lac de Vassivière time trial, where Indurain finished fourth, 1–41 ahead of Delgado. It emerged that Delgado had been suffering from an upset stomach, which explained his lack of apparent attentiveness at St. Etienne and later en route to Bordeaux, an error that would cost him a fourth podium finish in Paris in a row. But that, in turn, only gave more ammunition to those arguing that Indurain should have been the Banesto co-leader, at the very least, from the start, and that Echavarri and Unzue should have made a better call much earlier in the race.

The clearest argument in favour of Indurain came at Luz Ardiden, the last great mountain stage of the race. Whilst Delgado flailed yet again, losing a minute and a half, Indurain was the only one of the potential GC contenders able to follow a blistering attack by LeMond. Despite suffering badly on the climb, Indurain not only clung on to LeMond's back wheel, but was able to swing past at the finish for his second Tour summit victory in two years.

This victory provoked more comments of the ilk of Luis Ocaña's, the 1973 Tour winner and later an influential commentator for Spanish TV. 'Even if you start a race with one leader, when you have somebody so exceptional waiting in the wings, it's only fair to give them a chance too.'

For others, what really justified Banesto's caution in the Tour was Indurain's failure to impact in the 1990 Vuelta, where he *had* been given the role of team leader ahead of Delgado. Indeed, Spain's only weekly cycling magazine of the time, *Meta2Mil*, placed Indurain at the top of the ranking of pre-race favourites. But Banesto were – like the rest of the top names in the Vuelta that year – caught out when the underrated Marco Giovanetti gained time in a first week break then proved a far harder nut to crack than anticipated. Banesto placed Gorospe in the lead thanks to his participation in the same break, but the Basque cracked completely on the first mountain stage, whilst Giovanetti, with a string of top ten places in the Giro d'Italia to his name, then took over as leader.

Indurain and Delgado chipped away at Giovanetti's lead but on neither of the set-piece key stages, a time trial at Valderazcay and a mountain-top finish in Cerler, could they really dent his lead. The writing appeared on the wall with a vengeance at a long, flat time trial in Zaragoza on stage twenty. Both Indurain and Delgado picked up time on Giovanetti, but it was a fraction of what was needed to oust the Italian: whilst Delgado gained thirty-seven seconds and moved into third, Indurain was only eighteen seconds ahead. The real Spanish challenger, in fact, looked to be Pello Ruiz Cabestany, winner in Zaragoza whilst Anselmo Fuerte, a gifted climber, also had some cards to play. After Cabestany cracked on the last stage, Delgado moved into second, but the harsh truth was that the defending champion had never been in a position to threaten Giovanetti. With Indurain only finishing seventh, it would have taken a brave manager to opt for Indurain as sole leader in the Tour.

In his defence, Indurain was – once again – suffering from a cold throughout the Spanish Grand Tour. Indurain's underlying breathing problems were more severe than for other riders, too. In

December of 1989, doctors at a clinic at the University of Navarre – where Echavarri and Unzué regularly sent their riders for analysis and tests – had diagnosed Indurain with chronic sinusitis, brought on by a deformed nasal septum that partially blocked the airways in his nose. Thus, and in keeping with their conservative approach, Echavarri and Unzué argued that in comparison with the tried and tested Delgado, Indurain should, after his setback in the Vuelta, have a secondary role in July.

Delgado himself argues that this was what Indurain wanted: 'Maybe it was José Miguel's fault, but it was certain that Miguel was very wary and he didn't want to have responsibilities, no way. People always say that he should have not waited for me in Saint Étienne, but I said, OK, that's what the fans think, but Miguel didn't. He wasn't acting under orders, but he stopped to bring me back up to the bunch anyway.'

'The good thing about Miguel is that he is very generous, he's going to respect the team plan even if it goes against him. But then there was also the thought in his head, "And if I fail? I don't want that responsibility. Better I stay in the system, where I'm feeling more at ease with myself." That's why he preferred to do what he was told to, rather than look for his own solution.'

Certainly the public had not changed their minds about who they supported the most, as Juan Carlos González Salvador discovered when he signed with Banesto after his three-year stint in KAS. 'The whole *Perico*-mania thing was completely crazy,' he recalls. 'He was so popular nobody wanted to go in the same team car as him after a race because you knew the damn car would be mobbed and followed all the way to the hotel. It was completely nuts.'

That public vote of confidence in Delgado acted as indirect pressure on the team. 'We had Miguel, but we had the winner of the 1988 Tour and – in our eyes – the moral winner of the

1989 Tour,' argues Arnaud. 'On an individual level amongst the favourites, it was Delgado who had done the 1989 Tour the fastest. The idea that Miguel could have won the Tour in 1990 just didn't come up, or if we ever talked about it, it was behind his back.'

'He could have made it onto the podium on one stage after he dropped back to wait for Pedro [St. Étienne] and then afterwards there was an enormous media scandal about it all. And my answer to that question about whether Indurain should have been leader in 1990 is, he didn't lose the Tour that year: 1990 was the year he won the following five. That year, seeing what he could do, win on Luz Ardiden and put in good showings in the time trials, as well as being the go-to rider for doing all the spadework on the flatter stages, you could see he had all the ingredients you needed to be a Tour winner. That was when it became clear, not before.'

Asked after Luz Ardiden if it would have made more sense if he had been race leader in the Tour and Delgado in the Vuelta, Indurain argued, 'it would seem that way, looking at the results. But there's no way of knowing that beforehand.' He did not have an issue with the team hierarchy, either, arguing, 'I'm happy with the way it's worked out, because we share out the responsibility between us, and one of us doesn't get all the pressure.'

The questions on the Indurain–Delgado handover of power, though, continued to echo through the sport for years. Delgado once told *MARCA*, 'Could Indurain have won that year? Perhaps, although we'll never know. But any team that's worth its salt should begin a Grand Tour with clear ideas and at that point, I was the leader. At that moment, he could have won because the race was proving to be a very weird one and LeMond, as usual, was always in the right place at the right time, even if he wasn't the strongest. Both Chiappucci or Miguel could have won.'

However, it is also certain that thanks to Delgado's (and to a lesser but also important extent, Reynolds') pioneering work, the belief in Spain that victory in a Tour with one of their riders was a real possibility had taken root again. This was not a once-in-a-lifetime triumph as it had been with brilliant but erratic racers of the ilk of Federico Martín Bahamontes or Luis Ocaña (whose cycling background was in any case as much French as it was Spanish). Rather it was Delgado and Arroyo whose racing in the 1983 Tour for Reynolds had re-created the belief that victory in cycling's greatest Tour was possible more than once. The 'voyage in the dark' in the Tour for Reynolds that year had gone a long way to creating the team's internal cohesion for major stage races, too. Then whilst Delgado's victories in the 1988 Tour and 1989 Vuelta had ensured that the massive media interest created by the 1983 results and Spain's 'radio wars' – such as José María García's blanket coverage of the sport – remained intact, Indurain was able to continue to progress at his own pace. Without having any pressure to produce results, Indurain could come unscathed through Echavarri's erroneous dreams of making him a Spanish Francesco Moser and prove his worth in week-long stage racing and the Grand Tours.

Delgado agrees that the removal of those inferiority complexes about the Tour was one important factor. But so too was his 'being more of a rebel than Miguel, more restless. Miguel prefers to reach the finish with the other favourites in the same bunch rather than risk attacking and end up getting dropped by the rest. I helped push away those doubts, not just for Miguel but for Spanish cycling in general. In 1983, Reynolds was the only Spanish team in the Tour. But by 1985 or 1986 there were lots of Spanish teams there, and they were saying "heck, this is possible, these rivals are only human."'

'In the case of Miguel, it allowed him to be close to a rider who was winning the Tour without the responsibilities. For a young rider, that's a very different scenario to when you're in a team that is simply going into the Tour to grab whatever they can. This way, I think Miguel was in a position to experience, inside a team, what had happened and then he could use those experiences, in his own way, to his advantage.'

There could be little doubt, though, that Indurain was ready to take on a greater role in Reynolds. Whilst the period following the 1989 Tour had been fairly flat in terms of results, Indurain made much greater gains across the board in 1990, as his rise in the FICP ranking – the international classification of riders' all-round performance – would suggest. In 1989, he was twentieth in the classification; in 1990, he was fourth.

A second victory in Paris–Nice, this time crushing Roche on the Col d'Èze climb, confirmed that his previous year's win had been no fluke. Indurain also picked up stage wins in the Vuelta al País Vasco and Vuelta a Valencia. Yet outside the question marks over Indurain's role in the Tour and the doubts that had been created by the Vuelta a España, the most intriguing development was his continuing progress in the Classics. In August Indurain captured a stunning victory in the Clásica San Sebastián, Spain's biggest one-day race, and in April he had taken an all but unnoticed fourth place in the Flèche Wallonne, later upgraded to third after Gert-Jan Theunisse tested positive.

Indurain's victory in the Clásica made him the first Spaniard to win a one-day race in the recent World Cup series, which replaced the Super Prestige Pernod International, the unofficial points system. But as Unzué puts it, 'there was a lack of interest, of cycling culture, about those kinds of races outside Spain. We didn't see that we could really achieve something in them and at the same time, it has to form part of the team's culture. But back then we were pretty green, and still discovering the top events. The Vuelta took place at the same time, more or less. Back then, Spain didn't have the riders for it as we now do, with Alejandro [Valverde] and we weren't obliged to take part in them as we are in the WorldTour. Now, it's different.'

The ongoing debate of what Indurain might have done had his team been more focussed on the Classics was overshadowed by the imperious necessity to give the Navarran a much more important role in the Tour de France. After 1990, not even the perpetually cautious Echavarri and Unzué could deny him that. 'I don't know if that was the Tour he didn't win,' Unzué says, 'but I do know that the 1990 race was the one that made him see that he had a Tour victory in his legs. He wouldn't say I want to win this, that or the other. Ever. You had to interpret his silences, but a lot of the time it was so evident that he didn't need to say it.' What was evident, too, when compared to Delgado, Unzué says, 'was that the student had now begun to be better than the teacher.'

CHAPTER 6
Neither Monk Nor Martian

Halfway up the Tourmalet ascent in 1991, José Miguel Echavarri and Miguel Indurain had the conversation that would – finally – start the process of removing the last remaining obstacle between Indurain and victory in the Tour.

In a group that was already shredded to less than a dozen and which was lacking Pedro Delgado, Indurain's role as Banesto's leader for the Tour was, at long last, beyond all doubt. But the issue now was, with Indurain in sole command, how far the Navarran could go in his new position – and how soon? Indurain's question to Echavarri as the favourites inched their way up the Pyrenees' toughest climb went very much to the point on that score. The twenty-seven-year-old wanted to know how well his rivals were faring.

Referring to the race leader, Echavarri's first answer was '[Luc] Leblanc's not looking great.' But then he added the key phrase, 'and neither is LeMond.' That was all Indurain needed to hear to head to the front of the pack and, together with his key ally of that day, Claudio Chiappucci, step up the pace as much as he could. As they did so LeMond, the leading favourite, found himself carved out of the group, then slowly but surely shed behind.

One of the best photos of those crunch moments that saw Indurain move into top gear for the 1991 Tour was taken on a sweeping left-hand bend on the Tourmalet's upper slopes. To the right of the road, a white stone cliff gleams brightly in the intense heat, on the left there is a steeply dropping precipice. On each side of the broad, smoothly surfaced tarmac in between there is a long, thick line of fans, many dressed in singlets and shorts and waving Basque *ikurriña* flags as they cheer the riders on. In this improvised, swelteringly hot arena, as the riders strain forward, there is nowhere to go but upwards, nothing to face but pain.

The photo was taken just as the race was splitting apart, from behind LeMond's right shoulder, looking ahead at the backs of Chiappucci and Indurain as they lean over their bikes to force the pace on a group of six or eight riders. At the back of the group, visibly struggling, are yellow jersey Luc Leblanc and his compatriot Gerard Rue. But behind them – and presumably struggling even more – is LeMond, separated from the group by a mere five metres of shiny, graffitti-spattered grey tarmac, his head craned slightly to the left as he tries to look round the group to see exactly who it is causing him to suffer.

To judge by the photo, the distance between LeMond and the rear end of the group looks minimal, a pedal stroke at most. Yet it was the first time in the race that LeMond, winner of the 1989 and 1990 Tours, was in serious trouble. That pedal stroke that would have brought him back into contention might have lasted just a fraction of a second but there was no way LeMond could dig any deeper to resist. The last time Indurain had made a move like this, at Luz Ardiden the year before, the American and Spaniard had launched a joint attack for LeMond to take the yellow and Indurain the stage. This time, the boot was truly on the other foot.

By the summit, LeMond had lost seventeen seconds on this group of favourites. A fast descent on the first, toughest, hairpin corners of the Tourmalet was enough to let the triple Tour winner regain contact. But by then, Indurain had disappeared from the front group, attacking alone and riding the last stretch of the long road from Villava and his green, nameless, first bike of the late 1970s, all the way to the pinnacle of cycling's greatest race – and the *maillot jaune*.

That LeMond was the last obstacle Indurain needed to sweep aside to stake a claim on the yellow jersey had become very clear by that point in the 1990 Tour.

Two of the top contenders, Raúl Alcalá and Erik Breukink, had already headed for home after their team, PDM, was struck by what was first treated as a case of mass food poisoning, although rumours that the case was to do with something altogether different have circulated ever since. LeMond, on the other hand, had gained nearly two minutes on Banesto early on in the Tour and then had been the rider that resisted Indurain's first time trial win in Alençon the most tenaciously, losing only eight seconds. Thus whilst Indurain was lying fifth overall when the Tour reached the Spanish town of Jaca the night before the Tourmalet, LeMond was the only pre-race favourite still ahead of him. On top of that, LeMond had won the two previous Tours de France. Gambling it all on winning in the final time trial in Mâcon would have been too close a call for Indurain.

The latter, on the other hand, had not started the Tour as a top contender or even as a lone leader in the Banesto team. Instead Indurain had been designated co-leader alongside Delgado, whilst a new signing for Banesto, Jean-François Bernard, was waiting in the wings. Echavarri, the *Diario de Navarra* reported, said that a final decision on who received top protected status would only be taken after two stages in the Pyrenees.

Bernard's semi-privileged status in a team that seemed to have decided on its successor had several explanations. Firstly, after 1987, when he took third overall, Bernard had been considered France's most promising young Tour rider. Then in 1991, he had finished fourteenth in the Giro d'Italia, ahead of Delgado and with two second places on stages. Neither rider had truly shone in Italy, but Bernard's better performance confirmed that after two difficult years, the Frenchman – who had performed well in the 1988 Giro d'Italia too before crashing out injured – could be back on track.

It wasn't quite as simple as that, though. Bernard had specifically asked Echavarri when he broke his contract with Toshiba at the end of 1990 to join Banesto that, after years of pressure in the French team, he should not be considered a leader. But at the same time, should Bernard suddenly have found himself in a top position overall, Echavarri was hardly likely to have told a former Tour podium finisher to squeeze on the brakes.

Coincidentally or not, following Bernard's signing, Indurain had stepped up his Grand Tour game in the Vuelta a España that spring, taking second overall. That surely merited the Navarran a top position in Banesto's game plan for the Tour – except that bizarrely, the 1991 Vuelta showed that making Indurain an outright leader might well have been risky.

For Indurain, second in the Vuelta was his best ever Grand Tour result by a long chalk. The problem was that he had been clearly beaten in the 1991 Vuelta by a rider who, to put it mildly, had come out of nowhere. At the time of the race, Melcior Mauri was a promising twenty-five-year-old time triallist from Catalonia. But Mauri's Grand Tour record – with a best placing, out of five starts, of 71st in the 1990 Vuelta, and with no stage wins to his name – hardly suggested that he would suddenly leap into contention in 1991.

Yet Mauri's sudden rise to the top of the Spanish cycling hierarchy was by no means entirely fluky. Mauri was part of the formidable ONCE team, a Spanish squad created in 1989 and which was rapidly gaining a name as one of the most forward-thinking, cohesive outfits in professional cycling. ONCE manager Manolo Saiz's meticulously planned team time trial efforts – one area where Reynolds-Banesto had traditionally been weakest – saw Mauri move to the top of the leader board in the 1991 Vuelta on the race's first stage, a time trial formed by three-man teams. Then matters improved even more for Mauri after the Vuelta's first full team time trial on stage two netted ONCE another 1–40 over Banesto. The race had barely started, and Indurain was already nearly two minutes back. 'We are the best in the world at this,' Saiz argued, and it was hard to disagree.

On each subsequent time trial, Indurain lost ground to Mauri: 56 seconds in Mallorca on stage eight, 42 seconds at Valderazcay's hill-climb, 66 seconds on stage eighteen in Valladolid. The only points where Indurain could pull back time on Mauri, in fact, were in the mountain stages, such as Cerler, where he regained a minute, and the Lagos de Covadonga, where he clawed back 28 seconds. The suspension of the key mountain stage in the Pyrenees to Pla de Beret because of snowstorms meant a loss of a day's racing that might have turned the tables in Indurain's favour. But in terms of Indurain's strongest suit, the time trials, he had been defeated throughout.

According to Saiz, Banesto had underestimated Mauri, basing their strategy instead around trying to beat Marino Lejarreta, the far more experienced ONCE pre-Vuelta leader. 'There was never a battle between Mauri and Indurain, it was between Lejarreta and Indurain,' Saiz observes. 'Indurain had a huge amount of respect for Marino. So the only time that the Vuelta was in danger for ONCE in 1991 was when Indurain got ahead of Lejarreta overall, after the Valladolid time trial. And the only time Mauri was in difficulty in that Vuelta was the next day's stage. But whilst Lejarreta was second Mauri was never in danger. We all thought that Mauri would crack under the pressure. But he didn't.'

Indeed, Saiz had himself played a part of keeping Banesto overly interested in Lejarreta, by arguing mid-way through the Vuelta that Mauri would crumple on the climbs. Instead, Mauri's tenacity proved enough to deprive Indurain of the Vuelta victory in what turned out to be his best ever chance to win the race, and his prowess in time trialling saw him beat the unrivalled master of racing against the clock for the next five Tours de France.

How did what was to be Indurain's last defeat in a Grand Tour for three years actually happen? Part of the problem was Banesto failing to give Indurain the mountain support he needed. 'We'd done the Giro as well as the Vuelta, and I think the Vuelta team was weaker as a result. If you only have twenty riders in a squad, it's not possible to have two strong separate Grand Tour teams,' Dominique Arnaud observes. ONCE's ultra-strong start to the Vuelta and having two leaders in the GC battle was another factor in Mauri's favour. The rough winter weather in the Pyrenees and northern Spain, with 34 riders abandoning or outside the time limit on the Cerler stage alone, was a third reason, given Indurain's aversion to the cold and wet. The cancellation of the Pla de Beret stage was a fourth.

A fifth factor may well have been that Indurain had had an exceptionally difficult start to the season, being forced to stop training for three weeks with flu in February, and could have lacked some base form. But Indurain's fourth place in Liège–Bastogne–Liège – his best ever result in a Monument Classic – just before the Vuelta hardly suggested he was in poor shape. That was even if, with Ariostea team-mates Moreno Argentin and Rolf Sorensen dictating events in the front group in *La Doyenne,* Indurain had no chance of taking the victory in Liège.

Indurain put it very simply, as ever: 'Mauri was going really well, and on top of that, ONCE had options with Lejarreta.' Essentially, Indurain had been outgunned by a team as much as by a rider – a lesson that few, if any, other squads apart from ONCE appeared able to grasp in the Tours to come.

Delgado's analysis also sheds extra light on such a puzzling defeat: 'In theory the Vuelta was the best Grand Tour for Miguel – short climbs, not too many days in the mountains at that time, and long time trials. But, and I don't know why, there are some races that take a liking to you, others that don't, and the Vuelta was a race which never liked Miguel, right up to 1996.'

With Bernard now waiting in the wings should Delgado and Indurain both crack, Indurain started the 1991 Tour with a point to prove as much to his team as to the world in general. But his urgent need to define his role once and for all in the Tour was overshadowed by another near-disastrous start for Banesto. Just as in 1989 where Delgado's prologue delay was followed by a weak team time trial, the first two days saw Banesto experience a double whammy of potentially devastating proportions.

The first setback came on a seemingly inoffensive, 110-kilometre circuit round Lyon, the first part of a split sector stage. That Djamolidin Abdoujaparov, the Uzbek sprinter, should win on a flat circuit would have been viewed as normal. But that Abdoujaparov should only have seven riders with him, rather than leading home the whole bunch in a mass dash for the line, was unusual. And that two of those seven riders with 'Abdu' were GC contenders LeMond and Breukink was even stranger. The main bunch, including all the Banesto riders, completed the stage nearly two minutes down, representing a lot of egg on the Spanish team's face, a huge blow to their morale and a significant dent in their chances overall.

The usually laidback Echavarri was furious, to the point where whenever riders came back to the team car for water on the morning stage, he reportedly yelled at them, 'Your bidon's just been dropped on the ground, it's two minutes down!' The GC damage then worsened even further when Z, LeMond's team, gained a further sixteen seconds on Banesto in the afternoon's team time trial. In less than 48 hours, Delgado, Indurain and Bernard were all at nearly two and a half minutes down on the American.

Indurain's first time trial victory, at Alençon, by eight seconds on LeMond, did little more than limit the previous damage inflicted by the American. Gaining a minute on Breukink looked promising, but Breukink's exit with the rest of PDM did nothing to resolve the main issue, which was LeMond. On the first stage through the Pyrenees to Jaca in Spain, featuring two first category and one third category climb, Banesto failed to put in any attacks of importance and two potential outside threats, Luc Leblanc and Charly Mottet, gained ten minutes. After LeMond's triumphant first week, that this happened on the day a Tour stage finished on Spanish soil for the first time in fourteen years just added insult to injury. Indurain managed, with a timid late attack, to regain eight scant seconds on LeMond. But the American, whilst 2–35 down on the new leader Leblanc, still had more than two minutes on Indurain. After Delgado's disaster of 1989 and having the 'wrong' leader in 1990, Banesto, it seemed, were once again staring into the sporting abyss.

'The terrain didn't suit us,' Indurain argued afterwards. 'I think that Val Louron is a much better stage.' *El Mundo Deportivo,* one of the less belligerent newspapers in Spain that evening, argued that 'we have to give Banesto the benefit of the doubt' but still accused the team collectively of being 'apathetic' and 'exasperatingly passive.' 'They had five riders in the front group,' the paper pointed out. Although *El País* stated that Echavarri had already warned that he would not be firing off his heavy artillery, it added that, 'It was hardly wholly acceptable for there to be no big battle, just because the last climb is thirty kilometres from the finish.' Behind the scenes, elements of Banesto's upper management circles were so worried that, *MARCA*'s Josu Garai claimed, Echavarri's position 'was hanging by a thread ... and an internal communiqué was doing the rounds asking for him to be sacked.' Even the Spanish minister of sport, Javier Gómez Navarro, turned up at the Banesto hotel and told Echavarri to his face, 'I've been listening to the radio and you wouldn't believe what they [the Spanish media] are saying about you ... how's *Perico*? Going well?' Echavarri's answer was much quoted afterwards. Indeed, most reports of the stage would probably now precede it with a couple of imaginary drumrolls for added effect. '*Perico*'s going well,' Echavarri said, 'but Miguel is going really well.'

Indurain was indeed going so well that after the descent to the foot of the Tourmalet, his advantage on the chase group was up to forty-five seconds and counting. For the third year in a row, first on the Marie-Blanque in 1989, then the Madeleine in the Alps in 1990, and now the Tourmalet, Indurain had attacked on the downhill of a major Tour climb – but on this occasion the stakes could not have been higher. It was at this point, at the foot of the Tourmalet, that the man who would prove Indurain's key ally in his dash for glory reached his side: Chiappucci, who had taken off after Indurain. Aware that he had both the Aspin and the ascent to Val Louron left to tackle, and with Chiappucci more than four minutes down on Indurain overall, Banesto's directors instructed Indurain to wait until the Italian reached his side. The working alliance that was to lead to Indurain's taking over the *maillot jaune* was about to form and it immediately began working well. By the summit of the Aspin, the lead was up to 1–45 on the favourites, but crucially, LeMond was at three minutes. A major power shift in favour of Indurain was on the point of taking place.

Intriguingly for a rider frequently slated for being over-calculating in the five Tour victories that followed, this time there had been no prior plan to Indurain's downhill attack. It was only after Echavarri's conversation with Indurain on the Tourmalet that the wheels began to be set in motion. Indurain later commented, simply, that at the moment after the Tourmalet summit where the rest of the top names had eased slightly, to take on board food and newspapers to protect themselves from the chill factor on the descent, he had thought: 'I'm not stopping. Whoever wants to, can follow me.'

'*Tranquilo, va como Dios,*' commented José Miguel Echavarri to the rest of the management, a phrase that can only be translated badly, but clearly, as 'Relax, he's riding like he was God.' Certainly if Indurain needed some divine protection, it was arguably on that blistering downhill attack. Unzué recalls that in the team car behind Indurain he was driving at speeds of up to 100 kph and they took the corners so hard, one of the bikes on the roof rack loosened its stays and went flying into a ravine. Once Chiappucci had arrived, though, the tension in what was one of Indurain's most dramatic episodes ever in a Tour subsided and the alliance between the two was easy to form: the classic dividing up of the spoils was clear – the stage for one, the overall lead for the other. It was a strategy that was often to be repeated in the Indurain years.

At the finish at the top of the ascent of the Val Louron, Indurain's swinging, one-handed, uppercut punch in the air as he crossed the line a few yards behind Chiappucci – taken in some quarters as an 'up-yours' gesture to the Spanish media for their criticisms of Banesto – indicated he knew full well what he had achieved. Not only did he have the first yellow jersey, but also, with the exception of Gianni Bugno who had the strength to react in time and who only lost 88 seconds, this was a knock-out blow. With everybody from sixth downwards on the stage more than six minutes adrift, LeMond finally tottered across the line more than seven minutes behind Indurain. Indurain's overall advantage on his closest rival now stood at three minutes on France's Charly Mottet: a Tour-winning margin.

From this point onwards, Indurain's team, rather than his individual performances, were responsible for maintaining the status quo. By and large, the team held up. Jean-François Bernard gave him vital support on the mountain stages, both on the ascent to Alpe d'Huez, where the Frenchman rode most of the climb in the front of the group and again at Morzine two days later. To judge by the way RMO, looking to protect Mottet's second place overall, were willing to ride so hard for Banesto when LeMond went on the attack on the road to Gap, Indurain's lead was viewed as a solid one by his rivals, too.

It was not just the time advantage, as Arnaud and Delgado both saw it, that played in Reynolds' favour. There was also Indurain's tenacity and his seemingly limitless ability to handle almost all situations when under pressure. 'Miguel's only problem was getting the overall lead. Once he'd got it, he'd never let it go, because mentally he was very strong,' Delgado argues. 'I remember once in a Paris–Nice when he was leading, he was isolated from his team and he had Stephen Roche to handle, but he came through absolutely fine.'

'I tried to make the team see that once Miguel took the lead in Val Louron, then he wouldn't lose it afterwards,' Arnaud confirms. 'It wasn't just his strength, it was how incredibly serious he was about it all. He couldn't lose it. We had the sense that if he lost it afterwards, it would have been his team's fault, not his.' In that sense, fortunately, 'The 1991 Tour team was very strong. There had been a bit of a doubt over whether to send the riders belonging to *Perico*'s generation, to which I belonged, or whether to send in the newer, younger, riders, like Armand de las Cuevas. Finally they sent the experienced side of the team: older riders like Bernard, Magro, me, Julián, Delgado. It was a very powerful back-up.'

Whilst LeMond fell apart in the Alps on the stage to Morzine, the most dangerous moment for Indurain after grasping the lead in Val Louron came on the following stage, to Aix-les-Bains. 'It wasn't an exceptionally difficult stage, just a couple of minor Alpine climbs, but it was one which had seen a lot of attacks go clear,' Delgado once recalled. 'On one of the ascents, which we were going up using the big chainring so it wasn't so difficult, it was lined out, and first Bugno, and then Chiappucci managed to go clear. I went haring after them, but there was no sign of Miguel. I looked round for him and he was quite a way back, maybe twentieth or thirtieth in the line.'

'"I'm in trouble," Indurain said when I got to him, without moving a muscle of his face, but it was clearly a tricky situation. 'So I went up to Bernard, told him to go at a steady pace and only to follow Bugno and Chiappucci as best we could. Which we did and we fortunately pegged them back. When somebody starts to claim that Indurain didn't suffer on the bike, I always remember that.'

Indurain signed off from the Tour in decisive style, solidifying his already all but indestructible lead with another time trial victory in Mâcon. Although Chiappucci began by running him close in the first provisional time check, Indurain inexorably opened up his advantage on the two Italians who would join him on the final podium, showing beyond all doubt that he had the endurance as well as the power to go the distance for a Grand Tour win.

From thereon, Indurain's first Tour de France win, the one that he would regularly describe as his favourite, was a question of staying upright on the largely ceremonial final stage into Paris, en route to Banesto's first victory as a sponsor and the team's second in four years. Indurain was also Spain's fourth Tour winner after Delgado, Bahamontes and Ocaña, the country's youngest (at twenty-seven) and – one for trivia fanatics – at 1.88 m, the Tour's tallest ever until Sir Bradley Wiggins (two centimetres higher) in 2012. But if Indurain's progress to the top had been steady, there had been no sense, as there had been with Merckx and Hinault when they won their first Grand Boucle and whose Tour achievements he would eventually emulate, that he had been expected to win that July. Rather there was more talk, particularly internationally, of why more experienced riders had not been able to beat Indurain.

It was asked how it was possible that LeMond had failed to manoeuvre himself into a position of power as he had done in the previous two Tours. Another major topic of debate was how it was that neither Bugno nor Chiappucci were strong enough in the time trials and that Breukink, quite apart from the questions hanging over his PDM team, lacked the power to go clear of Indurain on the climbs. 'Nobody in their right mind,' argued one top director at the time, 'would have said Indurain could have won a Tour in 1991 until he did it. Waiting to help Delgado and winning a stage like he did in 1990 has nothing to do with winning a Tour.'

After his two dazzling time trial performances in the Tour, few amongst the thousands of Spanish fans who acclaimed him on the Champs Elysées, amongst them around 500 from Villava, would have remembered how Indurain had suffered against the clock in the 1991 Vuelta, either. But abroad, Indurain's win had been almost too opportunistic – the most memorable moment being attacking on a descent and gaining exactly the right ally that was needed to take the key mountain stage – for it to be given a huge amount of long-term significance. *L'Équipe* were probably the politest of the international media, calling Indurain 'a new arrival in the international peloton' and almost leaving it at that. 'It was not seen as the beginning of an era, in the way that Ullrich's win was in 1997 or Hinault's in 1978,' observes William Fotheringham, one of a handful of English-speaking journalists who covered the 1991 Tour de France. 'Instead, LeMond, with three wins already, was still seen as the big favourite for the following year's Tour, and there were plenty of other top names – Roche, Fignon, Chiappucci – who had been around for longer and who were likely to give Indurain a run for his money in 1992.' If the international press's muted reaction seems surprising, it is worth remembering how hard it is to repeat one Tour victory the following year. Indeed, once Lance Armstrong's results had been wiped, the next rider to do so in the Tour after Indurain would be Chris Froome in 2016.

There were also the criticisms – already – of Indurain for being too withdrawn, too inexpressive. *L'Équipe* even went so far as to cite a nameless journalist from Madrid who claimed that 'after twenty years, Indurain's wife would still have no idea of the man she shares her nights with ... Apart from a polite smile on each finishing podium, the only sign of any kind of emotion was that gesture at Val Louron,' the newspaper added. 'He has such a great character that he has no need to express it,' was Echavarri's polite, if ironic, explanation.

As for the man himself? Indurain did not, by any means, over-play his achievement, preferring to call the Tour 'a race like any other, except that it's more important.' Given Indurain's fondness both for stating the obvious and his dislike of spending more time in the limelight than was absolutely necessary, perhaps that was only to be expected.

Inside Spain, Indurain's Tour victory gained him automatic entry into the pantheon of the country's cycling greats. However, his team-mates are adamant that Indurain's elevated stature had no effect whatsoever on his personality. For all his innate conservatism, this was more surprising than it sounds, given the usual pernicious effects on young athletes of hitting the big time. Indurain, some-how, resisted all that – permanently.

'I've worked in all kinds of sport, from cycling to basketball, and I've never come across anybody like him. Fame didn't change him in the slightest,' says Juan Carlos González Salvador, who after retiring from cycling became an agent for riders and athletes. 'Unfortunately, just the opposite case is usually the truth. It's very unusual for anybody who suddenly earns shedloads of money – for kids of twenty, twenty-two, twenty-four, or even if you're forty or fifty – not to change. Suddenly you've got the obsession with photos, the fixation with constantly changing your hairstyle and getting it all gelled up or in a pointy quiff, the sudden snobbishness, the "I've got to be better-looking-than-anybody", all that bloody garbage. Miguel was the opposite, he didn't change, never has. [He thinks] "I'm not bothered what you think of me, I don't have to project any particular kind of image, I know what I am … " That, in my opinion, shows real self-confidence. But that's not to say he was weird, either. He was *ni monje ni marciano* – as the Spanish put it when trying to describe somebody conventional, but in a good way – "neither a monk nor a Martian".'

'When he won the Tour in 1991, he was the same Miguel Indurain as he had been in 1986,' comments Arnaud. 'You could ask him about the same things, talk to him about the same things. He is the same even now: much more of a person, more of a man, than interested in playing the champion.'

'He never saw himself as being the big star of the show,' Delgado argues, and nor was he fussy or even obtrusive as a team-mate. 'He's so quiet, you don't even hear him,' Jean-François Bernard once said. 'When he comes down to a team meal, you don't even hear him pull his chair away from the table.' There was a limited amount of 'special treatment': by the end of his career, Indurain had his own *soigneur* and for one season his own medic, after the team doctor, Sabino Padilla, decided to quit Banesto in 1995 and Indurain continued working with him. But for years he seems to have unintentionally made a point of not being different from his team-mates; he never insisted on priority for massages for example, nor made demands for special treatment for his bike from the mechanics or for special diets for himself. Indeed, he was so good at *not* standing out from the rest that Delgado recollects one occasion when Indurain could obviously have asked him to change something and instead it was Indurain who put himself out – quite considerably.

'When Miguel became race leader in the 1991 Tour, I started sharing rooms with him. I got put in charge of handling the room phone, making sure he got left alone and so on. And then one day I got up to the hotel room, after four or five nights of sharing and I see there's another team-mate sitting on what ought to be my bed. And I asked, "Hey, what's up with Miguel?" and the team-mate answered, "he doesn't want to be in the same room as you." My first reaction was "Whaaat?" but then I went to find Miguel and asked him, straight out, what had happened. Indurain answered, "Ufff, Pedro, I'm sorry but I'm having a really rough time with you in the room." Well, I always did read or go to bed a bit later than the others and I had said to him for the first few days we were sharing, if the light's bothering you or whatever, let me know. But Miguel said no, it wasn't that: "it's because you make me feel really hungry".'

'Miguel really had to watch his weight ... And imagine, you get to the room after the stage and there I am, stuffing myself on a sandwich, a beer, some cakes and maybe a big belch afterwards. And you're nibbling on some muesli. And on top of that I'd say to him, as a joke, "God I'm hungry!" As Miguel put it, "I've suffered enough on the bike to put up with you stuffing your face as well."'

But as Delgado says, what was really surprising was that Indurain had not insisted that Delgado, not he, change rooms. Nor, as was another option, had he made Delgado go into their shared bathroom every night to eat his snack. Instead, Indurain – the Tour de France leader – packed up his suitcase and went down to the hotel reception to find another room himself. It was not a question of low self-esteem, Delgado argues, just that Indurain was incapable of viewing himself as different in any way from the other riders in the team – and therefore it was up to him to sort out the situation: 'As a fan, you'd look at Miguel and you'd say, "He's not a normal person walking down the street, he's God." But Miguel looks at himself and sees himself as normal, and he found that kind of hero worship or idolatry hard to understand.'

Amongst the staff, Indurain's lack of fussiness and failure to insist on special treatment even as he grew more famous made him appreciated, but they were also – privately – marvelling at how little he had changed. 'I'm pretty sure I was the first person ever to give him a massage, and he didn't care, ever, if he was the first or the last in the queue,' says Manu Arrieta, a Reynolds and Banesto *soigneur* for more than twenty years. 'It reached the point where if you forgot to give him a massage one day, he wouldn't say anything. He never wanted anything different, not even after he had won the Tour or if he was really tired.' Arrieta sums up Indurain's personality perfectly, perhaps, when he says, 'As a person, Miguel was exceptionally normal,' meaning that for someone that special to be that normal at the same time was in itself bizarre, but surely worthy of admiration and respect, too.

If there was one way that Indurain was unusual, Arrieta says, it was in his failure to talk at length – as most riders do – whilst on the massage table, as part of their way of de-stressing from the day. 'If you asked him something, he'd answer, but he wouldn't volunteer information.' The one time Indurain showed any anger – or indeed any kind of intense emotion – came during a Giro d'Italia. 'It's engraved in my memory because it was so unusual. Chiappucci and [Marco] Saligari had gone on the attack and that was the only time on the massage table that he sounded pissed off. He said, "Fuck, I could have attacked them but then it'd have been tricky on the descent." Hearing Miguel saying that word, "fuck", and sounding angry, it was completely out of the ordinary, never happened before or since.'

'He'd be satisfied after a time trial, but he didn't let it show much. But it was the same with everything. I've known champions – and I'm not going to tell you who – whose wives would tell me how glad they were that their husband's gone off to the race because they were so picky about their food, their spaghetti, their pasta. But Miguel, there was never any fuss like that when he was with us. In that he was exceptional, too.'

Yet as Delgado says, Indurain was not only a humble champion, but one who could easily disconnect from his sport. 'He's not obsessed with cycling ... He likes it, he enjoys it, he was very good at it, it is his hobby, but he was never totally absorbed in it. It's still like that now ... he'll say, "If it's less than eighteen degrees centigrade, I'm not going out," "If the weather's such-and-such, I'm not going out." It was his job, and he really enjoyed doing it, and it wasn't as if he had to beat himself up to do it, he was so good at it that it was easy for him. When you talk about Miguel you're talking about somebody normal, but with incredible physical gifts and a capacity to read a race that was off the scale, too.'

'As a racer, he was the most natural human being in the world, very straightforward, very careful,' adds Juan Carlos González Salvador, who joined Banesto's professional team in 1990, after racing with Indurain in the amateur squad. 'He didn't take unnecessary risks. For example, he'd always have a spare pair of shoes in the front car and in the second car too. And he was famous in the peloton for how he used to get rid of the air conditioning in hotels.' At a time when hotel room temperature controls were unified under the receptionist's sole command and the clients just had to put up with it, Indurain would borrow a screwdriver from the mechanics to take out the ventilator completely. 'He didn't do it because he was fussy, it was just that he knew how important the Tour was, he didn't want to catch cold and Miguel knew he wouldn't really suffer because it was hot.' This was one of the very few areas when Indurain risked being unpopular with his team-mates for the sake of the Tour. As Unzué recalls, 'He'd be absolutely fine in a baking hot room and his poor room-mate would be frying.'

Team insiders also noted Indurain's exceptional powers of observation, both of his rivals and – even more unusually – his surroundings. It wasn't just that like most farmers, Indurain was a real appreciator of countrysides and landscapes, taking a note-book and pencil along with him when away from Navarre, to make sure he wrote down the names of towns and regions he liked so he could re-visit them after retiring. Indurain was, Arnaud says, very methodical in other ways, too: 'He'd always be sure to get that extra's hour sleep. Back then, the Tours were three and a half weeks long. So that made for an extra day's sleep.'

In general, Indurain proved to be an unremarkable team-mate to room with. Delgado says, 'He was neither very chaotic nor extra tidy, somewhere in the middle.' As for his outside interests on the race, the joke going round Banesto was that Indurain had taken the same book with him to the Tour for years, but that he never got further than about page 60. In a kind of literary Groundhog Day, Indurain once admitted, 'I'll read the one chapter, fall asleep, and then have to read it again the next night.' But he had no private superstitions of the kind so many riders end up half-believing in – such as putting on one sock before the other before races or pinning on the race number in a particular way – or at least none Delgado knew about. As he puts it, 'Miguel never told that sort of personal stuff to anybody.'

At the same time, his team-mates could appreciate that behind the amiable, unflappable and utterly unassuming exterior Indurain knew, very much, what he wanted and how to get it. 'Miguel wasn't one to say he'd studied a route, or to talk about his training, like some riders would do, talking. Miguel would just do it,' Juan Carlos González Salvador says. 'When a sponsor put out a kind of new teeth brake in the 1990s, Miguel refused to use them from the word go. Instead, he insisted on using a certain kind of disc brake, and it was that kind of disc brake or nothing.' He recounts an occasion when Indurain made the Banesto mechanic, Carlos Vidales, change his bike gears completely fifteen minutes before a time trial. 'But he did so quietly, never making a fuss. It was always a quiet battle. From the outside, everything seemed to be perfect for Miguel. But that wasn't the case.'

Equally, the claim that Indurain was not, actually, capable of experiencing pain – as some reporters would imply with all their talk that he was from another planet – is clearly rubbish. As Juan Carlos González Salvador insists, Indurain's secret was that he was more used to living in tough conditions than others thanks to his rural childhood. That was a huge advantage in the Tour, particularly in the early 1990s, when hotels and transport were nowhere near as comfortable as in modern-day racing.

'It would be totally wrong to say that Indurain didn't suffer. It was more that he was used to it, he'd had a tough upbringing, working all weathers in the countryside. So who cares if it's hot or cold? It's not a big deal.' Speaking as if he were Indurain, he continues, 'Why should I care if I'm hot in bed? Another thing would be working in a coal mine.'

For all Juan Carlos González Salvador insists that Miguel was *ni monje ni marciano,* Indurain's unwillingness to create a fuss did create a certain unearthly charisma about him – one that was to be pointed out, time and again, as he racked up the Tour wins. His natural quietness, particularly amongst the garrulous Spanish, helped reinforce this slightly other-worldly quality, too: the sense of silent strength. Delgado believes his quietness, despite the fame, gave him more of a presence, made Indurain somebody people were keen to get to know, but were somehow aware that it was never going to happen completely. During much of his career,

Indurain remained an amiable enigma, difficult to understand for his fellow-countrymen, and all but incomprehensible for those from outside Spain: possibly it has never been harder to tell what truly made a cycling champion tick.

'In 1988, when I met him, he would barely talk,' Delgado says. 'He'd listen though. But that almost made people like him more, because as he didn't talk, people would be more inclined to think of him as being a nice bloke, not like me – people see me talking a lot, and that gets them more annoyed.'

Unadventurous as he was, 'Miguel wouldn't even come to the door of the hotel on an evening in the Tour. Well, we might have gone out for a moment, but as he was so quiet, you'd not notice he was there. There'd be flashes of humour, but only when he was in a really secure situation. Miguel is more one to finish off a phrase, to confirm what somebody else had said.' As for riders' almost universal habit of recounting race anecdotes of an evening, 'Indurain was never one for doing that. It's only now he does it, but more than an anecdote, it's normally a small incident that forms part of an anecdote.' But for all Indurain's seriousness, that does not mean he is averse to being the subject of gentle rib-tickling: 'I take the Mick out of him about it, saying, "Wow, Miguel, just listen to all those stories you know,"' says Delgado with a grin. 'He doesn't mind.'

This accessibility, quietness and innate humility made Indurain hugely appealing to work for as a team leader. Yet the flipside, as Arnaud recalls, of not having a demanding boss was that Indurain was often not demanding enough. It reached the point, in fact, where he was so inarticulate about his requirements inside a race that episodes like when he told Delgado he was suffering in the 1991 Tour were real rarities. Rather it became necessary for his team-mates to read his expressions, instead of waiting for words that never came.

'It was difficult because Miguel didn't talk. Above all, we'd guess what the orders were by working out how he felt from the way he was looking at us,' Arnaud says. Indurain having been with Reynolds/Banesto all his career was a huge help. 'Above all, he'd been my team-mate before he'd been my team leader. I knew from his face if he was in a bad way or a good way. Things like that helped, but you had to be a good judge.'

Only the odd gentle Indurain-esque joke would render the process a little faster. 'Sometimes I'd ask him "How's it going?" And he'd answer "Mavic. Ma-vic." In those days we had Mavic wheels, and if he wasn't up to going so fast, he'd say, "Ma-vic." In other words, if you could read the words on the wheel as it went round slowly, he wasn't going so well.' For a good day, 'he wouldn't say anything. You could just see it for yourself.'

For his team-mates depending on Indurain to be in the mood for jokes even whilst he was suffering was, to say, the least, an unreliable method of knowing whether they should go flat out from the start of a stage or soft-pedal for the day. But there was not much to be done about it, and on the plus side, the image of a strong, silent, inexpressive type certainly had its benefits when it came to playing mindgames with his rivals. This was ironic, considering that Indurain was hardly scary as a person. He just *looked* scary, according to Arnaud.

'It helped, definitely. He was more intimidating that way. But that wasn't really intentional. It was part of his being a simple, straightforward sort of guy.' Furthermore, although his pollen allergies and cold weather were definitely chinks in his armour, Indurain not only appeared impregnable, he also gave a good impression of being indestructible. In a sport where crashes are relatively commonplace, his major injuries during his career, both amateur and professional, could be counted on the fingers of one hand: a fractured wrist in the amateur Spanish Nationals in 1981 and again in the Vuelta in 1989 and a fractured collarbone in the Volta a Catalunya in 1990. In the Tour – nothing. For someone who rode nearly 70,000 kilometres' worth of Grand Tours during his career – the equivalent of pedalling more than one and a half times round the planet, and without even counting probably the same distance again in lesser events – that is a remarkably low total. It also meant that virtually nobody in the peloton had actually seen Indurain fall off.

Indurain's unflappability, which Arnaud said was the thing that impressed him the most, never changed. Gerard Rue, Indurain's team-mate from 1993 onwards, once recalled being in an ultra-light aircraft en route to a criterium alongside Indurain, when a storm broke and the aircraft began bouncing around in the turbulence. Whilst everybody else, from the pilot to the passengers, began to panic, Indurain was the only person on board who held his nerve, repeating the phrase *tranquilo, tranquilo* to try and calm everybody down. The plane, thankfully, landed undamaged.

Given his mask-like lack of expressivity, refusal to panic and general air of invincibility, the only option for Indurain's rivals was to go on the attack – and hope that Indurain would crack. However, it was a daunting process. 'The only time you could really test out Miguel was if it was bad weather, but if it was good weather you had to test him 100,000 times to see if he was really having a bad day or not,' says Abraham Olano, later tipped as Indurain's successor but his rival during an earlier part of the 1990s. 'Generally, you got the feeling he could ride his bike without having to turn the pedals. His position on the bike was very hard to read, he didn't make any gestures to give anything away, ever. You could always tell when I was tired or suffering, ever since I'd broken one of my collarbones, it would slump a little. But with Miguel, the only time you knew he was in a bad way was when he got dropped.'

The unremitting, expressionless superiority he seemed to exude apparently played on the minds of some of Indurain's top rivals. 'Tony [Rominger] was a bit obsessed with Indurain,' claims Olano, 'but Bugno was even more so. Even in a smaller race like Bicicleta Vasca, it got to the point where Miguel would beat him in something like a sprint' – not an event that normally wins or loses you a race outright – 'and you could tell Bugno was fed up with even that, always a bit angry, grumbling about him a lot.' As for Rominger, according to Olano, his team-mate's fixation with Indurain expressed itself indirectly: 'he'd always want it to be raining' – which was when Indurain, in theory, was more vulnerable. But until 1996, the weather in the Tour almost always seemed to be on Indurain's side.

At the same time, as Juan Carlos González Salvador recollects, when he was racing against Banesto, as a rival Indurain's combination of general niceness with such inner and outer strength made matters worse, not better: 'I can remember in the Vuelta a Valencia, which would be the first race of the year that he'd do, Miguel would be there, ten kilos overweight from the winter. I'd have done Murcia and Andalucía and so on and when we'd get to a climb that I needed to get over to go for a bunch sprint, Miguel would start pushing me up it! And I was in another team! Can you imagine the class he had to have: six or ten kilos overweight and at the start of his season, being able to do that? Basically, he was playing in another league.'

The arrival of Bernard represented a considerable consolidation for Banesto in their Grand Tour line-up in the 1990s. But up until the 1991 Tour, in the stage races that were Banesto's top targets, another Frenchman in the team already had multiple roles as race captain, *domestique de luxe* and general wheeler-dealer: Dominique Arnaud.

'Dominique was one of the most important riders Reynolds ever had in their entire history as a teacher for the rest of the squad,' observes Manolo Saiz. 'As well as Indurain, he passed on his knowledge to Echavarri and Delgado, who in turn passed that on to Miguel. Echavarri learned a huge amount from him.'

'He was such a key part of the squad because he knew cycling through and through, right down to its bare roots,' Juan Carlos González Salvador adds. 'He was a veteran, was widely respected, was a professional racer from head to toe and he was a real teacher for Miguel. Miguel had him both as a reference point and at the same time if we needed allies, Dominique was a great negotiator. If there weren't any allies available, he would warn the rest of the team that they needed to be on their toes. [Tour team-mates] Marino Alonso was a shieldbearer, [José Ramón] Uriarte as well, good, noble guys, but they just did their job.'

'*Perico* was very sharp at seeing what kind of strategies were going to be needed, although personally I was a bit surprised he didn't rebel more against Miguel taking over. Bernard, too, was hugely important. Apart from being a great winner of races in his own right, he was more than capable of saving Miguel if he needed help in the middle of hilly stages. Arnaud wasn't quite as classy, but he knew the races inside out and he knew what to do.'

Arnaud's insight was such that he quickly realised, he says, that Indurain being *simpático* also gave Banesto a major advantage on the field of battle. 'He didn't get mixed up in problems.

He was widely liked. And that really, really helped, on occasions when there were echelons or when the racing got tough.' Assistance from rival teams would sometimes be provided, unasked for, or as Arnaud puts it in a very short-hand form, 'when it came down to the moments of elbow-shoving in the peloton, if it was Miguel, then it was Miguel. You'd *open the door* [slang for providing a gap in the line of riders chasing down an attack] for him. Not always, but often. People felt intimidated by him, but not in the same way as they did with Hinault, which was a very different kind of feeling.' The degree of appreciation for Indurain was such that personal enmity was never an issue. As Arnaud put it, 'Miguel couldn't have enemies.'

As early as Paris–Nice 1989, Indurain had begun to use the strategy of letting his rivals take as great a share of the glory as they could, provided it did not interfere with his main task of winning the race outright. The divide-and-rule tactic was nothing new in itself in cycling, but what is striking is the way Banesto turned it into a near-systematic practice during the five years of Indurain's Tour success. During that period, excluding time trials, Indurain's team did not take a single stage win in any of the Grand Tours he took part in. Sharing the glory was therefore a way of lowering the pressure on the team. Up to and including the 1991 Tour, Arnaud as team captain was responsible for overseeing which rivals would be able to go for the stage win – as in deciding which breaks Banesto would not try to close down.

As Arnaud says, 'The most important thing to remember was if a team had a rider in a break, that was one team less in your favour if it came to pulling back the move later on. So you didn't think about this rider or that rider, when it came to letting him go up the road, you looked at what his team could do if you needed them in an emergency.' Such an emergency, in Arnaud's time, never arose: 'It was my job to avoid that. Knowing how to do your job well on a bike,' he points out with a chuckle, 'is knowing how to make the other guys, the opposition, work.' For Indurain, whose entire strategy was based around racing conservatively, it was vital – and Arnaud was instrumental in letting him do that.

As for the day-to-day mechanics for Indurain's team-mates of ensuring they got him to Paris in yellow, a lot of the time was spent on patrol at the front of the bunch, not necessarily setting a pace, but observing the pack for potential signs of rebellion. Again this is anything but new in cycling, but it was much harder then than now: back then there was far less technological assistance and as Arnaud says, that made the 'look-out' work more important. 'You could never have less than two team-mates there, particularly as you didn't have radios in that era. There was no race director telling you through your ear-piece that there was a dangerous corner coming up in three kilometres. It was all done on talking, looks, and making damn sure you read the route book in the hotel room the night before. Jesús Rodríguez Magro was the other key "look-out" for the team and he was really good at it, very experienced. If he wasn't up there on the front, then it was me.'

With Bernard, Arnaud, Delgado, Rodríguez Magro and Alonso amongst the line-up, Arnaud says that Indurain's first Tour bid enjoyed considerable support. 'It was a hugely experienced, solid team, the only rider who was a little weaker was [Javier] Luquin.' Nor were Unzué and Echavarri in any sense, as Arnaud sees it and Delgado has already observed, overly prone to micro-managing. 'Generally, we were allowed to get on with it', with the only guaranteed point of contact 'a briefing at the start of the stage.' But the process of putting the team's objectives for the day was up to the riders, 100 per cent. 'They trusted us,' Arnaud says simply.

Unlike many other directors, 'They might come up a couple of times during the stage in the team car, but it wasn't systematic.' This again, he agrees, was an approach that suited Miguel, who could be *'más tranquilo'* – calmer, left to his own devices – without his bosses breathing down his neck.

After Arnaud left, the position of road captain in Banesto, and its multiple roles, were firmly established. Arnaud's successor was 'Jean-François Bernard, and to a much lesser degree, Gerard Rue and Armand de las Cuevas, although Armand proved difficult to handle. Jean-François, though, was very good at it.' But by this point, it was taken for granted – and a part of the Banesto organi-gram – that Indurain was content to defer the reins of responsibility to another rider further down in the hierarchy. 'It was very easy to work with Miguel, and also he was not a fan of giving orders. If somebody else could do that, then he felt more comfortable about it,' Unzué observes.

Yet Indurain's lack of communication could have become more frustrating to his team-mates than accepted. The insistence on remaining 'one of the crowd' could have provoked contempt rather than producing respect, and the delegation of responsibil-ities could have caused annoyance rather than simply reallocating respective workloads had it not been for one crucial factor: Indurain was not only widely liked as a person, he actively knew how to inspire loyalty, too.

It was, and is, standard practice for leaders to work for their *domestiques* in the early races that were of little importance long-term, but Indurain would take that tactic to levels that were almost unprecedented. ONCE director Manolo Saiz cites the time when his squad had tried to put Indurain and Banesto up against the wall on a hard early climb in the last stage of the Vuelta a Andalucía in 1991, when it was led by one of Indurain's team-mates, Robert

Lezaun. But instead of simply sitting up and easing back, 'like any other leader I've known would have done, instead Miguel worked his finger to the bone for Lezaun, suffering what it took to get up the first hard climb to the finish, to then guide him through to Granada. All the way.'

'It was the classic situation of a collective [ONCE] versus an individual [Lezaun] who'd never have won that race in his fucking life without a rider with the humanity of Miguel to work all the way through for him. That wasn't a Giro or a Tour, that was some small race. Any other leader I'd have known would have sat up and said "fuck them all."'

Indurain's hard work for Lezaun en route to Granada came immediately prior to his first Tour de France victory. But as team-mates like Julián Gorospe would discover in two other spring-time races, the 1993 Vuelta a Andalucía and Vuelta a Valencia, when Indurain did a similar amount of spadework to help his team-mate win, this attitude was something that did not change over the years. In this, as in all other facets of Indurain when a Tour champion, it seemed impossible for him to alter. What changed far more, in fact, was how the Spanish public perceived Indurain – and moulded his image into something that to a farm boy from Navarre must have seemed almost unrecognisable.

CHAPTER 7

1992: Indurain Is Spain

Some time during the mid-1990s, I was studying French at Granada University when I was asked by my teacher, a Spaniard – having found out what job I had – who I considered to be the greatest ever cyclist of all time.

'Eddy Merckx,' I answered, which drew some instant murmurs of disapproval from my classmates and a few mutters of 'Indurain, no?' So what, the French teacher asked me in a voice that brooked little opposition, did I consider Indurain to be? My mumbled answer about the sporting value of numbers of Tours won versus other 'minor' events like World Championships, Giros, Vueltas and Classics was simply ignored. Nobody cared.

The wider point this anecdote illustrated – as would countless other discussions I had across Spain at the time with friends and journalists from all walks of life – was simple. For the Spanish, Indurain was not only cycling's greatest ever racer but also, as one early Spanish biography of him put it, 'the athlete who has gone the furthest and highest in the history of our country.' And in 1992 Indurain became representative of Spain per se, the ultimate symbol of how successful the country's drive towards a modern, pro-European state was proving to be.

Everything Indurain did mattered hugely in Spain – and at times it seemed anybody who rode a bike who wasn't called Miguel and who hadn't worn a *maillot jaune* on the Champs Elysées at some point or another was written off as an irrelevance. It could have been predicted that on home soil, after winning a second Tour, Villava would name one of their plazas after Indurain or that in Pamplona during its famous 'Running of the Bulls' festival, his name would be chorused by chanting crowds between spells of dodging *toro*s and downing *Rioja*. But the Indu-mania extended across Spain to the point where for a brief spell in the early 1990s, cycling became second only to football in terms of popularity.

Long-term, it was arguably the sponsors of the time, not cycling, who reaped the benefits, given that most of the broader public's interest started and ended with Indurain and, at a stretch, Delgado. In 1992, *Cycle Sport* reported that thanks to their cycling team, public awareness of Banesto had increased seven-fold amongst the Spanish. And that was even before Indurain had won the Giro (which generated five million pounds worth of positive publicity for the bank in terms of television viewing hours alone) and the Tour that season.

Indurain's conversion into a living symbol of Spain in Europe wasn't only because he had won a Tour de France in 1992 that was deliberately designed to take in as many EEC countries as possible and simultaneously celebrate the creation of the EU single market and euro in the 1992 Maastricht Treaty. There was also what Indurain looked like – tall and lean, closer to the clichéd image of the northern European than the typical stockier, swarthier Spanish macho. But it was above all *how* he won: it might be a dull strategy, it might look unspectacular, but it was coolly calculated, business-like and above all efficiently captured. Put simply, Delgado might be far more charismatic and his victories far more dramatic, but he also turned up three minutes late for prologues, thereby fulfilling every Euro-cliché about the Spanish predilection for chaotic organisation, unpunctuality and *mañana, mañana*. Indurain, on the other hand, not only won the time trials, but also crushed the opposition in every *contrareloj* there was going: hence his representing a modern, forward-looking, new kind of Spain that, amongst other things, kept its emotions firmly under control.

'For the Spanish,' says Juan Carlos González Salvador, 'he invented a new style of cycling. When or where had we seen a rider like him get through the Pyrenees and Alps and win a Tour de France?' This kind of racing, and winning, felt like breaking a huge glass ceiling, one that had stood for decades between themselves and the rest of Europe. 'Historically, we – my parents and my grandparents, have always have had a sense of inferiority,' recounts Delgado. 'We always undervalue ourselves with regards to what comes from abroad. We're the poor ones, the ugly ducklings of Europe. With Miguel there's a change of mentality, a point when we realise that in the rest of Europe, they don't actually eat Spaniards for breakfast.'

The difference was, as Delgado says, that whilst Spain had won one Tour on three previous occasions, Indurain was the first to win two or more, and to prove – therefore – that this was no fluke. 'He showed us that Europe is Spain and Spain is Europe,' Delgado argues.

'We still had that sense of inferiority sometimes, but it was way weaker than before. Miguel broke the mould.' The year was already a boom one for Spain's international self-esteem with a hugely successful Olympic Games in Barcelona and a Universal Expo in Seville. But on an individual level, Indurain winning the Tour was proof positive that Spain had as much a right to a place in the gleaming new EU-format of Europe as everybody else.

In terms of the media, the foundations for Indurain's metamorphosis had been laid down by cycling's boom in popularity in the 1980s. The vast amount of coverage cycling garnered in the print media, live prime time mid-afternoon TV broadcasting – just when half of Spain was slumped on the sofa for a siesta – on state channels TVE1 and TVE2 and above all, unprecedented levels of reporting by most of the top radio stations had been established in the previous decade. All that was needed to maintain and justify that virtuous circle of public interest in cycling was high-level success, and Indurain certainly provided that.

Indurain and Reynolds' connections to Navarre were almost automatically deep-rooted, given the links on so many different levels – financial, sporting, historical, personal – between rider, team and area. But if we look at one event near the end of the Indurain era – the 1995 team presentation in Madrid – this shows how much Banesto the cycling team had woven its way into everyday Spain's social fabric, too. Traditionally an event for journalists and sponsors, on this occasion Banesto filled Madrid's main sports hall with nearly 10,000 fans for an evening's entertainment that simply re-introduced a team that by then needed very little introduction. The cost was estimated at around twenty million pesetas (€120,000). If Banesto were able to draw such a massive crowd on a week-day in early February in Madrid, the scale of nationwide support by the time July and the Tour rolled around beggared belief.

One of the most memorable events where I saw that for myself was in Granada in 1995, when Indurain, his brother Prudencio, Tony Rominger and 1994 Giro winner Evgeni Berzin participated in a Mountain-Biking exhibition. None of them were in any way experts on using MTBs, and the racing was anything but spirited.

But once again tickets – which were not cheap – in a vast sports palace that could hardly be further away geographically in Spain from Pamplona sold out instantly. Indurain's presence alone guaranteed that.

Nor was this the first time that a Spanish cyclist in winning the Tour de France became a figurehead for 'modern Spain'. In 1959, when Federico Martín Bahamontes won the Tour for the first time in Spain's history, he was seen as representative of the country breaking away from its economic, social and political isolation under Franco and moving into a new era. In 1992, Indurain had a similar role. 'He was a great hero in a Spain that was moving forward and where democracy was finally taking a firm hold,' says Manolo Saiz. 'He's the figure that shows us what Spain has become in the modern world.'

But as Delgado points out, this was curious in that Indurain himself was 'not a mould-breaker.' Nor, he agrees, was he privately the kind of 'modern city man' of Spain's 1990s, which in theory would be the country's closest relative to *Euro-hombre*. 'He's very rural, very traditional, nothing at all like the image that was projected of him.'

'He never gave a single headline to the press, but his rivals said so much about him, Indurain's personality was created by them,' his sports director Eusebio Unzué argues. And inside Spain, amongst his own people and friends? Indurain's sparsity of comments in public meant that no matter how much country and folk wisdom there was in him, no matter how little of the streetwise intellectual you could see in him, for the broader Spanish public it didn't matter. As the sporting conquerer of Europe, he was *Miguel el moderno,* the vanguard of forward-thinking Spain. As Manuel Vázquez Montalbán, one of Spain's most brilliant contemporary authors, journalists and political commentators wrote in *El País,* 'If, some day, Indurain no longer feels representative of Spain but only of Navarre or Villaba [sic], I think the Spaniards will live the longest dark night of the soul, when it comes to questioning their proper essence. Spain is Indurain, and whatever the *Financial Times* says we are, too.'

At the other end of the political spectrum, during the 1993 Tour, a heavyweight political columnist in the conservative daily, *ABC*, wrote, 'Once the Tour de France is over, we need Indurain to have a prime time television show to explain to the Spanish public the way he thinks, the way he acts, and the way he is … we can ill afford not to take the advice, experience, motivation and assistance of such an exceptional human being both on the sports field and off it.' Indurain was not just, then, a sports hero; as the *ABC* writer put it, Spain itself needed to be – as the made-up verb expressed it – *Indurainised*.

It was not only the broader public in Spain; the sporting glitterati also lined up to be associated with Indurain. As Unzué says, 'Tomba, Schumacher, Prost, Maradona – when we went down to the Expo '92, they all wanted to see Miguel, to be with him, and that association was something that shows you where cycling was and where Miguel had taken it. You could see how impressed these other top names were, you could see how much he was appreciated.'

Yet Indurain's broader appeal was partly because he remained very much the boy next door, whose idea of heaven, as he once said, was 'to live and live well', whose idea of hell was 'the bad things one has to live through', whose favourite music was 'songs where you can understand the words' and whose favourite food was 'whatever there is going, so you can put that down [as your answer]'. His simple, direct, unpolished answers made him come across as accessible and familiar as well as glamorous, fashionable and able to demolish the Europeans at their own game.

For much of the foreign press, what came across to the Spanish as irresistibly avant-garde in Indurain (and at the same time, bizarrely, very familiar), was just plain dull and about as charismatic as a brick. 'Do still waters run deep with Indurain?' the celebrated *New York Times* cycling writer Sam Abt argued before offering a classic punchline: 'Do they run at all?' Instead, the international press championed mountain challengers like Claudio Chiappucci. 'Against the steady, stoic, unflashy Miguel Indurain, Chiappucci was everything the Spaniard was not: unpredictable, aggressive, exciting. He was *El Diablo*, who so fully embraced his nickname that he rode time trials with a cartoon devil on his helmet,' Richard Moore wrote recently in his book on the Tour de France, *Étape*.

But the Spanish did not care. They would point to the risibly small amount of time Indurain had lost thanks to Chiappucci's breakaways, to Indurain crushing Chiappucci in the time trials. Panache might get the Italian a few good headlines, but it would be Indurain's name at the top of the overall classification in Paris. Chiappucci, in fact, was precisely the kind of rider – impetuous, inconsistent – that the Spanish did not, briefly, want to know about at all. They had seen too many of them in the past. After Indurain won the Volta a Catalunya in 1991 for a second time, a win achieved according to *El Mundo Deportivo* without 'a single lock of his hair falling out of place', the newspaper went on to say that, 'With [previous Tour winners] Ocaña, Delgado and Bahamontes we were dependent on their moods and risked the most absurd of defeats. Indurain is the most dependable rider in Spanish history.'

'Modern cycling has moved on, before it was all decided in the mountains,' Indurain argued when asked about how he felt about his new style of racing, 'now it's opened up to other options.' Had he adapted himself to modern cycling or is it the other way round, the paper asked? 'Let's say it's both, me changing towards a new type of racing and the racing adapting itself to a new generation, the era of Alcalá, Breukink, Bugno' – the latter described by Indurain as 'the new face of racing this year, along with me.'

Having established himself as the dominating force in the Tour de France, the question of what Indurain sought to conquer in the years to come was critical. But rather than divide his targets, Indurain made it clear that July was what mattered the most, even if he said: 'There's Milano–Sanremo, there's Liège–Bastogne–Liège, there's the Worlds. None of them is the Tour but I'd like to be up there. What's evident is you can't be up there in the Classics and the Vuelta and the Tour. You have to make some decisions.'

'I've tried to shape my body towards winning in any of the races there are. But you can't try to win everything. I have to select.' After the events of July 1991, it was clear which race Indurain had chosen to make his top priority. All that remained to be decided was the approach path.

What helped establish Indurain in 1992 as a modern-day hero in the eyes of the Spanish was, curiously enough, not so much his decision to race the Tour, but to do the Giro d'Italia instead of the Vuelta. Never won before by a Spaniard, Indurain's decision made it clear he was operating on a European racing programme, rather than sticking to more familiar home turf. Furthermore, in trying for a Giro–Tour double – the first Spaniard to do so seriously since Ocaña briefly toyed with the idea in 1974 – Indurain was raising the Euro-bar for the Spanish in style.

Paradoxically, the Giro at the time was an event with far less of an international flavour than it has attained in the last decade. 'In that era, the Giro was much more homely,' Indurain recalled in an interview I did with him for *ProCycling* a few years back. 'It was much more the Italians' own Grand Tour where foreign riders didn't have so much influence or, normally, have much effect on the racing. These days it's far more similar to the Tour de France.'

'From the start of each year it was clear that I'd be going for the double but the Giro wasn't ever my main objective. It was all about the Tour. If I did a good Giro, well, that was a bonus. The Giro–Tour double is definitely doable but you've got to have the right mentality and you have to know how to spend your energy and when. You can't just go rushing into the start of the season, for example; you have to take things a bit more slowly and get closer to your top level when you get closer to the start of the Giro itself.'

There were other advantages to his heading for Italy. Already, when they had first taken part in the Giro d'Italia with Pedro Delgado in 1988, Banesto had discovered that the first halves of the flat stages would be far less manic affairs than their equivalents in the Vuelta or Tour. 'It all fitted together a bit better than it would nowadays when the rivals come to the Giro in top form and the route in the first part of the Giro is much more complicated,' says Unzué.

'The easy Giro start was ideal, too, if you looked at it and the Tour as a whole. Plus there was the attraction for us of winning the Giro in any case.' There was pressure, Unzué says, for Indurain to ride the Vuelta, but fortunately having Delgado – a double Vuelta winner and very much in contention in 1992 and 1993 – to head their line-up there made it less of an issue. 'Banesto wanted Miguel to ride the Vuelta too, but fortunately they never questioned the calendar he had.'

The other option, of course, would have been to head to the spring Classics. But as Arnaud explains, Banesto saw drawbacks at the time in placing too much emphasis on these events. 'Miguel could have won Paris–Roubaix, physically he had it in his legs. But there were too many risks. Flèche and Liège were races for him. But we rarely went, year in, year out, to these races, so we didn't get the experience we needed.'

'We'd go to Milano–Sanremo, but more because of the prestige of the race than anything else. We didn't have the riders for it, and if you don't go to Paris–Roubaix to do something important, given how dangerous it is with crashes, there's no point. We'd go to the races we needed to.'

The strategy with Indurain in the Giro d'Italia was equally conservative. This was partly because he was only elevated to the role of sole leader because Jean-François Bernard, after a spectacularly successful spring winning Paris–Nice and the Critérium International, had had to pull out at the last minute with a bad back. But it was also because the Giro d'Italia was mainly raced by Indurain as a way of form-building for the Tour and so his race strategy was not to expend too much energy. As soon as he lost a Giro, in 1994, he never returned.

Unintentionally, the 1992 Giro became the prototype Grand Tour for the classic Indurain strategy: take time in the time trials and hold off the opposition in the mountains as best you could. The 1991 Tour had been won as a combination of strong time trials and a mountain attack – downhill, but a mountain attack all the same. What the 1992 Giro d'Italia confirmed was that from here on in the Grand Tours, just as they had done in the week-long races like Paris–Nice and the Volta a Catalunya, Banesto and Indurain were going to play it safe.

So there was no attacking for Indurain when he took Spain's first *maglia rosa* since Francisco Galdós, one of the few top Spanish racers in the 1970s, held it for over a week in 1975. He began the race by finishing second in the opening prologue behind France's short distance time trial specialist Thierry Marie: 'My gears broke,' he would tell Basque journalist Benito Urraburu in his typically laconic style a few months later, by way of explanation as to why he didn't win. Without that gearing issue, Indurain would have quite possibly worn the *maglia rosa* from start to finish. Instead, in singularly unspectacular style, Indurain moved into the Giro lead on a hilly first-week stage. That was prior to claiming a victory on stage four in the 38-kilometre time trial between Arezzo and Sansepolcro, albeit by the comparatively small margin of 32 seconds over French team-mate Armand de las Cuevas, and strengthening his overall advantage.

From thereon, as Indurain played a strictly defensive hand, on each mountain summit finish – the Terminillo on stage ten, the Bondone in the Dolomites on stage fourteen (where Indurain suffered a brief hunger knock halfway through the stage, brought on by the cold and rain of that day), the Monviso on stage eighteen and the Verbania on stage twenty – the gap between him and his rivals slowly but remorselessly yawned further open. Whether it was the 1991 Giro d'Italia winner – the ageing, hook-nosed Franco Chioccioli – or the fiery Chiappucci that took off up the road, Indurain shadowed them all, strangling whatever options they might have had. 'I killed myself just trying to attack,' Chiappucci said later. With such a level of domination, even one contemporary Spanish account, whilst rejoicing in Indurain's success, admitted that 'the race was almost boring'.

On the final stage into Milan, on the race's last time trial, Indurain finally turned the power back on in full. After coming down the start ramp three minutes behind Chiappucci, by the finish he had won by nearly the same margin on Guido Bontempi, his closest pursuer. Not only that, he had overtaken Chiappucci near the finish line, in what was to become the classic, trademark image of Indurain at the height of his time trial powers – an almost sinister-looking giant of a figure, unrecognisable and expressionless in his full-face helmet and skinsuit, sweeping past the opposition, en route to another victory against the clock, and another Grand Tour in the bag.

Did Indurain ever object on a personal level to this kind of strait-laced, efficient racing? 'I think the management made him much more conservative,' argues Juan Carlos González Salvador, whilst Delgado suggests that the tactics suited both the management and their lead rider. 'José Miguel was very cautious and he didn't like taking risks. He'd say, "this is how it is, this is what we've got, we shouldn't do more."' Although Delgado points out that 'Back then, the figure of director wasn't so relevant, anyway, as he is now. Often he was essentially a driver on a very good wage and decisions were taken by the riders. The director, therefore, tended to be very prudent.'

'That caution fits in very well with Indurain's approach, of taking as much time as he could in the time trials and then conserving his energy on the big mountain stages. When I left Reynolds for Orbea in 1985, Echavarri had already based his team around Julián Gorospe because he was a rider who rode very well in time trials and who could stay with the favourites in the mountains. He was absolutely in love with Miguel because he fitted the bill perfectly: Navarran, obedient, someone who listens. Me and Arroyo, we'd answer back, and argue. Miguel, he'd listen to what he'd say and get on with it.' Rather than being obliged to attack in the mountains, as they were with Delgado, therefore, Indurain's Giro d'Italia policy was a continuation of the previous strategy, and with a more adept pupil.

'Echavarri was the perfect director for Indurain,' claims Manolo Saiz. 'He had that kind of phlegmatic, imperturbable attitude that I hadn't got and which suited Indurain down to the ground. People talk about [Cyrille] Guimard, but in my opinion, Echavarri was cycling's best director in the last half century.'

Historically, Echavarri had had his reference points for this kind of strategy, too, dating from when he raced in BIC in 1969 as a first year pro, alongside Jacques Anquetil, the first rider ever to take five Tours de France. He was 'the rider that José Miguel admired the most,' claims Delgado. 'But when he was directing Gorospe José Miguel was less experienced. When Miguel began to stand out, José Miguel was more practised at what he did' – and able to see exactly how viable the Anquetil strategy was

From a foreign point of view, having to handle Indurain's obliteration of the opposition on the bike and painfully dull press conferences overloaded with bland clichés off it, it was easy to condemn the lack of panache in Indurain's victories, the absence of any recklessness in Banesto's strategy. But as Juan Carlos González Salvador observes, 'The strategy was neither good nor bad. Who has done that, win five Tours in the way that they did? They were basically racing for the Tour, nothing more, and even in the Tour they were ultra-cautious, sharing out the stages, just in case.' The same went for the Giro d'Italia, with José Miguel Echavarri telling Sam Abt that there were four riders, whom he refused to name, that knew that they owed their stage wins to Banesto. As for the next Giro–Tour double winner, Marco Pantani in 1998, his team-mate Mario Traversoni told me in *The End of the Road*, 'I remember Indurain because he was the man of the moment when he turned pro, he was the last *señor* to ride a bike, I've never known anyone as respectful as him … and he was more than capable of gifting stages to other riders. Marco wasn't like that, he was in a constant fight with himself and as part of that fight he had to be the first to reach the line.' Inside Indurain's head, there were no such mental conflicts.

Banesto were, González Salvador argues, somewhat cold-blooded in refusing to take even the most minimal of risks. 'They were prepared to base their whole game plan around the Tour. It was a political calculation: 'We fulfil our electoral promise, let's not get involved in other battles, we might do a little bit of mucking around on the side, but that's it. But can we say they're wrong? They could have found a different way of winning Tours with Miguel. But then Manolo [Saiz] tried doing that with his riders, and look what happened – he blew it.'

The answer to the question of what Indurain's *palmares* would have looked like had Banesto opted to use a different strategy is one which can only remain hypothetical. But the broader issue of what Indurain might have achieved with a different kind of director is one of the biggest question marks that remains over his career. As Juan Carlos González Salvador points out, 'Their philosophy from the start had been one of total protection, total caution, don't let anybody see what we've got. Pushing him a little harder, just a little, how many more races could they have won with him? With the tenth part of Merckx's ambition what would Indurain have won?'

According to 1970s pro Barry Hoban, for Eddy Merckx it was all about winning, no matter how small the race. 'Whenever someone waved a flag then Merckx would sprint for it,' Hoban said. For Unzué and Echavarri, when it came to guiding Indurain to Tour victory, the one key factor was arguably the much more mundane matter of Indurain's weight, and the consequences of it. 'There were ten to twelve kilos that made all the difference, you had to be really careful,' Unzué reflects.

Those ten to twelve kilos, the natural difference between a featherweight climber and a top time triallist like Indurain, were the key to their strategies – going right back to when, in late 1987, Indurain and Echavarri went to visit Francesco Conconi at Ferrara University in Italy. Although he became well-known at a later date as a sports doctor of dubious reputation, at the time Echavarri and Indurain were looking for a consultation from Conconi on a simple question with complex solutions. 'We were looking for the balance between weight and power output and how best to achieve it,' Unzué says. 'Indurain was a man with weight issues. Conconi was a bit of a guru at the time, and he gave us some advice on that. In time, we ended up seeing he was right.'

The contact was, in any case, relatively brief. 'We should have worked with him for two years,' Indurain once said in 1990 to Josu Garai, 'to know which training plans were the best for me, but finally we only went to see him for three months, from December 1987 to March 1988, just after Milano–Sanremo. We had to do a power threshold test and some lactic acid tests, in theory each month.'

Indurain says that the training plans were overly strict and did not work well for him. On the plus side, he says he learned a lot about 'taking responsibility for my training plans and my diet. But in general the training plans were too tough.' (Interestingly, at least one later piece of research suggested that Conconi's threshold test, once considered definitive, tended to over-estimate endurance athletes' strength.) In any case, with the Italian option closed, Echavarri and Unzué once again acted as his main training consultants.

'What we did was optimise his talents and help him not to lose what he'd gained in a time trial,' Unzué says. 'Maybe I was always excessively prudent with him, but that's because I didn't want to make too many mistakes. I work to win, not to put on a

Indurain, aged 12, with his brother and cousins at the CC Villavés team presentation in 1976. Bottom row, fifth from right Miguel Indurain, then to his left, his brother, Prudencio and cousins Javier, Luis and Daniel Indurain.

Pepe Barruso, co-founder and president of the CC Villavés, in front of the clubhouse with one of Miguel Indurain's first ever bikes.

Indurain and the rest of the Reynolds pro team let their hair down at their training camp in Panticosa, prior to the 1985 season. José Luis Laguia, the team's top rider, is seated on the far left, Indurain, just 20, third from left at the back.

Indurain leading the Tour de la CEE, his breakthrough race victory, in 1986. 1984 Olympic gold medallist Alexi Grewal of the USA is on the far left, KAS rider, Patrice Esnault, who ran Indurain the closest, on Indurain's right.

1990: Indurain with Banesto team-mate Pedro Delgado, the year before Indurain took over the leadership of the squad in the Tour de France. In many ways, Delgado acted as a trailblazer for Indurain.

En route to victory in the 1991 Tour de France, Indurain's first, alongside team-mate, Dominique Arnaud.

A crunch moment on the Galibier in the 1991 Tour de France when LeMond, the double defending champion, cracks on the climb. The final phase of Indurain's rise to power in the Tour is about to begin.

At the height of his power: Indurain blasts to victory in the 1992 Luxembourg time trial, the win that netted him that year's Tour de France and established him as the dominating force in the Grand Tours for the 1990s.

Banesto team-mate Prudencio Indurain (R) pulls the ear of his brother Miguel during the 12th stage of the Tour de France from Isola to Marseille, 16 July 1993. Prudencio was Indurain's room-mate for several of his Grand Tour wins.

1994: Moments after breaking the Hour Record in Bordeaux velodrome, Indurain stands holding the blackboard that indicates the distance he achieved.

18 July 1994: Indurain rides with Spanish national champion Abraham Olano during the 15th stage of the Tour de France cycling race. Olano was widely viewed as Indurain's successor but, despite a hugely successful career, did not live up to Spain's impossibly high expectations in the Tour de France.

Indurain leads a chase group behind Marco Pantani on the road to Guzet Neige during the 1995 Tour de France. Behind him is ONCE's Alex Zülle, second overall in that year's race, top mountain climbers Richard Virenque and Claudio Chiappucci, and (in green) Laurent Jalabert – arguably Indurain's toughest rival in that Tour.

Five out of five: Indurain, en route for Paris on the last stage of the 1995 Tour, his fifth and final Tour victory.

Indurain raises one arm to celebrate team-mate Abraham Olano's controversial victory in the 1995 World Championships. Indurain himself took silver ahead of Italy's Marco Pantani.

3 August 1996: Abraham Olano, Miguel Indurain and Chris Boardman stand on the medal rostrum for the men's time trial event. It was Indurain's last win, and revived hopes he might continue racing after his defeat in the Tour.

The end of the road: Miguel Indurain is helped back to his hotel, El Capitán in Asturias, after abandoning the 1996 Vuelta. His professional career was effectively over.

Indurain with the top three finishers in the eponymous Grand Prix in Navarre: [from left] Sergio Henao, second, Ion Izagirre, first, and Moreno Moser, third.

May 2016: La Perla hotel in Corvara, nestled between the jagged pinnacles of Alta Badia, where Indurain was hosting rides for customers of cycling tour operator In Gamba, which runs exclusive tours from the hotel.

performance, because you never know what'll happen the next day in a stage race.'

'Cycling is an exam where the circumstances change, every single day. From your body through to the weather conditions, there are so many variables. It's not at all similar to any other sport, it's pure, unadulterated improvisation. It's not a sport where there are eleven athletes against eleven or eight against eight. It's one team against twenty-one, one rider against two hundred. Then the field of battle changes, the weather, the opposition ...'

In that running battle against variety and unpredictability, and with a team leader whose stage racing gifts could be exploited deeply but in a very limited number of ways, strategically, Echavarri and Unzué were faced with few options. What was clearly divided during the Indurain years were their roles. Unzué, it emerges, was more often the director who would be in the team car, closest to the action behind the peloton or guiding Indurain in the time trials, 'because José Miguel was very respectful about that sort of thing and he said that as I'd known him for longer, right the way back to amateurs, it made more sense.' Echavarri, whilst sometimes in the team car, would often head off 'on scouting missions, to check out the terrain ahead.'

'It made sense for José Miguel to be the talker and me the doer. It was never discussed, we just both felt comfortable with it, in particular me,' Unzué says. Another of the team's strengths, in Unzué's eyes, was the way that Banesto and Indurain remained very much an all-Navarran project, 'a sort of continuation of those golden days of SuperSer. In 2012, when we won the team time trial in the Vuelta in Pamplona with Movistar, I couldn't help remembering being on the balcony of Pamplona town hall in 1991 and our reception there. So our roots have always been here and still are. It is a nice part of the story.'

Unzué points to the fact, too, that Indurain never moved from Pamplona to a place with a more favourable tax regime like Monaco, even though, as Indurain once said, 'one of my legs is owned by the Spanish Inland Revenue ...' 'He stuck to his roots, he was very loyal.' The one race Indurain said he was sure he would take part in every year was the GP Navarre, which would later be renamed – after he retired – the GP Miguel Indurain.

After ten years with its headquarters in Pamplona and more than twenty in Navarre, the team's structure and place in the local community was more than settled, it was all but set in stone. In an equally stolid fashion, when Unzué explains their yearly racing and training programme for Indurain, it sounds more like an insurance plan or pensions scheme than a master strategy to conquer the cycling world: 'it was basically to race somewhere between 70 and 90 days, a bit more than you would do now, mainly French and Spanish races barring the Giro. You'd mix in some training camps at altitude, and after the Tour, with no Vuelta, a much longer period off the bike than you'd have these days.'

It was an almost ridiculously simple, unadventurous strategy, but Unzué argues this is what Indurain needed to perform the best. 'Cycling is very straightforward, you need to race, you need to train and you need to rest. And this was what suited Miguel. This wasn't [a training and racing programme] for the Classics, in stage racing you're either aiming to gain time or not to lose time. There are so many talented riders who can shine occasionally, but here it was gaining consistency that mattered.' As a result, long rest periods outside racing (like after the Tour) and recovery – both during the race and after it – were central to the Banesto philosophy with Indurain. 'It's the key, the ability to handle one massive workload on one day, and again onto the next and the next. You don't just have to handle it physically, there's the media and psychological pressure which is vital too. In twenty-one days, so much can happen. Without that ability to recover, you're a dead man.'

Unzué and Echavarri's approach was adopted wholeheartedly by Indurain, to the point where the Spaniard used to turn down almost all of the post-Tour criteriums. 'He realised it was the worst way to try and recover for the following year. If you turned them down, then what did you lose? A couple of thousand euros for each one? You can't prove, ultimately, what it did or didn't achieve, but I always used to believe in getting a real rest after each Grand Tour. The criteriums just meant you would wring the last drops of energy out of your body when it's already been hung out to dry. Get some rest. Miguel discovered that racing another criterium was like adding another rival to the list.'

What Echavarri and Unzué realised was that using Indurain to win a Grand Tour was, in one sense, like using a man with a sledgehammer for a building demolition job. Whilst very effective at knocking down some extremely big walls, the only way to be certain you can fully exploit such a powerful and – in some ways – inappropriate tool without the man collapsing under the strain was to use it as sparingly as possible and when you were guaranteed maximum effect. The more rest between efforts, the better.

In Indurain, Echavarri and Unzué had a more than willing pupil when it came to collaborating in this strategy, but not because of the modern, pro-European image that the Spanish general public had decided he should have. Rather Indurain's typically rural caution and conservatism chimed perfectly with a strategy that minimised risks – as any farmer will try to do, given the degree of unpredictable and uncontrollable elements like the weather that have to be handled. Such is the strength of Indurain's link to his agricultural roots that urban legend claims that he was pulled out of the Tours in

1985 and 1986 in order to go and help his father with the harvest. 'That isn't true,' Unzué says with a smile, 'although it sounds like the kind of joke that would have been made at the time.'

Yet just as Indurain's team-mates would have been delighted by his lack of airs and graces, but were reduced to interpreting his looks to understand him, there was a flip-side to this seemingly perfect cooperation between directors and riders. The question that lurked behind Indurain's acceptance of his director's wishes was whether Indurain was too compliant. 'I think that more than once he should have put his foot down, because he accepted everything,' argues Delgado 'I would always tell him, "Miguel, you have to be more pro-active with your team-mates, you have to make your team, not José Miguel." Yes, he trusted him, but I remember there were a couple of riders that I told Miguel that he should tell José Miguel not to sign.'

'When they took [the notoriously individualistic] Armand de las Cuevas to the Tour, I warned Miguel that Armand was a rider who tended to ride in his own interests. It would have been better to have somebody not quite as sharp, but who you know will be loyal. Because if you don't, you're racing with one less rider. But instead Miguel gave José Miguel a free hand, even though he was the one who was out there suffering. Miguel's problem was, although he had a very clear idea what he wanted, he preferred to avoid that kind of responsibility.'

Whilst Indurain wholeheartedly swung behind Unzué and Echavarri's master-plan, that is not to say that he or his team were given to wringing every last drop of potential benefit out of his time trialling potential. That Banesto mechanics would sleep with Indurain's time trial bikes in their bedroom during a Grand Tour is indicative of how important the bikes were to the team's strategy. But Unzué says that Indurain never, to his knowledge, kept a time trial bike for training at home – something that is now de rigueur for top Grand Tour specialists.

'Time trialling was something of a little world of its own at the time, something that only a very few people were involved in. He would train on a time trial bike – and come round here [to team headquarters] to get one – but training on the TT bike wasn't something top racers automatically did.'

Equally (and something that once again debunks the robotic image he had abroad), Indurain was no techno-fiend in terms of his bike set-up or having the latest model. 'He prefers to let his team make the decisions on that,' *Cycle Sport* magazine observed in 1995 when comparing Indurain to Anquetil, Hinault and Merckx and their different approaches to the technical side of the sport. 'He had no computer or power meter, he didn't have special gearing for the mountains,' adds Unzué. 'But he knew how to interpret his body perfectly, how to read his own engine, when he should decelerate or how to climb. He knew he could take advantage of the rest on descents, which was one of his big specialities. But as the favourite, normally he had to defend what he had rather than attack.'

This is hardly an attitude to which Merckx or Hinault would give their approval – as favourites, they would argue that it was necessary to do exactly the opposite and sweep their rivals away at every opportunity. But as Andy Hampsten, the American climber who was briefly a Banesto team-mate, told Sam Abt, the point was that Unzué and Echavarri's conservative approach worked. 'It's classic,' Hampsten, who won the Giro d'Italia in 1988, told Abt. 'But it isn't easy. He [Indurain] makes it look easy.'

It was obvious, Unzué says, that Indurain had immense respect for and dedication to 'the daily work, the suffering, the training, all of those things you needed to get where he got to. But as for resting up, did he have the sense he was losing out by not going out with his friends or going on holiday or partying? No, he didn't.'

'When he married, of course he would go on holiday with his wife. But until he was twenty-eight, right back to when he was eighteen, and going into his living room to watch TV wearing his grandfather's coat, he knew about needing the time to recover. He worked for those results, but his recovery time was so important too, he was so serious about that as well.'

Indurain's suitability for the task in hand also added to his shunning of stressful situations, like having to make decisions on the road, or delegate. 'We consulted Miguel in all the important decisions, but he gave us carte blanche in that way. Miguel rarely would come in to say "bring me this rider". I can't actually remember him doing that even once.' Nor would he come to Unzué and Echavarri, Unzué says, and tell them a particular rider needed to be removed. 'We're back to that familiar story of interpreting his silences. Sometimes it's evident if a rider needs to go. You didn't have to wait until he said it, you simply sorted it out. In that sense, helping Miguel not to make decisions, that kept him calm.'

It got to the point where Echavarri and Unzué would always check with Indurain, prior to the team meeting on each stage, to be sure that whatever he wanted would then be carried out. Depending on him to tell the team during the meeting itself was not a reliable method: 'He's maybe been excessively hermetic but those characteristics contributed to his greatness. People still respect him now, and that's without having ever said much. His language has been the language of gestures.'

'More than his words, his *palmares* tell you more about his progression,' Unzué argues, and they also act as an advance warning. 'There was the way of saying, "Blokes, look what's coming at you, here's where I've beaten you. And here, and here." On top of that, there was the way he'd race even when he didn't win.'

Yet Unzué, as a team manager over nearly half a century, confirms that Indurain had a level of maturity when it came to racing that few, if any, other riders possess. He rarely got angry at races, with only three reported occasions in a career of twelve years: once when the team allegedly obliged him to stay for an extra day in Paris after the 1991 Tour (which Unzué denies happened), once in 1995 (of which more later) and once during a Tour de France when Danish racer Jesper Skibby trod on Indurain's foot. 'I remember seeing him get cross occasionally, but part of his greatness was how he accepted everything. When he was beaten, he was beaten. You might even say he was insensitive to what had happened. He was very ambitious, but that anger, that "fuck" and hammering your fist on the table that we all do when we lose – he didn't have that.'

'I very rarely saw him pissed off or angry, and then only towards the end of his career when things weren't working out as he wanted them to,' Delgado adds. 'He always wore that mask.' Given his superiority in time trialling, Indurain exuded a huge sense of impregnability. 'I never knew when Miguel was going to crack, never imagined it, I couldn't tell. Almost every other rider has a gesture that gives it away, but Miguel was a robot.'

'Behind that mask, he was suffering,' Unzué adds, 'but he was a good actor, and he was, and still is, a very good card player.' There was even one point in the 1992 Tour where Indurain fully exploited his ability to hide his feelings to hide a major crisis. The night before the rest day in Dole, Indurain began suffering badly with an infected tooth. His team talked it over with their *coureur regionale*, Jean-François Bernard, who recommended a local dentist he knew. Unzué and Indurain sneaked out of the back door of their hotel for two visits to the dentist during the rest day and solved the problem, caused by an infected filling.

It says a great deal about the team's ability to keep a secret, as well as Indurain's own hermetic nature, that this particular incident was never revealed to anyone outside Banesto until well after Indurain had retired, years later. As Chiappucci himself said, 'I've never seen a single sign of suffering appear on his face.' Combined with Indurain's capacities as a racer, it only made beating the Spaniard seem even more improbable.

The fates could hardly have chosen a better location for Indurain to produce what is widely considered the defining ride of his career – and in the process prove not only that he was a completely different class of racer compared to any other Spaniard, but also that he was the ideal sporting representative for modern Spain. Luxembourg was where Delgado had arrived more than three minutes late for the opening prologue in the 1989 Tour – and effectively lost it. This time round Luxembourg was where Indurain left no doubt as to who – barring accident or disaster – was heading to Paris in yellow. As Indurain's arch-rival Gianni Bugno said after the time trial, 'Miguel has won the Tour.' He also added, 'There were 180 riders in today's race and one extra-terrestrial.' 'I've never seen anything like that in my time as a bike racer,' added Stephen Roche.

Roche and Bugno weren't alone in their comments: after Indurain had obliterated his GC rivals in the Luxembourg time trial, there was a fair amount of comparing him with creatures from other planets. For the first time in his career, Indurain was labelled an 'extra-terrestrial'. As Sam Abt wrote so memorably and without any of the double-entendres that were later to blur such comparisons with aliens in cycling, 'anybody who wondered where Indurain had been hiding for the prior part of the Tour got the answer in Luxembourg. He was in a telephone booth changing into a bicycle racing jersey with a very big S on it.' Similarly, *Cycle Sport* headlined their July 1996 edition *'Is This Man a Robot?',* with a picture of an Indurain that was half-man, half-machine.

That the second best rider in Luxembourg was Indurain's team-mate, Armand de las Cuevas, only underlined the Spaniard's superiority. And that Indurain's margin on de las Cuevas was three minutes showed how far ahead of the rest of the field, team-mate or no team-mate, Indurain had been. Luxembourg 1992 was, in fact, the greatest ever margin recorded in a Tour time trial between the first and second rider, Indurain's time of three minutes beating the record set twice by – appropriately enough – his spiritual ancestor in the race, Jacques Anquetil, in 1962 at Lyon and in 1961 at Péri-gueux, by just one second.

Beyond that, the gaps were simply staggering. Bugno, himself a consummate time triallist, lost nearly four minutes. LeMond – who had won the 1989 Tour thanks to his time trialling skills – was over four minutes back. So too, was Stephen Roche, who had defeated Delgado in the final time trial in Dijon in the 1987 Tour, so clearly was no slouch in that speciality, either. Chiappucci, meanwhile, lost more than five minutes despite dumping the usual road bike – which arguably had cost him the 1990 Tour after he used it in the final time trial – and using an aerodynamic helmet, aerodynamic bars, a disc wheel and shift gears. Small wonder that the idea that Indurain was from another planet abounded. As Abt put it, 'Very rarely does a rider crush his opponents so thoroughly in a long time trial ... for all the good Chiappucci's extra gadgets did, he should have added a motor.'

In defence of those defeated so clearly by Indurain, you could argue that the Luxembourg course lent itself to displays of pure strength and clearly suited the Navarran down to the ground. In fact he had swept across the few technical parts of the course, like a stretch of cobbles mid-way through and a trickier, more exposed, section alongside the River Mossler, in such imperious style it was as though they barely registered. But either way, Indurain's time trial performance could not have been more intimidating. As *Nuestro Ciclismo* points out, Unzué, who usually acted as driver behind Indurain in time trials, had a crick in his neck and had to act as co-pilot. 'I had never seen him do anything like that before. Up until then, he'd always had at least one bad moment in each time trial where he had to ease off a bit. That day, he didn't. Apart from giving him ten or twelve time checks, the only thing I had to ask him was to stay calm. I was worried he would crack at any moment.' Indurain came up to Unzué afterwards to ask him why he had been so nervous, because he had been *tranquilo* all the way.

It barely goes without saying that Indurain registered the fastest time at each intermediate checkpoint, touching 90 km/h at times on descents, despite the relatively flat course. But that Bugno could lose eight seconds on Indurain in just two kilometres, that LeMond could have lost nearly two minutes two thirds of the way through the course, or that after Chiappucci in the Giro, this time the symbolic time trial victim – for Indurain to perceive in the distance, bear down upon and then zoom past with seemingly no effort at all – was double Tour winner, Laurent Fignon: all that placed Indurain's time trial in the realm of the exceptional.

Chiappucci had started three minutes before Indurain in the Giro's final time trial, this time Fignon had come down the starting ramp six minutes ahead. He was, in fact, the third rider that day to fall into Indurain's clutches, after Giancarlo Perini (Carrera) and Eddy Bouwmans (Panasonic), but by far the best-known. So much for Fignon's pre-Tour prediction that 'Indurain won't have it so easy this year,' or Bugno's claim that this year in the Tour, 'the moment I've been waiting for for so long has finally arrived.' As for LeMond, 'I thought I was riding well, really strong, but I kept losing time to him in every kilometre. It was unreal and I can't explain it. We will have to start thinking about who is going to finish second.' Fignon said, 'I was going at 53 kilometres an hour according to my speedometer. He must have gone past me at 60 kilometres an hour, and into a headwind. That was no plane, that was a missile.'

What must have made it more upsetting for LeMond was that up until that point, Indurain had been on the defensive in the Tour. True, Indurain had won the opening short prologue in San Sebastián, in front of tens of thousands of delighted Spanish fans – the first to be won by a Spaniard since Paco Errandonea, twenty-five years previously, unexpectedly outpowered Raymond Poulidor. But after the race skirted the Pyrenees for the first time since 1910, Banesto had only taken a relatively disappointing seventh in the stage four team time trial, albeit only losing around 30 seconds on Bugno's Gatorade squad. 'I'd have taken anything up to 90 seconds,' Echavarri commented, 'so it's not a tragedy.' Worse was to come en route to Brussels, when an ambush by LeMond and Chiappucci across the *pavés* had left Indurain trailing by over a minute. 'These roads should only be used in the Tour of Flanders,' Echavarri snapped at the finish.

But the stage nine Luxembourg time trial placed Indurain and Banesto in another galaxy. Banesto's pre-time trial estimate had been that Indurain would gain roughly a second per kilometre on his rivals. Averaging more than 49 kilometres an hour – and just a fraction short of 57 km/h in the first 22 kilometres – Indurain more than tripled that prediction. The sledgehammer effect had worked even without Indurain using exceptionally tough gearing – 54 x 46 on the rings, 12 x 19 on the sprocket. But it left the Spaniard more than three minutes ahead overall of all his main rivals, albeit still out of yellow on early race leader Pascal Lino, not considered, even in Lino's own estimation, as capable of winning the Tour. 'Now it's up to my rivals to start getting worried,' was Indurain's wry comment afterwards. Echavarri's analysis made it clear that from here on, the Tour's time trials were going to be where 'Indurain has to attack, not on the descents, or in the rain or on the *pavé*. This [time trialling] is his terrain.'

'He's made for time trialling,' Echavarri said, recalling that in 1984 he and Unzué had already thought that Indurain should focus on a future bid on the Hour Record, recently beaten by Francesco Moser. Echoing Unzué's comments that Indurain never had a time trial bike in his home, he added, 'There have been no aerodynamic studies … his position on the time trial bike is what it should be naturally. When the athlete's tribars started to be used, he was one of the first. Apart from his exceptional cardiovascular qualities' – his resting heart rate was a very low 42 bpm – 'he also has exceptionally long femurs, just like many of the champions before him.' Echavarri also mentioned Indurain's height as something that made him stand out, from the Spanish crowd at least. 'At 1.88 m, that's the complete opposite to what we've always had in Spanish cycling.'

The bike that Indurain used was his standard time trial machine, with the cranks of 180 millimetres one of the few areas that stood out as radically different – a consequence of those long femurs – as well as a smaller front wheel (a type now banned by the UCI) to give a more aerodynamic position. Indurain tended to use a normal saddle in time trials, not liking those with extra padding. But the tri-spoke front wheel and rear discwheel, the aerobars, the slightly more oval-shaped, aerodynamic frame – all of these were standard fare. It was only the athlete that was truly different.

Such a colossal contrast between Indurain and the rest of the field not only set him up for Spain's first Giro–Tour double, it also felt like the start of an era, of not one but many Tours. 'To describe what Indurain did is a question of getting the Spanish Royal Academy Dictionary [Spain's equivalent to the *OED*] and finding every possible adjective that is equivalent to spectacular,' said *El Mundo Deportivo*. 'Only Eddy Merckx or Jacques Anquetil are on a similar level. It's not just that Indurain has won every time trial in the last three Grand Tours he has raced, as well as the prologue in the Tour and the time trial in the Tour de Romandie, it's the how.'

If the Giro had acted as the testing ground for the prototype of Indurain's time trial strategy for Grand Tours, then the 1992 Tour was the first time that strategy was launched in full. What is curious is that Luxembourg marked the high point of its effectiveness. Never again would Indurain produce such a dominating time trial ride in the Tour de France and never again would his rivals be crushed so completely. The return of the Pyrenees in their fullest format, rather than a couple of brief incursions, gave the climbers more opportunities to test Indurain's strength. But the inroads the opposition made in the years to come were, at first, so comparatively minimal, it barely mattered. Indurain, Luxembourg made clear, was here to stay.

The creation in Spain of the image of Indurain as the modern European racer who had left behind his country's former limitations and who symbolised a new, Euro-centric *España* reached fever pitch. *El Mundo Deportivo* and just about every other Spanish newspaper highlighted that Indurain was not just in a league of his own in the Tour, he was also in a league of his own when it came to Spanish cycling. 'Our champions have always been mercurial types, capable of one great gesture one day and three days of childish errors. Not Indurain. He is our most secure winner ever,' the paper said. 'He is totally different.'

Whenever Indurain was asked who his most dangerous rival was, up until the middle of 1994, he would invariably answer 'Chiappucci'. The reason was simple: Chiappucci's breakaway to Sestriere, soloing across the Alps for 125 kilometres, in a move that, as Richard Moore observed, contained everything Indurain's time trialling approach seemed to lack. Above all, it had a sense of spontaneity and foolhardiness, a death-or-glory approach that had no place in Indurain or Banesto's race manual of the time. It was the kind of move that Delgado would have been more than proud to make, had he not been Indurain's team-mate. Because if Indurain had wound back the clock to the greatest days of Anquetil or Merckx in his time trial at Luxembourg, Chiappucci had arguably done even more than that. His lone flight over the Iseran, the highest point of the Tour, then the Mont-Cenix and finally up to Sestriere had more than an air of mountain geniuses like Charly Gaul, something from cycling's golden era, about it.

Chiappucci's place in the history books was even more clearly guaranteed given that the last rider to soar to victory in Sestriere in the Tour had been Fausto Coppi, forty years earlier, with a margin of more than seven minutes on closest pursuer Bernardo Ruiz of Spain. This time, Chiappucci's gap on the closest Spaniard behind him, Indurain, was just one minute and forty seconds, but to the tens of thousands of *tifosi* who egged the Italian up on the final twelve-kilometre climb, it didn't matter. Chiappucci's effort, as *La Gazzetta dello Sport*, Italy's leading sports daily, put it so eloquently the next day, 'had made us go crazy'.

After breaking away from the tiny peloton of chasers, Indurain's relentless pursuit of Chiappucci on the ascent to Sestriere had initially brought, as I recall it, chanting of the theme music from *Jaws* from parts of the foreign media in the Tour's press rooms. Yet that image of Indurain the cold-eyed reptile began to blur a little when, with three kilometres to go, he visibly began to crack. Rather than having a gigantic 'S' on his back like in Luxembourg, Indurain started weaving long, stuttering 'S'-bends in the middle in the road as his strength began to reach its limit. When he came to the line, for all this was the moment when Indurain finally took the overall lead from France's Pascal Lino, press officer Francis Lafargue refused to let Indurain speak to the media after the winner's ceremonies, convinced the Spanish star – 'cross-eyed and only able to repeat the words "I'm hungry"' – was on the edge of total collapse. 'It was the one night of the Tour I saw him in difficulty going up the stairs,' recalls Jean-François Bernard. It also happened to be the one night that Indurain was due to talk to *Cycling Weekly*, the magazine I was writing for at the time. But when we reached the team hotel – given what had happened, we knew our chances of getting an interview were slim – nobody was about and it was enveloped in a ghostly silence.

Chiappucci's move had clearly caused some damage, but the huge poster at the start next day borne by two *tifosi* – 'Today – do it like yesterday' – showed no sign of coming true. Instead, as Indurain shadowed Chiappucci all the way up the Alpe d'Huez, there was no sign of any more moments of weakness. Even with a week of racing left to go, Indurain's second outright Tour victory was in the bag. From then on, it would be only slightly exaggerating to say that the only moment Indurain seemed to be in any sort of difficulty – although his dental problems, later revealed, proved otherwise – was on the Paris podium, when he tried to hold the cub-sized Credit Lyonnais cuddly toy lion the race leader received each day with one hand, and almost dropped it.

'Two exploits will remain in people's memories from this year's Tour,' Echavarri observed on the eve of the final 64-kilometre time trial in Blois. 'Miguel in Luxembourg and Chiappucci in the Alps.' That last time trial was also won by Indurain, this time by a 'mere' 40 seconds over Bugno, although his average speed of 52.349 km/h set an as yet unbeaten record average speed for a Tour time trial of over 60 kilometres. Hinting strongly at the idea that Indurain would not be keen on winning at all costs – and thereby creating enemies on all sides, rather than adopt a strategy of letting his rivals take their share of the glory – Echavarri added, 'But Indurain needs Chiappucci and Chiappucci needs Indurain. It never makes sense to humiliate people with whom you share something.'

However, Echavarri was clear, too, about what he wanted to achieve with Indurain. 'When they talk about Indurain's lack of panache, that makes me laugh. Miguel races with his head, to win, Chiappucci is operating on another level, which we admire. But he doesn't win.'

That was perhaps the key lesson from Chiappucci's lone break-away: it looked good, but it failed to do more than cause a ripple in Indurain's smooth, steady progress towards his second Tour de France victory. Indurain had set out his stall at Luxembourg for the years to come and in the Tour raced at a new record average speed of 39.5 km/h; Chiappucci's response had fallen far short of doing more than shake him. If this was the best the peloton's most rebellious individual could achieve, what was the point of trying?

After the Tour de France, the Indurain show went on. In 1990, the flurry of questions around his potential Tour win had overshadowed his superb lone victory in the Clásica San Sebastián. Two years on, Indurain's back-to-back Grand Tour wins – the first in the Giro and Tour since Stephen Roche in 1987 – saw two other impressive triumphs all but completely eclipsed. The first had come in June, in the one day's racing he took part in between the Giro and Tour, when he outgunned Iñaki Gastón by less than half a wheel for his first (and only) National Championships Road Title. The second was in September when, for the third time in five years, Indurain triumphed in the Volta a Catalunya, after losing a time trial against Alex Zülle – the first since the Vuelta a Aragón that spring – but then applying a ferociously steady pace on the race's toughest ascent, to Valter. Zülle, still in his rookie year as a pro, was unable to handle the pace and Indurain rounded off his season with another overall victory that confirmed his leadership, for the first time in his career, in the UCI's Individual World Ranking.

In many ways, Indurain's 1993 Tour de France victory felt like an extension of his triumph in 1992. Not just because, with Indurain at the height of his powers, barring accidents it was so widely seen as a foregone conclusion, but also because the format used was a carbon copy of the previous July. A prediction by one of French cycling's leading figures, former director and racer Raphaël Géminiani, that 'only a mass attack in the first week can prevent Indurain from winning this year's Tour' proved to be uncannily correct.

Victory in the opening prologue of Le Puy de Fou theme park, despite its hillier format, instantly gave Indurain the upper hand. After ceding the yellow to a series of sprinters, Chiappucci's Carrera squad gained thirty-five seconds on Indurain in the time trial, but Banesto proved superior to Bugno's Gatorade team by twelve seconds and – above all, given subsequent developments in the Alps – the Spaniards gained nearly two minutes on a newly emerging rival, Tony Rominger and his Clas-Cajastur team. There was no sign, though, of Geminiani's mass attack on Indurain.

The stage nine time trial at Lac de Madine was not as much of a knock-out blow as Luxembourg, partly because Indurain punctured, but it was a gamechanger nonetheless. Indurain's closest rival Bugno finished at over two minutes down, Rominger at nearly three and Chiappucci more than five minutes off the pace. 'It is a pity that I have coincided with Indurain, it may end up being the same as [Italy's 1960s Grand Tour hero Felice] Gimondi with Merckx,' Chiappucci concluded. 'When I attack, maybe the rest of my rivals won't be able to regain contact. But Miguel always will.' Possibly the greatest point of interest at Lac de Madine was that Indurain's puncture and subsequent minor delay meant that his brother Prudencio, last on the stage, was saved from being eliminated on the time cut. With the first and last names on the results sheet, this curious occurrence was dubbed an Indurain *bocata* (sandwich) by his team-mates. But that such incidents were given major media coverage is an indication of how predictable the result itself had been.

The following two weeks proved to be anything but nailbitingly dramatic as Chiappucci, Bugno and the rivals of 1992 and earlier fell by the wayside on the first Alpine stage, to be replaced by a new host of secondary actors to Indurain's lead part in proceedings: Rominger, Poland's Zenon Jaskula and Colombia's Álvaro Mejía. The greatest threat, Rominger, made much of the running in the Alps, taking two back-to-back stages, but there was a yellow-clad Spaniard shadowing his every move. Rather than dispute the first victory, Indurain reportedly allowed Rominger to claim his slice of glory, which defused, at least at this point in the game, any potential rebellion. On the second stage, Indurain fought harder for the win, but Rominger still managed to outstrip him. Given that with each Rominger victory, Indurain's own position on general classification had become increasingly secure, this was simply a wall-to-wall application of a standard practice between the two strongest riders in a race. At no point did Rominger even hint that he could win the Tour that year, saying his main enemies were Mejía and Jaskula in the fight for the podium. Good news for Indurain, perhaps, but for anybody barring the Spanish media, tedious to watch.

The final week of the Tour saw a few, insignificant chinks appear in Indurain's armour. Briefly dropped by Jaskula and Rominger at the race's final summit finish, in the Pyrenean ski resort of Saint Lary Soulon, Indurain then had considerably more difficulty in following Rominger on the Tourmalet the next day. Rominger had opened up a 50-second gap on Indurain by the summit, but sterling work by Julián Gorospe on the opening part of the climb to limit the damage and a breakneck descent by Indurain rapidly quashed that particular rebellion. Combined with Tony Rominger's victory in the final time trial of the race, beating Indurain by 42 seconds, these minor difficulties were the original snowball in the avalanche of speculation by the following June that Indurain might, at last, have met his match. But Indurain's defenders pointed to his falling ill with a high fever the night before the time trial and racing it when he was off-form. If Indurain – who kept his condition secret until after the Tour – only lost so little time when he was sick, how much more unlikely was it that Rominger would beat him when he was at the top of his game?

Indurain later revealed that the 1993 Tour had been a little more of a touch and go affair than he would have liked, with a severe chill threatening to wreck his race from the second rest day at Andorra onwards. He had, he told *Nuestro Ciclismo*, only let team doctor Sabino Padilla and his room-mate and brother Prudencio in on his illness: 'We treated the Tourmalet stage as if it was the last one in the race, and by the final time trial, everything was under control.' Like his secret trip to the dentist in 1992 at Dole, nobody outside the team had got wind of Indurain's vulnerability: yet again, he appeared impregnable, and given his ability to chase down Rominger and defend himself in the time trials even when ill, ultimately that was all that counted.

In the record books, Indurain's third Tour de France lifted him into a select circle of seven riders that had taken a hat-trick or more of wins in cycling's showcase event. He also became the first rider in history to do a 'double-double' of two Giros and two Tours in as many years, and the first to win five Grand Tours in five straight participations. By this point, Eddy Merckx's grumblings that Indurain was 'too limited in what he does to satisfy me totally' no longer seemed to matter.

Yet for all his superstar status, Indurain refused, as he always had, to be overly captivated by the trappings of success, preferring to stay loyal to his roots and keep his private life as much out of the public eye as possible. In 1992, he turned down an offer to be flown from Paris to the start of the Olympic Games in Barcelona to be Spain's final torchbearer of the Olympic flame. Instead he went back to Pamplona and Villava, where he held up a yellow jersey, in triumph, from the two town hall balconies to the thousands of fans below who had gathered to celebrate his victory. Equally, when he got married that November, whilst the wedding was not held in secret, there was no question of any exclusives of the ceremony being sold to any of Spain's gossip magazines, despite numerous offers.

It helped that Indurain's wife, Marisa López de Goicoechea, was equally determined to keep their private life private: she has never, for example, given an interview to the press and was only occasionally seen at races. Born in the Basque Country in 1964, she and Indurain met at the celebrations after what used to be the area's traditional end-of-season bike race, the Txitxarro hill-climb, in 1988. The two got to know each other better when she began working in the offices of the University Clinic in Pamplona, where Indurain would drop in for the team's medical check-ups, and, after a visit to the Pope to receive his blessing in Rome (Indurain gifted the Pope a mountain bike after the mass), they were married in November 1992. Echavarri and Unzué were witnesses, along with Indurain's sister, at the wedding ceremony held at a church in Pamplona – another indication of how deeply Indurain's personal life and work loyalties remained intertwined at the time. Yet as Unzué says, 'We never wanted him to be media material, because it wouldn't have helped. When that happens to athletes, somewhere along the line you end up breaking apart.'

In races, Unzué was greatly helped in this area by Banesto's press officer, Francis Lafargue. At the time a real rarity amongst teams, Lafargue was initially signed to help Echavarri and Unzué with the logistical side of things. Amongst his media 'skills' was occasionally stonewalling journalists for requests for interviews with Indurain or other riders. With time, most Spanish-speaking journalists, including myself, that needed interviews with Indurain would learn to go to races where Lafargue was guaranteed not to be present and talk directly to Indurain for some time. He would invariably co-operate, with my annual twenty-minute interview with Indurain at the Vuelta a Valencia only needing a 'see you tomorrow then' and a double check at the next morning's start for his tall, tracksuited figure to come out of a hotel lobby lift that evening, ready to talk.

'Surviving as a person when you've hit fame is the hardest part of it all,' reflects Unzué, 'no matter who it is. It's outside racing that it all can go wrong, because "real life" gives you the chances to make real mistakes. There are some lads who self-destruct at that moment, others who change, and others, a very few, like Miguel. I'd known Miguel for fifteen years and in all those he would say goodbye in exactly the same way, from the first time to the last time our paths crossed. Nothing changed, despite all that could have happened. There was never a PR department telling him what he should or shouldn't do. Miguel is Miguel.'

'If you take cycling's top fifteen figures, all of them have their own characteristics, their own personality, their own survival tactics. None of them are the same. But Miguel is unique. It's not that I haven't come across other people like him, I just don't think they exist.' Or as the Spanish would say, *Miguel es Miguel*. Although in 1992, as their standard-bearer in Europe, their most emblematic of modern-day figures, for a while Indurain became much more than Indurain.

CHAPTER 8

1993–94: A Strip of Sandpaper

A few years ago, former 1990s British professional Chris Boardman went to pay the Pinarello bike manufacturers a visit. The Italian company had all of their previous top bike models on display, including the time trial bike that Indurain used in his assault on the Hour Record, the *Espada*. What caught Boardman's attention, though, was not so much the machine per se as the strip of sandpaper someone had stuck down the leading edge of the frame's front tubes.

'It was very old tech, but somebody in there must have known what they were doing. You create roughness there, and by manipulating the air flow on the drag, you can gain quite a bit of time,' Boardman, a time trial specialist and Hour Record breaker, amongst multiple achievements, recounts. 'They'd done it crudely, but they did something. It was something we did with the Team GB track team clothing during the Olympics when I was working for them – not with sandpaper, but the principle was the same.' However, he was probably as much surprised as he was impressed.

Boardman, himself a triple prologue winner in the Tour, readily describes Indurain as 'one of the greatest time triallists in history.'

However, when it came to technological advances, '[Indurain would] use new kit and a few bits and pieces, but he was very much of the Old Guard. I don't wish to sound disrespectful, but he carried on doing his own thing. He was the last of an era.'

Indurain's successful Hour Record bid in 1994 came at the tail end of a time when as Boardman sees it, 'generally in the sport there was little to no understanding of aerodynamics, at best it was scrappy. Indurain was fortunate to be in a period when everybody was as ignorant as each other.' As the newcomer, taking his own first Hour Record in 1993, winning the Tour prologue in 1994 at a record average speed and very much at the cutting edge of what Unzué describes as the 'underworld' of time trial specialists, Boardman says, 'for me it was brilliant. I'd done the wind tunnel with Lotus [a fundamental element in Boardman's Individual Pursuit victory in the 1992 Olympics] and I knew what mattered.'

Boardman describes himself as an unwitting catalyst for change, 'because I was the newbie, I battered everybody; they actually took a closer look at what I was doing: a compact body position, very low gears, prologues at 120 rpm, dress rehearsals for absolutely everything. It was all just done in a completely different way. But they' – the opposition including Indurain – 'didn't understand the dynamics of the event, for them it was all about having a big engine and that was it. He was a big guy with his elbows out, grinding along. They didn't know that moving your body as little as three millimetres can change your whole aerodynamic silhouette. Back then it was all about power production. I'm not sure if Indurain even went to a wind tunnel. But I'm not sure if he was that bothered, either. He got his name in the history books – and ultimately all records will get beaten.'

Boardman is at pains to emphasise that Indurain was far from being the only one who relied more on strength than aerodynamics to make a difference. He cites the case of Luc Leblanc, the French-man whom he memorably overtook in the short opening prologue of the Tour in 1994, and says, 'He was going on a bike you could genuinely go into a Decathlon shop and buy, with his 44-centimetre bars so he could breathe better. It was a very inefficient system, for him and for Miguel. Put these people in the same races now with the same methodology and even with the same power and they wouldn't feature.'

What impressed Boardman about Indurain the most, in the eyes of one top specialist observing another, was Indurain's 'consistency. It's almost on a Team Sky level, because it's one thing to get to the top, it's a wholly different thing to stay there. It's different circumstances for you, it's different in your team, there are no "oh, you've done a good ride there". From then on, you win or you lose. So to be that good, for that long, that's special.'

Notwithstanding speculation very early in his career that he might one day make a bid for it himself, Indurain's first brief appreciation of cycling's most famous Record and the aura of prestige surrounding it probably came when a pale-faced British athlete was allowed onto the winner's podium at the end of a Tour de France stage into Bordeaux in 1993. The athlete in question was Boardman and his presence in the Tour ceremony was a homage from ASO to his having taken the Hour Record a few hours before in the nearby Bordeaux velodrome.

However, Boardman's impromptu appearance in red-and-yellow Kodak sponsored kit on the Tour leader's podium made it clear he was not a Tour rider. And that in turn summed up the yawning gap between Indurain, by that point well en route to his third Tour win, and the track specialists like Graeme Obree, who were currently reviving interest in the Hour Record with their repeated bids. Obree, in particular, had captured the media's imagination with reports of his Record bike being partly built out of bits of his old washing machine, and his oh-so-British diet of marmalade sandwiches and cornflakes prior to going out and hammering the Record to bits.

Indurain's unexpected interest began to filter through to the media in early 1994, courtesy of Echavarri and Unzué. 'It will be the cherry on the cake of his *palmares*,' argued Echavarri. That year's World Road Championships was skipped in favour of a post-Tour Record bid in Bordeaux, conveniently close to Indurain's home region of Navarre and as early as the end of 1993, Echavarri had already began sounding out Pinarello to produce a specific, ultra-light Hour Record bike for Indurain.

After four years of Tour de France wins and a strong focus on the Grand Tours, Indurain's Hour Record bid had a hugely exotic appeal to the Spanish media, and sumptuous TV contracts were reportedly offered to broadcast it. *MARCA*'s lead cycling reporter, Josu Garai, spent the entire month of August in Pamplona, doorstepping Indurain each morning as he headed out for training. Yet the Record bid was also handicapped by Indurain's almost complete lack of track racing experience – since 1986, he had raced fewer than half a dozen times in the velodrome – and by his focus on road-racing, in particular the Tour. Team doctor Sabino Padilla estimated that Indurain's peak of Tour form would begin to fade by 9 September by the latest, which called for a rapid period of adaptation from road to track. On top of that, Indurain finished the 1994 Tour under the weather, and needed to recover.

Arguably the biggest issue of all, though, should have been Indurain's physique. Given his height, 1 metre 88 and weighing 75–80 kilos when in form, ensuring he adopted as aerodynamic a position as possible was critical. Yet with such a tight time frame for Indurain to operate in – and with limited real knowledge of aerodynamics – endless testing of different positions was hardly an option.

The time schedule and his closest velodrome being 100 kilometres away meant Indurain, initially lacking the *Espada* [Sword] time trial bike that had been specially built by Pinarello until August, had to improvise his Hour Record assault in the most unsuspected of ways. As the *Diario de Navarra's* longstanding cycling journalist Luis Guinea recounts, using a standard Pinarello TT frame, Banesto mechanic Luis Sanz built Indurain a to-spec replica of the Sword. Until he received his real 'weapon', Indurain used this replica on a 22-kilometre stretch of ultra-flat highway running from outside his house to the town of Aioaz, riding time and again each day in the same gear and always following the white line in the centre.

Despite the somewhat homespun preparation, there was no reason to be overly pessimistic about his chances. Indurain began testing his track form on 19 August in Anoeta stadium in San Sebastián, clocking an average of 52.715 km/h over 5,000 metres. That was a fraction ahead of the time needed for the current Hour Record distance of 52.713 kilometres, clocked by Obree that April in Bordeaux. Indurain's performance, however, was for over less than a tenth of that distance, in a discipline where one of the biggest challenges was maintaining a rigidly aerodynamic position for a full sixty minutes. On 21 August, Indurain therefore began intensive work in Bordeaux to try to adapt as quickly as possible, with two hours track riding in the morning and another two in the afternoon. Four days later, he produced record-winning times over a half-hour period, but reports were filtering through, too, that muscles on his right side, due to the centrifugal pressures of cornering on the track, were beginning to suffer badly. Indeed, after the record, Unzué would recall how Indurain's fingers were so stiff, the masseurs had to unclaw them from the handlebars one by one. 'The last ten minutes of the Record are going to last a lifetime,' Indurain warned.

Matters were further complicated when late in the evening of 28 August, a news agency dropped a bombshell: Indurain, the report claimed, had tested positive in an anti-doping test in France. The positive had been recorded on 15 May, during the Tour de L'Oise, a minor stage race in France that Indurain had won. The substance was Salbutamol, a substance used to treat asthma and other breathing difficulties under the commercial name of Ventolin.

The Spanish media instantly cried foul, starting with the timing of the announcement, less than a week before Indurain's Hour Record attempt, and coming the day after the Record attempt was definitively confirmed as taking place. They pointed to the recent history of Delgado in the 1988 Tour and his positive-test-that-wasn't, and highlighted Indurain's long medical history as an asthmatic and hay fever sufferer. Furthermore, Banesto had in fact notified the race doctor at the Tour de L'Oise that Indurain was using Salbutamol and had the medical certificate from the UCI that authorised his use of Ventolin. Indurain also received the backing of the IOC, with Alexandre de Merode, president of the Olympic Medical Commission, arguing that 'there is no reason whatsoever for Indurain to receive any kind of sanction. UCI rules permit the use of Salbutamol under medical supervision and authorisation.'

According to the magazine *Jotdown*, Banesto already knew about the pending positive result shortly before the Tour. Echavarri mentioned, perhaps predictably, the idea that the French were simply bad losers. 'They want to damage Miguel's image. I don't want to think badly of them and start criticising. But it seems like the French are upset that we've won five Tours in seven years,' Echavarri said. Indurain put it down to the rules being misinterpreted and called it 'a pretty strange incident'.

Although the incident soured the good atmosphere surrounding the Hour Record attempt in Bordeaux – there were rumours the location would be changed at the last minute to Mexico – Echavarri warned of a boomerang effect. Indurain, he said, 'had been pretty upset when we told him about this before the Tour and that was perhaps why he raced so much harder in certain stages. Maybe the same thing will happen now.' Indurain also enjoyed support in some unlikely quarters, such as Bernard Hinault, traditionally critical of the Spaniard for his lack of attacking spirit. 'Why is he being judged?' Hinault asked. 'The law should be the same in all quarters. If he had been racing abroad this substance wouldn't even have been detected. Why doesn't France use the same list [of banned products] as the rest?'

In the event, Indurain was completely exonerated by the disciplinary committee of the French Professional Cycling League. The committee said there was 'no proof to show the substance in question had been used inappropriately', observed that a second medical dossier later provided by Banesto had further clarified Indurain's use and even criticised discrepancies between French anti-doping regulations and those of the UCI. The case was dropped. Indurain, on a motorbike holiday with his wife in the Pyrenees at the time he was cleared, was his usual silent self about it all. (By the time the news of the 'positive' had broken on the evening of the 28th, he said, he had been in bed, asleep.)

The 1994 positive-that-wasn't story was by far the most serious brush with suspicions of doping that Indurain had during his career. What speculation there has been afterwards has centred on the likelihood that drug use, particularly of EPO, was increasingly intense in that era in cycling rather than on any specific evidence linked to Indurain.

The most damaging accusation was made in 2000 by one of Indurain's French team-mates Thomas Davy, that during his time there in 1995 and 1996 Banesto as a team had used EPO. This claim was never substantiated and was categorically denied by Unzué. Equally, Indurain worked at certain points in his career with Francesco Conconi to use his anaerobic threshold test and, in the 1980s, for recommendations on his diet to reduce his weight. Conconi's reputation is mixed, to say the least: he is a sports doctor who was investigated for allegedly giving EPO to professional athletes for research purposes, but is also considered a founding father of modern sports physiology, in part thanks to his ground-breaking anaerobic threshold test. Sandro Donati, a respected anti-doping expert, once claimed that there had been large quantities of money paid by Banesto to Conconi and that 'I don't think Banesto paid that much to get the riders tested.' But this claim was never backed up. According to the website *Cyclingnews*, Erwin Nijboer, a Dutch rider with Banesto, confirmed the contact with the doctor, but said that it 'was only to do the Conconi test'.

After less than three weeks of specific preparation – far shorter than for either Boardman or Obree – the Hour Record attempt itself on the afternoon of Friday 2 September was a resounding success, pushing the limit beyond 53 kilometres, albeit by just 40 metres, for the first time in history. 'Magical Miguel,' was Echavarri's summary of Indurain's success at adding 327 metres to Obree's record, viewed in the Spanish sporting media as a way of wrenching the Record away from the 'laboratory cyclists', as *El Mundo Deportivo* put it. 'He has followed in Merckx's wheeltracks,' the newspaper solemnly pronounced. Possibly one key was Indurain's rapid acceleration on his 59 x 14 gearing to the required speed: 25 seconds in the first lap, 16 seconds in the second. By the 20th kilometre, despite Padilla's urging him to ease back and a painful ruck in his shorts, Indurain was already ahead of schedule and ahead of Obree. He continued to gain time steadily, at the rate of a second per kilometre, and by the 40th kilometre, barring disaster the Record was in the bag. By the time he passed Obree's mark, and still ignoring his mentor's pleas to slow down, he still had a further 22 seconds to push the distance as far as he could, in what finally totalled 5,949 pedal strokes in one hour.

'It went better than I expected,' Indurain said in his typically understated style, adding that barring the pain of having to maintain the same posture for such a long period of time, 'it almost felt like doing a time trial in the Tour.' *El Mundo Deportivo's* editor proclaimed it 'A triumph of man over machine,' as if the aerodynamics somehow detracted from the spectacle. 'Pretty boring until the last part and we didn't know if Miguel was used enough to track riding to do it,' Indurain's father, refreshingly unprepared, as ever, to toe the party line, said afterwards. 'I thought that he couldn't surprise me, but he managed to do it,' added Unzué. Even Francesco Moser, who had indirectly fuelled Unzué and Echavarri's earliest discussions that Indurain might go for the Hour ten years before, had a cameo role in the celebrations when a journalist managed to get him on the phone after Indurain's triumph. (Moser was, interestingly, one of the few insiders who had been convinced that Indurain had no chance of taking the Record.) Although physical power obviously played a crucial role, Delgado attributed a fair part of the triumph to Indurain's mental strength: 'When Miguel gets an idea of what he wants inside his head, it's very hard to stop him from doing it.'

Indurain's record sparked, briefly, reports of an Obree–Boardman-like rivalry with Tony Rominger for the Hour, given that

Rominger also went for the Record that autumn – twice. This was far more media hype than real, and unlike the Tour, it was 'won' by the Swiss rider, again on power rather than expertise or aerodynamics. Rominger was less experienced in track racing than Indurain, and the photos of his first venture onto the Bordeaux track that October, when he wobbled his way to a halt after half a lap and all but fell off, were widely published. Yet despite his lack of trackcraft, by the time he wheeled to a halt on his second Record attempt that November, Rominger had taken the maximum distance to 55,291 kilometres. That in turn was smashed by Boardman, in 1996, with a distance of 56.375 kilometres, before an absurd series of rule changes by the UCI in 2000 concerning the legality of different positions rendered all of these achievements, in the history books, all but null and void.

Although Rominger's new records overshadowed Indurain's effort internationally, at least initially, what concern in Banesto there was in regaining the Record seemed to have exhausted itself in 1994 at least with a one-off effort by Indurain. Amongst the broader Spanish public, that much of their interest in cycling began and ended with Indurain was once again evident. With no access in my flat to the pay-per-view TV channel that was featuring it, I went to watch the Record in a local bar in Granada heaving with Indurain fans cheering their hero on. A few weeks later, when Rominger beat Indurain's Record for the first time, there was so little interest in the same place I had to ask the barman – who had no idea it was happening – to change the channel so I could watch it.

It would be tempting to see the Hour Record as the culmination of the central period of Indurain's domination of Grand Tour racing – the 'cherry on the cake' as Echavarri had put it – but this would not be at all accurate.

Certainly Indurain continued to flatten the opposition in the Tour de France, with *L'Équipe* concluding that his fourth straight victory that July 'was probably the easiest of them all so far ... his rivals might have been new, but they seemed less dangerous than his previous rivals.' But in the Giro d'Italia, Indurain's near-perfect domination of the 1992 race represented a high point to which he would never return, and after finishing third in the 1994 edition, the race was quietly dropped from his programme and in 1996, it disappeared from Banesto's as well.

After 1992's double success, though, it only made sense that Indurain return to the Giro d'Italia in 1993, but on this occasion things were not so straightforward even before the race had started. A hurricane in the Alps when Indurain was reconnoitring a potentially decisive Giro time trial in Sestriere left him stranded without air transport. He finally got a ride in the Banesto team truck, arriving at the start on Elba by ferry, just one day before the race began.

It wasn't just the weather that no longer appeared to be on Indurain's side. The 1993 route featured far less time trialling and what little there was of it was much hillier: the tough mountain stage after that last – uphill – mountain time trial in Sestriere added to its 'anti-Indurain' nature. There were minor irritations, too, such as the clown hired by an unknown media outlet in the first week to let down the Spaniard's tyres at every start and then beat a hasty retreat amongst the spectators after his prank. In Spain, Indurain's conversion from cycling hero to folk hero was confirmed when Tele 5, the most gaudily commercial station of the time, bought the Giro's broadcasting rights. In what seemed to be an attempt to treat the Giro as a chat show rather than a race, Tele 5's coverage shocked longstanding cycling fans by sometimes including a mini commercial break one kilometre from the finishing line.

Indurain's bid to end the first day in the leader's jersey failed, too, after Classics specialist Moreno Argentin broke away and opened up such a considerable time gap on the first stage's opening mass start sector that it was impossible for the Spaniard to pull back enough time in the afternoon's first, short, time trial. In the event, Indurain finished second behind Maurizio Fondriest and then only moved into pink briefly in the mid-race time trial in Senigallia before ceding it to Italy's Bruno Leali.

However, in what all but turned into a re-run of the 1991 Tour, right down to his breakaway companion in the decisive move, having accelerated hard on the race's toughest pass, the Marmolada, Indurain moved away with Chiappucci in a break of five that saw Chiappucci claim a rain-soaked stage win and Indurain the *maglia rosa*. Victory for Indurain in the Sestriere time trial further strengthened his lead, but the Spaniard then, uncharacteristically, stumbled at the last fence. On the ascent to Oropa on stage twenty, the last major climb of the entire Giro d'Italia, Argentin – who Echavarri nicknamed *The Devil* for his strategic skills – shredded the field, then his team-mate, Lithuania's Piotr Ugrumov, launched a series of devastating attacks. As Chiappucci and his Carrera team-mate Stephen Roche made their own brief challenges, rather than overstretching himself, Indurain sat up and continued at his own pace. All he could do was hope that would prove enough to keep Ugrumov from gaining more than the 1–34 he had on the Lithuanian, a previously little-known rider who most observers thought would have settled for an unprecedented second place overall behind Indurain.

Echavarri lost the plot completely, shooting past the rest of the race convoy in spectacularly illegal style to bellow at Indurain, 'Relax, you can lose 30 seconds.' In the event Indurain lost 36 seconds but the final overall difference between himself and Ugrumov of

58 seconds, compared to over five minutes on Chiappucci twelve months earlier in Milan, made it clear how close the final gap had been. Echavarri was fined a sizeable 24,500 pesetas (€147 in today's money) for his reckless driving, but he said later that, with Oropa the last obstacle prior to celebrating the win in Milan, 'it was not important. I'm about to spend more on champagne.'

Multiple concerns had arisen for Echavarri in the Giro d'Italia, and not just Indurain being somewhat on the back foot in one stage: Banesto as a team had delivered a poor collective performance, accentuated when Fabrice Philipot and Stéphane Heulot both quit with sunstroke in the first week. Armand de las Cuevas, a talented but eccentric Frenchman, was expected to step into the breach, but instead opted to race in his own interests, not Indurain's. Banesto seemed to rely on theoretical rivals Festina to do much of their spadework in the early part of the stages – an alleged favour that was later to cost the Festina team manager, Jan Giesbers, his job – and it had an unexpected knock-on effect that winter, as Banesto underwent a major overhaul.

Echavarri's first attempt to reinforce Banesto by signing the bulk of the Ariostea squad alongside Gianni Bugno and Zenon Jaskula, two of Indurain's top rivals in the Tour, failed to work out. So did a bizarre proposal from, of all people, Italian tycoon Silvio Berlusconi for one of his companies to take over as main sponsor from Banesto at the end of 1994, with a possible fusion with an Italian squad part of the deal. Instead in November, Banesto and one of the country's most powerful middle-ranking teams, Seguros Amaya, announced that the two squads were fusing. Banesto very much remained the senior partner, but gained some strong support riders, including 1991 Vuelta a España winner Melcior Mauri and 1992 Vuelta runner-up Jesús Montoya. On top of that, two of the most promising young riders of the Spanish peloton, Mikel Zarrabeitia and

Antonio Martín, also joined the Banesto line-up, as did two of the top directors of the time: Javier Mínguez, later to direct the Spanish national team; and José Luis López Cerrón, later president of the Spanish Cycling Federation.

'The fusion was more a shock for the team staff than for anybody else,' Delgado reflects. 'What had been a very quiet team suddenly became a place with people yelling their heads off at each other. Miguel didn't participate so much in the running of the team, so I think it didn't affect him much, and if it did, he'd never say anything about it anyway.'

'There was a bit more of a dynamic feel in the team,' Delgado reflects. 'Some things were better. For example, Cerrón was very well-organised, he sent you the list of the races you'd be doing in advance. Before I'd only come across that in PDM.' However, Delgado insists that the squad had not changed excessively, and that Unzué and Echavarri were still very much the senior partners.

What seemed more likely to cause major turbulence in the team came when Banesto, at the time Spain's third largest bank with seven million clients, teetered on the edge of collapse in December 1993 following the exposure of a multi-billion pound deficit. Head director Mario Conde was fired for gross negligence as allegations spread that he had created companies to buy and sell assets within the Banesto group. At this point the Bank of Spain took over Banesto's management and Conde's dramatic exit, along with that of Arturo Romani, created a huge ripple effect. Trading in its shares, which had plummeted, was suspended, and inevitably questions about the viability of Banesto's considerable investments in newspapers and television stations, not to mention the long-term future of a certain bike team, began to spread.

The bank was subsequently salvaged by Banco Santander in one of the biggest bank rescue operations ever mounted in Spain, and Alfredo Saenz, the new director, took great care to ensure messages reached the team in mid-January that Banesto's cycling team – just weeks after the Amaya fusion had seen it expand its budget for 1994 – had a secure future. Conde was later imprisoned amidst counter-allegations that he had been the victim of an undercover political campaign, and the team pushed on regardless. The scandals, though, did no good to Banesto's public image. 'For many months,' Josu Garai wrote, 'the only good thing, at least in the public's eyes, that Banesto had going for it was the bike team, although, like everything in this life, there was a "before" and "after" with Pedro Delgado, and, above all, with Miguel Indurain.'

As Indurain's sporting achievements became more and more identified with Spain rather than the team, it became increasingly complicated for Banesto to justify his repeated absence from the Vuelta, which after all was (and is) Spain's biggest bike race. By early 1994 Unipublic, after two years of victories for Rominger, one of Indurain's top rivals, announced that from henceforth teams would have to provide a line-up worth 60 per cent of their FICP points. Banesto refused point-blank to comply and the stand-off reached a point where the question of Indurain's participation was briefly the subject of debate in the Spanish parliament and the Spanish Sports Council – the country's equivalent to a Ministry of Sport – was brought in as a mediator. Finally it was agreed that barring exceptional circumstances Indurain would race the Vuelta in 1995. But in 1994, for the third year running, Spain's greatest Grand Tour specialist and the sport's top rider did not take part in the Vuelta.

Indurain's track record in the Giro d'Italia (two wins out of two starts) and in the Vuelta (one second place overall, no stage wins and three abandons from seven starts) made the Italian race the logical choice. However, after five Grand Tour wins, the 1994 Giro d'Italia turned out to the first where Indurain's strategy of dominating the time trials then defending that lead in the mountains went seriously awry.

The first issue was that Indurain's approach of using the early part of the Giro d'Italia as a build-up to ride himself into form was already out of kilter before he started. Pollen allergies and colds had hit him harder than usual in a cold, wet Spanish spring, with decidedly mixed messages coming from the Vuelta al País Vasco. In his most important head-to-head duel against Tony Rominger, looking set to be his top challenger in the Tour, Indurain launched a dramatic attack on one stage, scattering the peloton, prior to abandoning the next. Rominger, meanwhile, not only won País Vasco, but took the Vuelta a España for a third time, where neither Banesto's Mikel Zarrabeitia nor Pedro Delgado, second and third overall, placed the Swiss rider under any serious pressure.

Third in the 1994 Giro's opening prologue for Indurain, five seconds off the pace behind his former team-mate Armand de las Cuevas, looked promising enough, although the Spanish were under a collective cloud following the suicide of one of their cycling icons, 1973 Tour winner Luis Ocaña, a few days before at his home in France. Then when young Russian Evgeni Berzin won at the first week summit finish of Campitello Matese by nearly a minute, given the second-year pro's 90th place in the previous Giro, it was hardly going to set off any alarm bells.

What did set the cat amongst the pigeons was Indurain's seriously poor time trial on stage eight, where he was beaten not only by Berzin by two and a half minutes, but where even Gianni Bugno managed to gain time on the Spaniard. Padilla attributed Indurain's poor showing to pollen allergies, whilst Indurain said he was unable to find an explanation but that 'if the Russian goes on racing like this, he'll be unbeatable.' *L'Équipe* called it 'the worst day of Indurain's career on a stage that he should have dominated.'

A 3–39 minute time gap on GC and the lack of any flat time trials in the remainder of the Giro left Indurain with no choice but to attack in the terrain where he had previously raced most conservatively: the mountains. 'I don't like to attack there for a very simple reason,' Indurain argued, 'I'm heavier than the rest.' However, he concluded that 'three minutes in a Giro like this one is no difference at all.' Echavarri, fond as ever of his religious reference points, said that 'two masses have been heard in the Giro so far – referring to the first two Sundays of the race with their respective time trials – 'and there are two more masses to come.' Here, he meant at Aprica on stage 15, over the notoriously difficult Stelvio and Mortirolo passes and the final ceremonial stage into Milan. In other words, there was still time to turn the Giro round for Indurain.

Indurain had rightly predicted that were the climbers to begin the process of fragmenting the race, he might well be able to take advantage of that, by following wheels when the roads steepened and wearing out the younger, less resilient racers, like Berzin, in the process. What he could not have expected was that instead, the critical weekend of the Giro d'Italia would see a new, more explosive kind of climber, emerge – for the first time during Indurain's Grand Tour domination.

Marco Pantani's devastating attack over the Jaufenpass on stage 14, the longest climb of the Giro d'Italia, and then on the long descent in an ultradynamic position, with 'his backside off the back of the saddle [and] within millimetres of the tyre' as Matt Rendell writes in *The Death of Marco Pantani*, had 'attracted huge public attention in Italy and abroad.' But whilst reminiscent of Claudio Chiappucci in Sestriere in the 1992 Tour, Pantani was far more consistent than his Carrera team-mate and one-time mentor, and that made him much more dangerous. When Pantani charged away on the lower slopes of the Mortirolo for a record-setting ascent of the climb, Berzin's panic and attempt to follow the Italian at all cost was comprehensible. Indurain, meanwhile, opted to let both riders go, and his steadier pace initially paid dividends: whilst Pantani shot over the summit 50 seconds ahead, by then Indurain was 47 seconds in front of Berzin. When he and the Italian, who waited for Indurain on the descent, then tore through the finish town of Aprica for the first time, at one point their advantage over Berzin had doubled to two minutes. At the least expected moment and in the least expected fashion, Indurain had turned the tables on his younger rival. A third Giro d'Italia victory seemed to be beckoning.

However, on the final, seemingly inoffensive Valico di Santa Cristina, a much shorter second category climb, Indurain ended up paying a high price for his colossal effort over the Mortirolo. He initially attacked but was first caught, then dropped, by Pantani. Suffering terribly on a theoretically less difficult climb, by the finish Indurain had lost three and a half minutes on the young Italian, and his advantage over Berzin shrank to a mere thirty-six seconds. It had been, without a shadow of a doubt, the most dramatic of Indurain's performances in any of his Grand Tours, yet it was one of the least beneficial. The double Giro d'Italia winner was now third overall, but Berzin had effectively raced like Indurain – panning his rivals in the time trial, then defending in the mountains as best he could – and was now en route to victory in Milan.

'I gave it everything, but that last part of the race was one of the worst moments of my career,' Indurain said at the finish line. He blamed his last minute collapse on, possibly, wearing too much protective gear on the rain- and snow-soaked Stelvio, the first mountain pass, and overheating. 'Miguel lost the Giro that year because he felt too sure of himself,' Unzué now says. 'He didn't need to go so hard. Miguel was great at calculating the times he needed to be sure of winning, and he had to do that on the Mortirolo. But [on the final climb] he should have gone steadier, and the Giro would have been won. He went from losing the Giro to winning it to losing it again. Imagine how mixed up your emotions would be then. But at times, to be almost perfect like Miguel, you have to make mistakes.'

There was also the question of the team's weakness in the Giro, with Indurain lacking support in the high mountains. 'It's like a third-division Italian side,' Chiappucci said scornfully. Indurain did not comment on the question but his brother Prudencio confirmed that they had expected stronger performances in the climbs from Montoya and Gerard Rue.

Indurain's last, faint, hope was that he could recoup his losses in the final, very hilly time trial on stage eighteen. But by that point in the game, Berzin was able to open up the throttle again, winning the stage and setting the seal on his victory. Indurain's second place, twenty seconds behind, both enabled him to consolidate his third place overall and strongly suggested he was closing the gap on the Russian intruder. However, his rising form came too late: after five consecutive Grand Tour wins, he was forced to settle for third in Milan. Indurain had, in effect, been *out-Indurained*.

Indurain's difficulties in the 1994 Giro d'Italia, contrasting with Rominger's third win in the Vuelta in as many years, led *L'Équipe* to give the Swiss rider five stars as their maximum favourite for the Tour de France, and Indurain four. After three years of unbroken domination in the Tour, it must have been tempting for a news-paper to predict that Indurain's increasing difficulties in the Giro were a prelude for a battle royale in the Tour. Rominger's medical entourage even went on record as predicting that Indurain would be dropped by the Swiss rider in the mountains. In fact, this turned out to be wishful thinking, even if losing the prologue in Lille to Chris Boardman by a whopping fifteen seconds acted as ample confirmation that the Briton's much-derided 'scientific' racing approach had more than a few merits. Indurain's strategy, designed by Unzué and Echavarri following the Giro d'Italia, was far simpler: a great deal of rest, with just one day's racing, the Spanish Nationals in Sabiñánigo, which he abandoned.

On the stage nine time trial to Bergerac, though, Indurain eliminated a considerable part of the doubts surrounding his condition, as he pulverised the opposition with what was his best performance against the clock since Luxembourg two years before. Only Rominger came off relatively lightly, losing a 'mere' two minutes on the 64-kilometre course along the rolling roads of the Dordogne. Beyond that, De Las Cuevas – one of those who had beaten Indurain in the Spaniard's near-debacle in Follonica in the Giro – had the honour of being the 'best of the rest', more than four minutes and twenty seconds down, whilst the rest of the field was truly kicked into touch. Ugrumov, his 1993 Giro d'Italia challenger, was more than six minutes behind, and Marco Pantani, nearly eleven.

The one potential fly in the ointment for Indurain's latest reign in yellow was Rominger, still less than three minutes down overall. But seven kilometres from the summit of Hautacam, the race's first major mountain-top finish, the Swiss rider was, as *L'Équipe* put it, 'executed' by the Spanish champion. Noticing Rominger was near the back of the steadily shortening line – 'a position he would not normally be in,' the ever-observant Indurain pointed out – the Tour leader first ordered team-mate Jean-François Bernard to step up the pace, then pulled away himself.

Metre by metre, pedal stroke by pedal stroke, Indurain's ferocious increase in pace was the first time since the Tourmalet in 1991 where he had really exploited his ability to keep a steady, relentlessly high rhythm on the climb in a Grand Tour. But this time the damage was far greater. The born climbers might well be able to accelerate at a higher speed. But after giving them time to waste their energy, Indurain's relentless pace behind slowly but surely shredded the opposition who had tried to stay on his wheel and, like fish on a line, he wound back in the few, the very few, who had tried to outplay him by anticipating his move.

With only Luc Leblanc for company, Indurain sailed past the last and most rebellious of his rivals, Pantani, 500 metres from the line. It seemingly mattered little that Lebanc then tore past for the stage win: once again Indurain had asked a rival for collaboration in the last two kilometres and this was his reward. 'I didn't care that he outsprinted me. All I want to retain from this day is the time I've taken on Rominger, De Las Cuevas and the rest,' Indurain said. De Las Cuevas lost nearly a minute; Rominger, his closest rival but suffering from illness, lost over two, meaning the gap between Indurain and the rider who was, on paper, his major threat was nearly five minutes. With ten stages to go, the Tour was effectively over.

'Hautacam was a surprise for me,' Unzué recognises. 'I had never seen him fighting *mano a mano* like that with the climbers. Then again, he was inside his "magic triangle"' – an area in the Pyrenees that had seen Indurain do well time and again. 'Miguel's time trial victories in the Tour de l'Avenir [Tour de la CEE] were from [nearby] Lourdes to Tarbes. We'd go past the foot of Hautacam on the warm-ups for those time trials. And then he won his first stage in Cauterets, he went up Luz Ardiden with LeMond, and on the Tourmalet and then at Val Louron he got his first yellow. It's very near the area where he trains and knows the best. Even if it was in the mountains, the area always inspired him.'

There were two narrow escapes for Indurain after Hautacam, the first being when he came within a whisker of suffering one of his rare crashes, on the descent of the Ventoux. 'I was in the first car behind Indurain as we came off the Ventoux and there was a left-hand bend. His brake blocked and he skidded further and further out,' recalls Manolo Saiz, the ONCE director. 'At the last possible moment, his brake unblocked and he could continue. But two more centimetres further out and he'd have come off and at that speed, goodness knows what could have happened.' Watching in the pressroom in Carpentras, used as we were to Indurain's apparent impregnability, I can still remember the collective gasp of disbelief that Indurain, the seemingly indestructible, could have come so close to disaster.

'But how many times did he have punctures or wheel changes in the years when he was dominating the Tour?' Saiz asked rhetorically. 'None, or maybe once at most. Why do we all remember that skid on the Ventoux? Because it was so rare. He had the luck of champions, or even more than that. Hinault, Merckx, Anquetil, they all had strokes of good luck, like, say, when Ocaña crashed out in the Tour in 1971 and so Merckx could win. Not Miguel. He never needed that kind of luck. Who ends up puncturing? The rider who's not strong enough to be up at the front and not riding on the edge of the road. Who doesn't crash? The rider who's most alert. That was always Miguel.'

Yet as Unzué now reveals, behind closed doors and for the fourth year running, Indurain's seemingly straightforward third week of the Tour was not as easy as it looked either. 'He suffered more than most in the cold weather and wet. I can remember in 1994 we lost a heck of a lot of time on the stage nineteen time trial to Avoriaz because coming out of Cluses it started to hail and Miguel was losing time [on stage winner Piotr Ugrumov] really fast. It was only when the sun came out again that he began to act a lot better. We were almost on the point of ... there was a margin, but it wasn't that big.'

In fact, Ugrumov's time trial win in Cluses, combined with a lone stage victory the day before, had allowed the Lithuanian to reclaim five minutes overall on Indurain. Yet that still left him more than five minutes down on the Spaniard in second place, allowing Indurain to notch up what *L'Équipe* grudgingly conceded was his most *'tranquille'* of Tour wins, and which put him just one rung below Hinault, Merckx and Anquetil, the all-time greatest of the race.

The Spanish media highlighted that for the third year running, Indurain's podium companions in Paris were once again different, but what had been, in fact, most unusual, was his strategy. Rather than seeing the mountains as an area where he would border purely on the defensive, he had now used his relentlessly steady pace on the climbs as a new method of gaining time as well.

'It was a great strategy, really courageous,' Boardman argues. 'They'd just wait and wait and wait, you didn't use your troops right up until the end of the climb, then he'd do the last few kilometres. It was a setpiece format, ride a devastating time trial then on the last three kilometres [of a mountain]: bang.'

Was Hautacam possibly a sign of increasing insecurity about his time trialling ability? That theory might hold water if Indurain had, say, lost the Bergerac time trial to Rominger in the same way he had been defeated by Berzin in the Giro in Follonica. But if he had felt any need to prove a point to his rivals, he would surely have fought far harder against Luc Leblanc to take the stage win on Hautacam. Rather this was improvisation, a spontaneous reaction to observing that his toughest rival was in difficulties, and would, in fact, abandon ill a few days later. What Hautacam showed was that for the first time, Indurain was no longer simply adhering to the conservative Grand Tour script previously written for him by Unzué and Echavarri. It would not be the last.

CHAPTER 9

Le Tour du Record

As plotlines go, it feels appropriate that of all his Tours, the one which saw Indurain take the record of victories won successively in cycling's toughest stage race was the one he was at the greatest risk of losing. The 1995 Tour was also the one in which Indurain displayed a skill set far beyond that of 'merely' being the Tour's (and perhaps cycling's) greatest ever time triallist. 'This was the Tour,' says Eusebio Unzué, 'where Miguel surprised me the most ... where we saw the day he came closest to racing like Eddy Merckx.' It was also, though, the Tour in which Unzue says Banesto experienced 'the hardest day of all the five,' where 'for many hours, it seemed as though something [an Indurain defeat] could happen ... the Tour was slipping through our fingers.' All this in a Tour where Indurain struck the first blow – and the hardest – of all five of his victories.

The opening salvo of Indurain's assault on the 1995 Tour, on roads made famous by their repeated presence in the Ardennes Classics, could not have been more unexpected. As Indurain's move unfurled, Eurosport commentator David Duffield reported that two of the Tour's most famous pundits, Laurent Fignon and the recently retired Stephen Roche, had looked across at each other in the commentators' boxes in frank disbelief at what they were seeing.

What was so unprecedented was Indurain's surging move on the Mont Theux climb, some 25 kilometres from the finish in Liège, passing through a little breakaway containing Lance Armstrong and Laurent Jalabert and across to attackers Éric Boyer and Johan Bruyneel. At a point where it was expected that the Spaniard would play his usual conservative game, waiting for the time trial the following day, Indurain tore up his own script with a vengeance.

Over the Côte des Forges, out of the Ardennes foothills and along the banks of the River Meuse into Liège, Indurain pushed on and on remorselessly, heedless that Boyer had dropped back and Bruyneel was glued to his back wheel. Indurain was going so hard that Jalabert, in theory due to become race leader after picking up enough bonus points on the stage, gave up his frustrated counter-attack and allowed himself to be absorbed by the peloton. Bruyneel was only able to come past at the last minute, and take the yellow. But Indurain's gestures of authority did not stop once he stopped pedalling. The Belgian later told colleagues that Indurain put one arm around him after the stage and told him 'don't worry, tomorrow, that [the yellow jersey] will be mine.'

Indurain's gaining fifty seconds at this point in the race was a devastating psychological blow. For years, the peloton had accepted that the Spaniard would automatically out-match them in the time trials. Then at Hautacam in 1994, he had added another string to his bow by burning the bunch off his back wheel on a very difficult mountain climb. Outpowering the field on a rolling stage, though, was another kind of demonstration of strength, but not necessarily because Indurain had wanted to intimidate the bunch: he simply did it because he could. Yet years later, it has emerged that Indurain's attack at Liège was anything but spontaneous.

'When we went to look at the time trial route, after the Spring Classics that April, we came and looked at this part of the road stage too,' Manu Arrieta explains. 'And Indurain told me, as I was doing his massage that evening, "You'll see, people are going to wait for the mountains and more than one of them is going to get a surprise that day." I never told anybody and then I wasn't selected for that year's Tour staff and once the Tour had started I thought, "Sod it, I'll take my car and go see what the surprise is." So I drove all the way from Spain up to Belgium and parked on the side of the road outside Liège, just to wait and see the stage go past and what would happen. He had planned it – but it certainly took quite a few people aback.'

That did not just include Indurain's rivals. 'What surprised me the most about his winning the Tour in any year was the time when he attacked at the end of the Liège–Bastogne–Liège route,' Unzué says. 'It was a Miguel Indurain that I didn't know, the day before a time trial, what did he need to do that for?' Juan Carlos González Salvador adds, 'Miguel was getting too predictable, and he switched strategies because he knew what his rivals were expecting from him. Apart from anything else, he did it because it was within his power to do so.'

Indurain's second major blow to the opposition came on more familiar terrain in the stage nine time trial, but he paid for the effort of the previous day, up to a point. Rival Bjarne Riis' loss of twelve seconds on the rolling course was the closest Indurain had been run in a time trial victory since 1990. But the rest of his rivals, ranging from third-placed Rominger at 58 seconds through to Jalabert at 2–36, Breukink and Zülle at almost four minutes and Pantani at nearly eight, were all duly quelled. Indurain, needless to say, had kept his word to Bruyneel, and was in yellow.

The third part of Indurain's rise to power was arguably the most impressive of all. A long-distance attack by Zülle on the first Alpine stage saw the Swiss rider nearly five minutes ahead of Indurain and the much depleted field at the foot of the final ascent, to La Plagne. This not only converted Zülle into race leader on the road, but obliged Indurain to chase the Swiss rider all the way up the seventeen-kilometre climb.

La Plagne may be one of the longer Alpine ascents, but it is one of the smoothest and steadiest. In theory therefore, riding the opposition off your wheel is all but impossible. Indurain, though, having received brief assistance from two team-mates, Rue and Vicente Aparicio, nonetheless blew the field apart in the space of half a kilometre before settling down to a lone pursuit of the Swiss.

Zülle initially had few problems on the gradually rising gradients. But the higher up the climb, the more noticeable the difference in riding styles became. Indurain was impassive behind his sunglasses and cap, jersey zipped up in the warm weather, hands on the top of the bars, pounding out the steadiest of rhythms with barely the slightest rocking of his shoulders. Zülle rode with his jersey opened, upper body heaving from side to side, mouth open and bareheaded as he lunged backwards and forwards on the pedals. Only in the last kilometre, where the gradient briefly steepened, did Indurain's mouth open in a grimace of suffering as he held onto the drops and accelerated hard. By then Zülle's advantage was down to two minutes, and the rest of the field – climbers, time triallists and GC rivals alike – was scattered across the Alpine ascent. Six rivals, prior to La Plagne, had been at less than three minutes and the closest, Riis, had been at a mere 23 seconds. Afterwards, only Zülle, 2–23 down, was left at anything less than five minutes. 'It was Hautacam all over again,' observed Delgado and Indurain appeared, once more, to have the 1995 Tour completely resolved, ten days out.

At this point in the game, it seemed Indurain's first significant change of race programme in the first half of the season since

1991 had worked wonders. Opting to avoid the Giro d'Italia was seen as a way of reducing the risks of Indurain suffering a tough final week of the Tour de France as his peak form began to fade. The alternative option as a build-up for the Tour therefore lay in racing the Midi Libre and the Critérium du Dauphiné, week-long events where he would have more time to recover. Indurain also started his build-up later than usual, with his first victory of the year coming on 15 April, a short time trial in the lowly Vuelta a Aragón.

The latter part of May and early June left no doubt that Indurain was as strong as, if not stronger than, when he had raced in Italy. Whilst top rival Tony Rominger finished the Giro d'Italia as he had started it, wearing the *maglia rosa* of leader, but physically drained to the point that the rest of his season looked to be at risk, Indurain scooped up win after win, first in Aragón and Asturias, and then – much more significantly – in races as tough as the Midi Libre and France's key warm-up race to the Tour, the Dauphiné Libéré.

'I haven't chosen the Dauphiné for training, I've chosen it to suffer,' Indurain told the eponymous organising newspaper's reporters. But if so, for Indurain it was a form of cycling masochism that produced excellent results. In a miniature re-run of the 1994 Tour de France, he began by finishing slightly off the pace in the opening prologue, won (as in the Tour) by Chris Boardman, then crushed the opposition, just like in the '94 Tour in Bergerac, in the mid-week time trial to move into the lead. Where Indurain proved, conclusively, that Hautacam in the 1994 Tour had been no flash in the pan was on the Ventoux, destroying the field in an alliance with Richard Virenque that saw the Frenchman take the stage and Indurain become the overall winner in all but name. Carlos Arribas, a member of the Spanish press corps watching the race on the Ventoux, reported in *El País* that when Indurain passed him, having dropped all of the field bar Virenque and an exhausted Álvaro Mejía, he had the poise to wink at them as he passed. Clearly, not a man on the point of collapse. 'Coming here was the right choice,' Indurain, the first Spaniard to win the Dauphiné since Luis Ocaña twenty-two years earlier, said after his victory. 'I am in better shape than I was this time last year.'

The first ten days of the Tour represented a new phase in Indurain's relentless domination. But where there had been cracks in Indurain's armour, they were in terms of his team. This was clear as soon as the Tour hit the mountains, when Delgado, commentating for Spanish TV, observed at La Plagne that 'Zülle has placed Banesto in serious trouble, leaving Miguel very isolated.' After Julián Gorospe moved on to the fledgling Euskadi squad at the end of 1993, the 1994–5 off-season had once more seen a series of ultra-experienced racers such as Jean-François Bernard and Pedro Delgado retire or move on from Banesto. Marino Alonso, the only Banesto team-mate to take part in all of Indurain's five Tour wins, was a strong force on the flatter and hillier stages, but the remainder of Indurain's climbing back-up were too thin on the ground. One new marquee signing, Andy Hampsten, proved to be a complete flop and given the strong performance of riders like Aparicio and Ramón González Arrieta in the Dauphiné a month before – Aparicio placed third overall – there were concerns that they had peaked too early in the year. Ever since 1988 Banesto had remained amongst the top three teams in terms of firepower for Grand Tours. But by 1995, they were getting overly dependent on their star rider.

The problem for Indurain was that fielding a weaker team could not have come at a worse moment for Banesto, given that rather than take on firebrand individuals like Chiappucci or Pantani, in the 1995 Tour Indurain was to find himself facing a very new kind of threat, a mass attack by a single squad. And to quell that challenge, even Indurain needed a team in top condition – particularly given who his rivals were this time round.

When Manolo Saiz and ONCE started out in the late 1980s, the team commanded so little respect that as Saiz puts it, 'there would be directors in other squads that wouldn't even bother to say good morning to me.' This was partly due to Saiz's rookie status, but partly, too, there was increasing awareness that – rather like Boardman in time trialling – Saiz was blazing a trail in his approach to professional racing that threatened to upset the established order.

It wasn't just that Saiz's background as a team manager was not, highly unusually in those days, as a former pro. Or even that rather than being backed by a business, his ONCE team was sponsored by Spain's Association for the Visually Impaired, a kind of public charity that is Spain's equivalent to the RNIB. What made Saiz so unconventional in a sport where tradition and conservatism has always tended to dominate was his relentless interest in both the latest technological developments and in developing a team spirit above and beyond any individual success. 'This team is different,' he told *Cycle Sport* magazine in the mid-1990s, 'because this team has got a soul.'

'We weren't the most powerful team, we were the best structured,' Saiz now claims, and this despite ONCE's home terrain being Spain, he adds, 'where we're addicted to personality cults.' Saiz defined his own situation in the peloton as a voice in the wilderness in other ways. 'Myself, I have probably got more in common with Boardman than with other teams.'

Where Indurain's overriding focus of each season was the Tour de France, ONCE made a point of winning across the board, in as many different races as possible. Team time trialling was one of Saiz's obsessions, too, and from the early 1990s, ONCE became by far cycling's most consistently successful squad in that speciality. It's no coincidence that they were one of the few Spanish teams ever to show any real interest in one-day Classics. Thanks to one of their top racers, France's Laurent Jalabert, they were the first squad from Spain ever to win the Giro di Lombardia Monument, the second to win Milano–Sanremo. Banesto were unmatchable with Indurain in the Tour. But ONCE were as ambitious in the smallest events in Spain as they were in cycling's top international events, crushing the opposition from the tiny Challenge of Mallorca race in February and the Ruta del Sol in March through to the Subida a Montjuic, for many years the event that brought down the curtain on Spanish racing, in October.

This radically different approach to racing created fertile ground for the creation of an ONCE–Banesto conflict, further fuelled by Saiz and Echavarri's fondness for launching verbal missiles at one another. But the one area where ONCE proved consistently less successful than Banesto was the overall classification of Grand Tours. ONCE had triumphed in 1991 against Indurain in the Vuelta and won it again in 1995, 1996 and 1997. 'The Vuelta was the one Grand Tour where collectives like ONCE had the edge on individuals, because the mountains in the Vuelta at that time were not so tough as in the Giro and Tour,' Saiz observes. 'Now, it's a very different story.' But whilst they were indomitable on home soil, both the Giro and the Tour proved always to be beyond his squad's reach.

'Our philosophy was that as we were the National Association for the Blind, we could not ignore any of our national races,' Saiz explains. 'The Banesto–ONCE war was simply something in the press. We had a huge amount of respect for each other as teams and there was a bit of sniping, but if there's a sector of the Spanish press that attacks me for finishing sixth and fourth in the Tour, then I have to respond because that's just misunderstanding sport.'

With the exception of Rominger in 1993, when he was racing for an all-out Spanish squad, Clas-Cajastur, ONCE were the only Spanish team to continually challenge Indurain. 'The rest were on a level below us,' Saiz argues. 'Before us, there were man-to-man combats with Indurain – Chiappucci, Rominger and so on. We were the only one to fight him as a collective.' As a manager, rather than a rider, Saiz had one advantage – his riders might be defeated, but not Saiz himself. 'There were days when I'd go to bed saying to myself that Indurain was unbeatable,' he recollects, 'but that didn't stop me from waking up the next morning and trying to work out how to do it all over again.'

However, on Mont Theux on the road to Liège, Saiz's master-plan singularly failed to work out. 'Had it done so, we'd have surrounded Indurain with a host of ONCE riders, we could have won the Tour that day. But Mauri made a tactical mistake; he let a gap open on the climb and Indurain was able to get across to Bruyneel. The idea had been to keep lots of riders with Miguel. Bruyneel sat on his wheel because behind, we were the ones driving to try and catch him.'

After a disastrous time trial for ONCE's riders, Saiz returned to the attack with Zülle on the road to La Plagne. 'That was planned. We'd had a rest day and a bad day and I said to myself, let's give it another whirl. So we went for it from the start and when Zülle moved away, I told him to go for it. I also told him not to go past more than such-and-such a percentage of his full effort and that all but cleared out the peloton. But not Indurain, although up to the moment Miguel attacked, Zülle maintained that time gap. Then there was a great battle between the two champions. Zülle could take out time on Indurain's *domestiques* but when Indurain moved he was faster than Zülle.'

Saiz does not agree with the idea that Indurain eclipsed ONCE's triumphs, like Zülle's stage victory at La Plagne that day, with his overall wins in the Tour. 'I never felt that, more that it magnified our success, because if Indurain represented individual success, ONCE represented success as a collective. Indurain was never seen as a team success [but] ONCE won the team time trial in the Tour de France, and then we went to Ruta del Sol [in February] and won, and then in Montjuic [in October] we won, which meant we were up there fighting for the win with different riders across a greater period of time. During the months of June and July, the passion [Spanish] people felt for Indurain was blind to anything else. But the Indurain–ONCE situation was one where we complemented each other, which was brilliant for Spain.' Nowhere, though, was the conflict between cycling's most powerful team and cycling's top stage racer set to become more dramatic than on stage twelve of the 1995 Tour de France.

Dominique Arnaud, retired from Banesto at the end of 1991, was driving guest cars for the 1995 and was a ringside witness to what was Banesto's greatest ever debacle in the Tour de France. Mistake number one, he says, came even before the Mende stage had got underway. 'Any team that is defending the *maillot jaune* can't possibly, ever, have its riders leave the start right at the back of the bunch. Right from the start. It's a black mark in any serious professional's copybook. Only Miguel went ahead in the bunch in the *zone fictif* [the neutralised pre-racing section of the stage prior to the *départ réel*]. The rest of the team, they were all over the place.'

'It's the same as if you go into the feed zone, above all where the roads are narrow, without the whole team surrounding the team leader in case of surprise attacks.' This also, he claimed, had happened to Banesto in that year's Tour, but had fortunately passed off without any incident: the 222-kilometre stage 12 from Saint Étienne to Mende, though, was another story.

Like a large feline waiting outside a mousehole, sitting behind the steering wheel of his ONCE team car, Manolo Saiz was poised, as he had been ever since the start of the Tour, to pounce. Saiz was, more than his riders, the brainwave behind ONCE's attack. 'The reason we chose that stage was simple,' he recounts, 'it had a climb early on. A little like in La Plagne, in fact, but this was the only stage with one right at the start.' That Banesto were caught napping tipped the balance even further in ONCE's favour.

Interestingly for those who argue that race radio has killed off innovative racing, the fuse to the greatest rebellion against Indurain's domination was lit thanks to ONCE's riders being equipped with them. Saiz says that 'Mende is proof of how important it can be in these situations, it would have been impossible without them, because it was me who knew Miguel's team wasn't working well and that he could be isolated.' Saiz's proof can be seen in the results: apart from Indurain, the first Banesto team-mate to appear on the classification is in 60th place, more than fourteen minutes down.

'Everybody was saying at the start that it was going to be a day for the backmarkers, but in the first twenty kilometres there were bodies everywhere,' Stephen Roche commented on Eurosport. Yet interestingly enough, even if Banesto were in disarray – early footage shows no fewer than five Banesto riders driving along desperately hard in a second group – Jalabert, the hero of the day, was not amongst the most aggressive riders right from the start. Instead, the first big attack came from Sergui Outschakov, a talented Russian breakaway specialist. And Jalabert? 'I wasn't feeling so motivated,' he told French TV later although interestingly, he had had one brief dig the day before going into St. Étienne, with the idea of testing the waters for the following day and seeing if Indurain would react – which he did.

As for the Mende move, 'The initial attack itself was purely by chance. Instead, early on I was chatting at the team car, then I stopped for a pee. It was only when I came back through the bunch and went after the breaks that I decided to go on the attack.' Even then, the key move of the day over the summit of the second climb was not initially engineered by Jalabert himself. Rather the *tête de la course* at kilometre 27 was Dario Bottaro, an Italian *domestique* and Classics specialist with Gewiss although Jalabert, having chased down one counter-attack containing his longstanding enemy Lance Armstrong, then promptly stormed across.

Where Saiz was crucial was firing riders up the road to join Jalabert. 'Alex Zülle had a knee problem that day so we had to have Herminio Díaz Zabala [one of ONCE's best *domestiques* for ultra-hilly stages like the Mende route] and Johan Bruyneel stay with him,' Saiz explained in an interview with *El Diario Vasco*. 'I told them to talk to Alex as much as possible about anything and everything – except his knee. Finally Alex got a bit better and he even went on the attack on the final ascent to Mende. It just goes to show you could never tell what would happen with him.'

Saiz radioed through for 1991 Vuelta winner Melcior Mauri to bridge across to Jalabert, which the Catalan duly did. As two more Italians, Massimo Podenzana and Andrea Peron, joined Botaro, Saiz ordered another top ONCE *domestique*, Neil Stephens, to bridge over to Mauri and the Frenchman. With a well-forged reputation as one of the toughest racers in the peloton, Stephens also brought a gritty Australian black humour with him to a breakaway that, with nearly 200 kilometres left to race, seemed doomed to failure. At one point, Jalabert complained that he could do with another tooth on his chainring in order to pedal a little harder: Stephens instantly shot back to his French leader – who had hurt his mouth and jaw badly in an appalling accident the year before in the Tour – 'I think you need more than one tooth, eh, Laurent?'

Jalabert, at 9–16 behind Indurain on GC, hardly constituted one of his major threats. But with only three team-mates initially left to support Indurain in the first chase group behind and three ONCE riders, two of them well placed on GC, ahead on twisting, narrow roads with barely a metre of flat, suddenly he was hugely vulnerable. 'We've got a rider in sixth overall, and another in eighth, I think it's normal we try and attack the leader,' Saiz said in one live French TV interview during the stage.

'I knew it was a sort of suicide to attack 200 kilometres from the end,' *Cyclingnews* reported Jalabert as saying afterwards, 'but in ten days the Tour will be over and if you let others break away there go the stage victories. I had lost nine minutes since the start of the Tour so I told myself to go for it. I thought that if I cracked then it was just too bad. I started the Tour thinking that I had already had a wonderful season and that anything I got out of it would be a bonus.'

'When I attacked, Indurain came after me,' Stephens told me in an interview for *Cycle Sport* during the Tour. 'Then Bruyneel attacked and Miguel went after him too. Echavarri came up and yelled, "Miguel, don't panic, don't panic. The guys behind are full on to get back." He had to calm Indurain down, so they thought they'd let the group go up the road, then bring it back later on.'

'A lot of the Banesto riders were failing to react and Miguel was absolutely determined to be ahead,' Saiz argues. 'But the more determined he was to be ahead, the more and more of his

team-mates he was wiping out. Miguel was all but alone in a peloton of twenty or thirty riders whilst we were attacking and that's
when I got them to go for it even more. Miguel wasn't able to find
a calm enough moment so he could ease back and stop, and that
way we could open a gap.'

Saiz himself knew that Jalabert was not, in himself, a born Tour
winner like Indurain. But as a team, he believed ONCE had the
wherewithal to pull off the seemingly impossible task. 'That day,
Bruyneel could have got into the break, but I was lucky to have
Jalabert there, because he was the bravest of them all.' It sounds
like a contradiction, but as Saiz sees it, 'Jalabert was clever enough
to know that he could never beat Indurain in a Tour. But even so,
he said, give me a battle to fight, and I'll have a try. Just like we
could have won the Tour that day in Liège, as a collective, we could
have won the Tour in Mende. This was the ideal strategy to beat
Indurain: isolate him and then attack.'

As Banesto attempted to limit the damage, the road reared and
fell across miles and miles of wild, Massif Central moorland and
broad valleys, and the gap rose remorselessly. Despite a puncture
for Jalabert, the six riders' advantage rose to a maximum of ten
minutes and eighteen seconds, at which point Jalabert was race
leader on the road. On the region's constantly twisting, narrow
roads, with tarmac so heavy and sticky from the hot weather that as
Roche graphically put it, 'you feel like you're slowing down even
when you're going downhill', Indurain's chase must have been
atrociously difficult. Yet he refused to give in.

From the Banesto point of view, Unzué recognises the race
could well have been lost that day. 'Time went past, the kilometres
went past, and there were some very complicated moments, very
tense moments. We saw the Tour was slipping through our fingers.
It was certainly one of the most historic days of the race, where it

seemed for many hours as if it [defeat] could happen, and which fortunately for us, it did not. It was a spectacular stage, our rivals played their hand very well and then a moment arrived when we could only count on half the team. The Tour had broken apart.'

For that, Unzué said, 'there was no remedy, the only solution being to pick up the pieces and see what you can resolve.' One way out, simply accepting that time would be lost, was not possible. ONCE and Jalabert had played their hand too well: 'Sometimes you can be patient, but this was not a stage to stay calm and say, "OK, let's let them get two or three minutes." There were too many good quality riders up the road and we had to go after them and see who could face them down.'

Indurain himself was in no way prepared to allow the Tour to go under. With his tenacity tested to the core, he responded brilliantly and with exactly the kind of stubborn, never-say-die resistance such circumstances require. TV images showed him already driving from the earliest moments onwards, shadowed by Stephens – before the Australian bridged across to the breakaway and further compounded Indurain's problems. By the last twenty kilometres, when team-mates Rue and Ramon González Arrieta were finally able, together with Novell, to give some more support, Indurain was constantly zipping to the front, urging the shattered peloton onwards. On the last part of the climb, having shaken off the bulk of the chasing peloton when Indurain overhauled a mountain specialist of the calibre of Pantani, only Riis could follow the Spaniard.

Indurain had another hugely important factor on his side: his popularity. Seeing Indurain was isolated and taking a battering, a number of allies came, requested and unrequested, to his aid. What proportion of assistance had been preceded by direct negotiations and what proportion was provided with no prior conversation at all cannot really be resolved. Yet if the breadth of teams willing to help Indurain save the day seems surprising – in decreasing order of apparent logic: Gewiss, Carrera, MG-Technogym and even Novell, a team fighting mostly for sprints and with virtually nothing to gain – seems surprising, was that really the case? Indurain was so widely appreciated, Manolo Saiz recalls, there was at least one stage of the Tour when ONCE, despite being the supposed arch-enemy of Banesto, was willing to help early on, 'although we did that,' he says, 'because it was Miguel, not for the team.' Indurain's team-mates and the ONCE riders got on well, too. As Delgado argues, 'The rivalry was more between Echavarri, Unzué and Manolo than it was between the teams' riders. We weren't so involved.' As Boardman says, 'Miguel was one of the few people at the time with no enemies at all, he wouldn't piss anybody off.' That factor, too, may well have helped at Mende, or at the very least would have done him no harm.

There will be those who argue that Indurain's willingness to let the opposition take their share of the glory in the shape of stage wins had its effect. But that was a straightforward, unspoken agreement that has always had its place in the peloton, even if Indurain was more likely to reach such agreements than Merckx or Hinault. A wholly different fact is that Indurain was genuinely liked by his colleagues, rivals or not: 'There were moments where Miguel found the support and collaboration of various riders who backed us [Banesto] up,' Unzué recognised. 'There was collaboration ahead [in the break] and collaboration behind. It's true, though, that for us in the car that day was possibly the hardest stage of all of the five Tours.'

Nor will Saiz criticise Indurain and Banesto for doing what they had to: 'Indurain saved the day ... by being professional and pacting with others. As he should have.' By the time the breakaway sped across the River Lot in Mende's valley before the final climb to its airfield, the gap had shrunk to 6–50 and Stephens, having ridden himself into the ground, finally cracked. Mauri and Jalabert continued to battle, as they had done with Stephens, to keep the gap the highest, with the trio of Italians, as was logical, waiting for the Frenchman and Spaniard to crack.

Instead, as Mauri finally peeled off at the foot of the three-kilometre ascent, his job done, Jalabert launched a searing attack on a straightaway that only Bottaro could briefly attempt to follow. After two early zig-zags, Mende's steep, straight ascent – 'like riding up the side of a house,' as the *Guardian* once described it – clearly suited Jalabert to perfection. Still ahead of Bottaro and Peron by the false flat at the summit, all that remained was a long, hard final kilometre on the flat runway to the line. Even though Indurain had ripped ahead of the chasing group at the foot of Mende, Jalabert was still nearly six minutes ahead of the Spanish champion. The Banesto leader had saved the day, but for many kilometres, it looked as if he would have been forced to cede the *maillot jaune* at the very least.

'At first I doubted whether it would work, with a gap of just thirty seconds for nearly twenty kilometres,' Jalabert told Spanish TV channel TVE. 'First Melcior got across, then Neil, and that changed things a lot.' Jalabert recognised elsewhere that 'Logically, Indurain has to be the favourite to win the Tour ... but that's no reason to give him presents.' He added wryly to TVE that he thought, though, it would be 'impossible for me to get [into a] breakaway again.'

Overall, his advantage was such that he and Zülle were now both on the provisional podium, Mauri had moved into fifth and the only downside for ONCE was that the Swiss rider had lost a little time on the Mende ascent after being squeezed out of the chase group. It mattered little. Coming on Bastille Day, Jalabert's success was the first for the French on their National Holiday since

Vincent Barteau in Marseilles five years before: a triumph which, after a decade of foreign domination in the Tour, felt like a massive breath of fresh air for the host nation.

It wasn't just the French who were overjoyed. The sense that Indurain could be pulled far closer to the precipice than had ever been imagined possible gripped the pressroom and the Tour. It proved that even the most consistently strong racer that the Tour had ever known could be virtually toppled from his throne. Yet although *El Diario Vasco* argues that 'Indurain never had such a tough day as the one at Mende,' Indurain himself did not come in for criticism as much as his squad. *L'Équipe* described Mende as 'the one occasion in five years where Indurain was up against the ropes because ... Banesto's Tour-winning strategy had become too predictable.' Nor was it only Banesto under fire: ONCE found themselves blasted by the pro-Indurain media in Spain, amidst claims – which Saiz denies – that ONCE's main telephone switchboard in Madrid was bombarded with so many hostile callers, accusing the team of 'betraying Spain', that the lines went down completely. 'The fans that didn't understand what ONCE were doing took it as an affront,' Delgado argues. 'They were saying "this guy [Saiz] doesn't want a Spaniard to win."'

'We were slaughtered over Mende by the sectarian elements of the Spanish press and that sectarian press still exists, even now, but they don't pay any attention to cycling,' Saiz says. He even goes so far as to argue that the calls to the ONCE head offices were exaggerated 'because that's what the media wanted people to believe. The important thing in sport is not who wins, the important thing is to have a sporting spectacle.'

'We were that much better as racers because we were battling against Miguel and possibly he was a bit better because he was battling against us,' Saiz said. 'We have much more to be grateful for to him, than vice versa. But we were necessary.' Indurain, however, was still viewed by much of Spanish society as being greater than any mere sports event. Any hostility towards ONCE would surely have stemmed from that – and whatever the more jingoistic elements of the Spanish press could whip up.

Could ONCE have actually won the Tour? Saiz is convinced that it would have been possible, had not the fates intervened in the most terrible of ways with the death of Tour rider Fabio Casartelli on stage fifteen. The young Italian's fatal crash on the descent of Portet d'Aspet did not just leave the Tour numbed in collective pain. It also ensured that the following day's racing, the last in the Pyrenees and where Indurain could have been vulnerable, was suspended as the peloton paid homage to the young Italian and slow-pedalled for the whole stage.

'If it hadn't been for the death of Casartelli, either we'd have won the Tour or we'd have messed it up completely,' Saiz argues. 'Riis was getting stronger, too.' Whilst ONCE kept quiet at the time, Riis was one of the very few voices who argued that the whole stage after Casartelli's death should not have been suspended. 'But I don't think he'd have ever beaten Zülle,' Saiz says. 'The only way he could have was if Indurain and ONCE had had a battle of egos and he could have taken advantage of that.'

'To my way of thinking that day, we didn't care if we were second or fifth, that day after Casartelli's death we were due to attack and maybe we'd have blown ourselves out, and not taken second, fourth or sixth as we did in Paris that year. But I didn't care. We'd have attacked to win the Tour de France. I can't conceive of cycling without attacking to win.'

Indurain's road to his fifth Tour might well have been more complicated than intended, but it ended with another time trial stage win for Indurain, outpowering the field at Lac de Vassivière by forty-eight seconds on Riis, with Jalabert at nearly two minutes. For many, rounding off his fifth Tour with a time trial victory summed up Indurain's path to a niche of his own in the history of the Tour. Yet not everybody felt it fully reflected the 'new' Indurain. 'I think he's lost a bit in his time trialling, but he's better on the climbs,' Tony Rominger told *El País*. 'He's definitely improved,' added Chiappucci, 'Now he's really gone out of everybody's reach.'

In one sense Indurain was clearly in a league of his own: taking five Tours in a row was a new record, inaccessible to any of the previous Tour greats. There were no more points of comparison in the 1990s: Tony Rominger's run of three consecutive Vueltas was a record, but all he would be asked at the end of the Spanish race was how he would fare in the Tour de France against Indurain. Tour routes that had lengthy time trials – distances of fifty or sixty kilometres that would seem enormous now, but which were in fact shorter than some in the 1980s – were criticised or praised depending on your preferences. On a UK front, specialist magazines like *Cycle Sport* would publish special features on 'The Death of the Climber', or 'Is This Man A Robot?' in reference to Indurain's exceptional physique. Indurain in Spain was, as we have seen, a phenomenon that went way beyond sport. No matter what the topic, if it was related to Tour de France success, only one rider could be the absolute reference point from now on – and that remains the case today.

The biggest difference in Indurain's path to the pantheon of the Tour's most successful champions was how long it had taken him. All three of the previous five-Tour winners – Anquetil in 1957, Merckx in 1969 and Hinault in 1978 – had taken yellow on their first try. Indurain, 31 by the time he won his fifth, had raced six Tours before even wearing the *maillot jaune* for the first time and his first top ten place – in tenth – came in 1990, a year before the first triumph. This measured approach led to a much more stable domination of the Tour when Indurain reached there, but it also meant the pressure on Indurain and Banesto to continue to win was much more wearing. No rider has won so many Tours so quickly, either – Anquetil's run of Tours was from 1957 to 1963, Merckx from 1969 until 1974 and Hinault from 1978 to 1985 – but none, as it was to emerge in 1996, would face defeat in the battle for yellow so abruptly, either.

It wasn't just Indurain who was paying the price of taking a seemingly unbreakable run of victories in cycling's hardest race. 'The first two or three Tours that Miguel won were fantastic, but the last three he raced we suffered a lot because nothing that wasn't winning made any sense,' observes Unzué. 'In the last few Tours, there was a huge amount of tension, knowing that if you didn't make any mistakes, if you got it totally right inside the team, then he wouldn't let you down. He was almost perfect.'

'So you had to check everything time and again, make sure it was all going to work perfectly. And what was the first thing you did when you got to Paris? Breathe easy again. When did you start to enjoy the Tours? When you got here in Pamplona or anywhere in Spain, and saw what all of that had meant to the people. That was when you could appreciate the real dimension of what Miguel had done.'

It was also striking that Indurain's consistency was such that no other contender finished second more than once, either, from 1991 through to 1995, behind him. As Tour de France win followed Tour de France win, what kind of limits such a lengthy run of success must have increasingly laid on the shoulders of one rider and one rider alone. Even before the race had started each year, the Tour was Indurain's to lose.

CHAPTER 10

1995–96: The House of Cards

At first sight, the only thing about the Hotel El Capitán that makes the Spanish out-of-town hotel remarkable is its location – although if you simply walked across the forecourt towards the line of traffic roaring past on the main A-road in front, that might not be so obvious.

A single glance upwards, in any direction, though, suddenly helps explain why El Capitán is such a popular destination, and its forecourt almost always full. On all sides, the mountains of Asturias tower over the sturdy-looking two-storey building with its large, wooden timbered windows, making the area a dream location for any nature lover. The most famous mountains are the Picos de Europa, which surround the Lagos de Covadonga climb, the most emblematic of all the Vuelta a España ascents.

If not the lap of modern luxury, behind the hotel's large main door, the lobby furnishings are comfortable, clean-looking and unpretentious. On the right, there is a receptionist's cubbyhole with rows of wood-lined pigeonholes for room-keys behind, on the left a long bar-room containing a huge number of chairs and tables. Not the most avant-garde of places, then, but solid and homely. It's only on entering the bar-room that you notice something a little out of place, perched on a large, metallic extractor fan that runs half the length of the bar itself. It is a paper plaque, complete with an advertising campaign photo showing a retired Miguel Indurain holding an anti-cholesterol yoghurt. After listing Indurain's achievements, the text goes on to say that 'on the afternoon of September 21st, 1996, this is where he ended his sporting life.'

Nothing much, staff say, has changed in the Hotel El Capitán since one early autumn afternoon of 1996, when Miguel Indurain peeled off that year's Vuelta a España route along the A-road, pedalled past the Banesto team vehicles assembled in the front courtyard, dismounted and walked through El Capitán's main door. TV cameras followed him as far as the door, but when it swung shut, that was it. Game over.

In fact, Indurain's abandon from the Vuelta and disappearance behind El Capitán's doors proved – as the plaque says and, barring a couple of criteriums, the last near Valencia that autumn – to be his exit from professional cycling. In the process, a year after standing on the Champs Elysées in yellow for the fifth straight July, Indurain's relationship with Banesto, Echavarri and Unzué, one of the most stable and longstanding between any professional team and rider in modern cycling, collapsed completely. The Hotel El Capitán gained itself a footnote in the annals of modern cycling, as the place where Banesto's house of cards – a relationship with Indurain so strong-looking on the outside but with its foundations eaten away – finally disintegrated for good.

According to Unzué, the first clear sign that Indurain was thinking of retiring came on the evening of the 1995 Clásica San Sebastián, held in early August. Traditionally that was the point in the year when he and Indurain would renew his contract with the team, but this time round, there was a surprise.

'It was a fortnight after winning the Tour, we were there with [Vicente] Iza [team *soigneur*], talking about the future, and normally his contract would be for two years. But Miguel said, "No, just for one." He was only 31, it's not like he was 35 or 36, and I said, "Dammit Miguel, only one season?" And he said, "I don't want to endure the effort and sacrifice it takes to train and race properly if I am not convinced I can go on winning the Tour. I'd quit. So from now on, we'll do it year by year." He was able to go on. He did 1996 and then that was it. But I think he intuited that his decline was close and that's why he chose only to sign for one season. He didn't want to take a risk if he wasn't in a position to win the Tour.'

Indurain's next objective, and the point where his relationship with Unzué and Echavarri began to hit turbulent water for the first time, was not, in any case, the Tour, or even a stage race. The 1995 Road World Championships, held in Colombia that October in the mountainous city of Duitama, 2,500 metres above sea level, were designed to be the toughest in history as a combined result of the altitude and an exceptionally hilly road-race circuit. It is a sign of how seriously Indurain took the Worlds that he and three Banesto team-mates, José María Jiménez, Santi Blanco and Andy Hampsten – the latter acting partly as a guide to the area – travelled to Colorado to train for a month in order to be prepared to race at such a high altitude. Furthermore, Echavarri felt that Colombia's altitude offered the perfect opportunity for Indurain to try to recapture the Hour Record, held by Tony Rominger since November of the year before.

The idea that Indurain could suddenly switch from being a top stage racer to one-day racing was in no way as ridiculous as it sounds. 'He can win Paris–Roubaix, he can win Liège–Bastogne–Liège, he can win every race there is, I'm 200 per cent certain of that,' Eddy Merckx said after Indurain took his fifth Tour – and he was already discussing going for the sixth as his principal objective.

For all of the final part of his career, Indurain was far and away the best and most consistent Spanish one-day rider of the era. It is true there was much less competition for that unofficial title at the time, with only Fede Echave, winner of the now-defunct GP Americas, and Marino Lejarreta, close to retirement, coming anywhere close. But Indurain's Tour triumphs had focussed the spotlight on his stage racing so strongly they eclipsed not only his victory in the Clásica San Sebastián in 1990, Spain's biggest one-day race, and in the National Championships in 1992: Indurain's consistently good performances in the World Championships were too often overlooked as well.

In more than one way, Indurain's Worlds' participations reflected his Tour success given that, like Delgado at Banesto, rather than being plunged into the deep end, Indurain had a long, steady initiation into the event with Spanish cycling's top Worlds' racer of the time. Indurain's senior Worlds' experience began in 1987 as a team-mate and room-mate for Juan Fernández, later a top sports director, but at the time a repeat bronze medallist (on no fewer than three occasions) in the Worlds for Spain. Indurain repeated his role of team worker for the early Worlds circuits in 1988, with Fernández still the leader of the squad. But in 1989 and 1990, when Fernández had retired, neither Indurain nor Spain impacted greatly on the Worlds. 'We weren't too convinced of our chances,' he recounted in *Historias del Arco Iris.*

Stuttgart, in 1991, was another story altogether as Indurain, now in the role of team leader, stepped up to the breach. 'I saw Indurain just before I abandoned' – on the seventh lap – 'and he looked so good, he wasn't even sweating,' Juan Carlos González Salvador recollected. Sharp enough to respond to an attack by Gianni Bugno in the last lap, only Steven Rooks of Holland and Indurain managed to bridge across, followed shortly by Colombia's Álvaro Mejía. Bugno's obsession with Indurain saw him close down the Spaniard on the right-hand side of the route, which allowed Rooks to overtake Indurain and gain the silver. But Indurain's bronze medal, in the same year as he won the Tour, made him one of just two Spaniards, alongside Luis Ocaña in 1973, with a top three World Championships result and a Tour de France in his *palmares*. Indurain, speaking to the few Spanish media who had managed to make it to the press conference after a series of misdirections, was his usual laconic self. 'Better this [the bronze] than fourth,' he said, before making a point of thanking Pedro Delgado for his hard work in the closing laps. Summing up his year, Indurain was equally low-key about his most successful season to date: 'It's not been too bad. I've got to keep progressing.'

The 1992 Worlds, held on home terrain in Benidorm and close to where Miguel Indurain and his wife had a summer second home, was a disappointment, although Indurain's sixth place behind Gianni Bugno at least showed that after the previous year's bronze the Tour champion continued to raise his – and Spain's – game. A searing attack by Indurain prior to the finish had created a select breakaway of Jalabert, Rominger, Chiappucci and Indurain himself over the Finiestrat, the decisive climb. But the group was brought back. Then, as neither the heat was as extreme nor the climb as tough as expected, and to cap it all, the roads had been resurfaced and made easier to race over, the 1992 Worlds was all but doomed to come down to a mass dash of a few dozen riders for the line. 'The guys who could sprint had an easy day,' Indurain ruefully reflected.

Indurain might have failed in 1992 to follow Stephen Roche's wheeltracks in 1987 and take Giro, Tour and World's, the so-called Triple Crown, in the same year. But in 1993 at the Oslo World Championships he could not have come closer, with silver behind the then almost completely unknown Lance Armstrong – who had attacked late on and stayed ahead of the bunch. Surprisingly, Indurain's silver medal was netted in a sprint, theoretically his weakest suit, against Classics specialists and fastmen of the calibre of Olaf Ludwig and Johan Museeuw. To make the result even more impressive for Indurain, it had been raining heavily, and on a crash-ridden course with a dangerous descent, 'which decided the race more than the climb,' Indurain observed, four riders ended up in hospital. He himself had come close to abandoning mid-way through, it later emerged. Instead, Indurain netted Spain's best result in a Worlds in fifty-eight years and the country's second silver ever in the category.

Indurain later admitted that the Spanish, like the rest of the field, had underestimated Armstrong's strength on the Oslo course. But he also argued that the Swedish road circuit, which Delgado blasted as being 'horrible and not worthy of the Worlds', had been too flat to favour him. However, the 1995 World Championships, with 5,115 metres of vertical climbing, more than in all but the most difficult Alpine stages of the Tour de France and at an altitude of 2,500 metres above sea level, was a different proposition. Given the Duitama course's fearsome reputation, it was perhaps just as well the UCI turned down the original route, which tackled the Cogollo, the single hardest climb of the 17-kilometre circuit with gradients of up to 20 per cent, in the opposite direction on its tougher side. As it was there were still only 20 finishers.

Expectations as to how Indurain might fare rose dramatically thanks to his performance in the World Time Trial Championships four days earlier, which he won easily ahead of Abraham Olano. Only in its second year of existence, in 1995 the World Time Trial title was widely considered a form guide for the much more keenly anticipated road race, and clinching both gold and silver suggested Spain had a winning hand for the following Sunday.

On a hilly but not exceptionally difficult time trial course and churning a hefty 54 x 12 gear, Indurain clocked all of the best provisional times, and there were only two briefest of reminders that his superiority against the clock could not be taken for granted. The first came mid-course when he overtook Maurizio Fondriest and struggled a little as he did so, and the second occurred at the very end, where Indurain eased back slightly and his advantage on Olano only flicked up a bare second in the closing few kilometres, to a final margin of 49 seconds.

However, the time gaps – beginning at four seconds ahead of Olano after five kilometres of racing and a staggering 20 seconds over his closest non-Spanish rival, Uwe Peschel of Germany – intensified the pressure on Indurain for Sunday's road race, a title that, as he saw it, 'has much greater prestige than this one.' Far from celebrating the silver in the World's Time Trial, for example, 90 minutes after the podium ceremony Olano was back out on his bike doing a 50-kilometre training ride, in preparation for the road race. He received a call from his wife Karmele, suggesting that having taken a silver medal he should come home and not wait to take part in Sunday's road race. Fortunately for the Spanish, he opted to stay.

The time trial victory made it clear that if Indurain was top favourite for the road race, he was also in great shape for the Hour Record. 'He'll beat it,' Eddy Merckx said categorically. However, oddly enough, when Indurain discussed his upcoming projects in Colombia he tended to focus purely on the World Championships.

There was little to no mention of the Hour Record and when the subject was brought up during the Worlds, he would seem to diplomatically avoid the question and say he was looking specifically at Sunday's road race, 'for which I've spent the last month preparing.' Not for the Hour.

Tactically, it was a masterstroke. On a personal level, for Miguel Indurain it represented a huge act of generosity. Yet when Abraham Olano darted out of the shattered remnants of the pack to solo to victory in the 1995 Road World Championships, whilst Indurain kept control of the peloton behind, it generated no small amount of controversy. It barely mattered that the Spanish media, by and large, attempted to present Olano's attack on the second last lap for what it was: a textbook breakaway by a second-ranking rider in a team whilst the top contender – in this case Indurain – crushed any counter-move. Much of the public saw it completely differently.

As Pedro Delgado points out, 'We fans remember it as a historic, enthralling moment, but the man in the street has forgotten: he just thinks of Olano as the "man who wanted Indurain to lose".' Josu Garai commented that, 'Half of Spain accused Olano of being a traitor,' although he himself, 'trying to be objective,' wrote a column in *MARCA* supporting Olano's attack. But he also suggested that Banesto were unhappy at the result. If so, it was the first time since 1991 there had been such leaks of a disagreement between the sponsor and top rider over their objectives and results, and not in one of cycling's lowest-profile events, either.

Had Indurain had an off-day and finished, say seventeenth, Olano would surely have been forgiven more quickly for his 'treachery' and Banesto would not have been, as Echavarri said later, 'disappointed at the result'. But expectations had been sky-high that Indurain would take the win and his time trial result had already proved he was the strongest rider individually in the Spanish squad. Finishing second made it look as if the only thing standing between Spain's greatest athlete and gold was ... another Spaniard. On top of that, the 'treacherous' Spaniard in question was widely tipped as Indurain's successor and had taken silver a few days earlier behind Indurain in the time trial. As a result, it was easy for the Spanish public, particularly in view of their severely limited knowledge of one-day racing as opposed to stage racing, to interpret Olano's attack as jumping the gun for his own benefit.

Yet Unzué has repeatedly said that the best way to understand Indurain and what Olano's victory meant to him is to look at his gestures, rather than expect Indurain to articulate his feelings in words. And there can be no mistaking the way Indurain's arm is raised in triumph as he crossed the line in Duitama for a silver medal, just as it had been four years before at Val Louron when he finished behind Chiappucci en route to the Tour, but this time with a huge difference in the overall outcome.

'Making that gesture of joy in Colombia that day when he came second was more than for him, it was for a team-mate, for a team-mate's victory,' Delgado says. 'At Val Louron, when he punches the air after finishing second behind Chiappucci, there was a reward for him, there was a yellow jersey. But in Colombia there was nothing. His joy, his satisfaction, was not for himself.'

'The leader was Miguel, everything about that Worlds made it Indurain's Worlds,' Olano says. 'He had prepared for it at altitude, and we were racing for him. But in races you have to be calculating. Better that a team-mate win, than a rival wins because of a mistake you have made. Just look at what happened with [Alejandro] Valverde and [Joaquim] Rodríguez' – in the 2013 Worlds, a lack of co-ordination between the two Spaniards saw Rodríguez lose the Championships to Portugal's Rui Costa. 'That could have happened to us, because the situation was very similar.'

Echoing Unzué's words, Olano says, 'The Banesto fans and Indurain fans criticised me, and all I can say to those people who – still – continue to hammer on about it, is to tell them to look at the Worlds video and the look of satisfaction on Indurain's face. It's not there because somebody's treated him badly, it's there because we won the Worlds.'

From a Spanish point of view, taking the first ever World Championships with Olano acted as a breakthrough. After 1995, Spain took the professional rainbow jersey of World Road Champion on no fewer than five occasions in less than a decade: once in the Time Trial and four times on the road race. '1995 was the first Worlds we went to with the objective of winning, it marked a new chapter,' Olano says.

But for Indurain? The final chapter of his 'American adventure', as the press nicknamed his six-week stint on the far side of the Atlantic in Colorado and Colombia, consisted of his second bid on the Hour Record in the velodrome in Bogotá, exactly one week after the World Championships. Given the extremely limited preparation time this gave him to adapt from the road to the track, even less than in 1994, it was an unusually ambitious target for the Spaniard. But Banesto presumably gambled on Indurain having strong enough form from the Worlds to bludgeon his way through any problems he might have. Like at Bordeaux, this was going to be more about power than aerodynamics.

The initial times, as Indurain pounded round the open-air Bogotá velodrome at the ungodly hour of 6 a.m. – to avoid possible strong winds – looked promising. After four kilometres, he was almost two seconds ahead of Rominger's record. But from that point on, he slumped further and further behind. After twenty kilometres, Indurain was over thirty seconds slower, and by the twenty-eight-kilometre mark, the distance had stretched to nearly a minute. Although Indurain was losing ground less quickly by this point, he was rapidly running out of energy and had no time left, even if he had managed to reverse his losses. Shortly before reaching thirty kilometres, not even the cheers of the 5,000-strong crowd who had braved the early hours and chilly night air to urge him on could keep him from pulling over and ending his effort.

The causes of such an unexpected defeat were multiple. There were those quick to point to an almost ridiculously low preparation and adaptation time of just four days, compared to the three weeks that Rominger had taken back in 1994. Nor was Indurain's build-up for a road event ideal. Weight-wise he was at the top of his game for the road but to get an idea of how inappropriate being so light for the track was, it's worth remembering that Bradley Wiggins put on ten kilos in weight between winning the Tour and focussing on racing in the velodrome. Rominger, Colombian newspaper *El Tiempo* reported, was three kilos 'overweight' when he beat the Hour Record in November 1994.

Another possible error made by Indurain and his entourage included riding in cold temperatures, when the air pressure is much higher and air resistance consequently denser. When Wiggins beat the Hour Record in London in 2015, the temperatures in the indoor velodrome in Stratford were set at 28 degrees, warm enough to give a performance advantage, given that every increase in temperature of three degrees results in a one per cent increase in speed.

The cold also, possibly, affects a rider's anaerobic threshold. By avoiding the wind 'issue', therefore, Banesto risked aggravating others. 'He did not get defeated when he was at his "real" level,' argued *El Tiempo*, 'but at this level of performance, you pay for any error.' Indurain himself blamed a mixture of starting too fast, gusts of wind and insufficient time – just twenty-four hours – between the 'dress rehearsal' and trying for the Record in earnest, given that both involved getting up in the middle of the night for a 4 a.m. breakfast. On top of that, after a strong start, he began losing his cadence, 'which led to me losing my ideal posture, which led to me moving around to try to get it back. But it's not the end of the world, sometimes you lose in races. I may try it again.'

Another Hour Record bid was quickly ruled out after a four-hour crisis meeting was held between Echavarri, Unzué and Padilla to decide whether he could repeat the Hour Record a week later in another Colombian velodrome, in Cali at sea level. That proposal collapsed when Indurain himself put his foot down and insisted that it was time for him to return home.

What should have been a hugely triumphant end to the season that saw Indurain enter the history books as the Tour's most successful racer, therefore ended, rather unexpectedly, on a duff note, with an abandon in the Hour Record and what was – to the broader public, if not to Indurain – the second duff note of a silver medal at the Worlds Road Race. Part of the problem was, as both Boardman and Unzué have observed, that anything less than total success was no longer judged as a triumph for Indurain. Nor can he have been unaware of speculation in the press that Banesto were displeased at his result, if not his racing approach in the Worlds.

None of this was a major setback, given that Indurain had a fifth Tour in the bag and was the dominating force in cycling by a long way. But at the same time after such a lengthy, harmonious relationship between Indurain and his team, even the rumour of an argument or a disagreement over objectives was far more notice-able. On top of that, he had finished the season much later than usual – this was the first Worlds to be held in October rather than August and Indurain's last race tended to be the Volta in the second week of September – and with a full month's less rest. 'That Hour Record was the first time,' Olano says, 'that I began to get the feeling that Indurain could be getting burned out.'

'Miguel wanted to go home and they said he had to stay on to do the Hour Record,' claims Delgado. 'But the Hour Record, mentally, is a brutal exercise. Physically, it's an hour of going round and round and your head's saying "What am I doing here?"' It was a question, it seems, that was already in Indurain's head both inside the velodrome and outside it. Delgado agrees that Indurain was exhausted, mentally if not physically, and concludes, 'I never understood that final assault on the Hour Record.'

'It wasn't a question of us wanting him to do the Hour Record, it was a question of proposing it,' argues Unzué. 'It was about making the most of the work we'd done in Colombia, being at altitude, and seeing how he'd raced seven days before, he clearly wasn't going badly.' However, 'There was a series of circumstances, and he was getting exhausted. He'd come from a training camp, gone onto the Worlds, gone on to the Hour Record, it was logical he was close to KO by then, but it'd all been set up. It was at a point where you couldn't stop everything. We knew how hard it would be, but we tried.'

'There was a discussion about trying it in Cali, at sea level. That was when Miguel said, "I'm fed up, I'm tired," and nothing more was possible.' There were some further, semi-secret tests in Bordeaux after his return to Europe, but it was more a symbolic effort than a real attempt to start up the process again.

Even if the rumours of Indurain slamming the door of his hotel room in Colombia when it was proposed he repeat his Hour Record bid in Cali, or – as Olano claims – of Padilla walking out of the Bogotá Hour Record velodrome before Indurain had quit, were never proved to be true, that such rumours existed did not augur well. A more tangible split between team and rider occurred with the definitive exit of Sabino Padilla, the team doctor and one of Indurain's greatest confidants in Banesto. Padilla's departure, to work with Basque football team Athletic Bilbao, did not stop him from working with Indurain in the future. However he only did so in a private capacity, with Indurain paying the doctor out of his own pocket, and Padilla using his private car to accompany Indurain on the Tour in 1996. Once again, this was hardly a major parting of the ways, but it was a parting of the ways, nonetheless – and that, in the history of Indurain and Banesto, was both unprecedented and unsettling.

None of the rumours of turbulence between Indurain and his team would have been remotely significant, of course, had it not been for the events of Saturday 6 July, 1996. After five years of domination in the Tour de France, three and a half kilometres from the summit of Les Arcs in the Alps, Indurain's era suddenly appeared to be in serious danger of crumbling away completely. As I wrote in Britain's *Cycling Weekly* in their report on the stage, and I was only half-joking, some day a monument should be erected at the exact point on the side of the road where Indurain finally did what had, for five years in the Tour, seemed inconceivable. He cracked.

The Mende stage in 1995 had been a defeat for Banesto as a team. This time it was Indurain himself who fell apart, weaving across the road, emphatically waving his hand in a typical rider's gesture to indicate he wanted something to drink. At the foot of Les Arcs, he later said, he had been thinking of attacking. But by a little over two thirds of the way up, Indurain found himself drained of energy, shoulders slumping as he grimly ploughed up the climb and at a point where he 'could barely think about finishing the stage.' Such a radical change in the most consistent Tour winner the race had ever known, a rider who, as Olano puts it, had such an effortless style he did not seem to be pedalling, bordered on the unreal.

At the end of the stage, a waterlogged slog through the Alps where the defending yellow jersey Stephane Heulot abandoned with tendinitis and several top riders crashed, Indurain had lost more than four minutes on winner Luc Leblanc and over three and a half minutes on Tony Rominger. Rominger was the rider who had said after Indurain's final stage victory the previous July that he 'knew he would never win the Tour.' But Rominger's excellent second place, despite crashing twice on the stage – 'he'd changed his brake levers so they would be turned upwards, like the brakes on a new scooter he'd bought and he couldn't control the bike properly,' his team-mate Olano reported – was totally eclipsed by Indurain's dramatic difficulties and attempts to find out what had caused them.

'I was shocked, surprised that he was not there any more,' Riis, finally the overall winner of the 1996 Tour, commented to *Cyclingnews*' Daniel Benson. 'I was like, "Wow, what now?" I actually think I lost a lot of focus on the climb, I would have been strong enough to follow Leblanc, but I think I was just a little shocked. My hero, the one I want to beat, he's getting dropped ...'

No single explanation at the time managed to provide a full picture of why it had happened. Indurain might have turned thirty-two, and was therefore approaching a point when he was bound to give way to a younger generation, but there had been no real signs it was going to happen that July. Quite apart from his track record in the Tour, Indurain had repeated 1995's approach path to the Tour and it had proved equally successful. A maiden victory in the low-key Tour of the Alentejo in Portugal in early May ahead of his brother Prudencio was a more unexpected footnote to his *palmares*. But from that point onwards, wins in the rugged Vuelta a Asturias against a solid line-up of Spanish contenders and for a second year running in the Dauphiné Libéré hardly indicated that his build-up had been anything but business as usual.

Furthermore, when Indurain had said that spring that he had been training harder in the mountains in anticipation of a harder Tour route, the evidence was there. A memorable victory on the Mount Arrate, the most emblematic of all Basque summit finishes, albeit not a hard one, had enabled him to fend off Zülle and ONCE team-mate Marcelino García in the Bizicleta Vasca. But what had really counted was Indurain's blistering performance in the Dauphiné Libére, first across the Izoard and into Briançon. As Indurain pedalled towards victory on the Col de la Bastille he reportedly patted Tony Rominger – a fine second – on the shoulder and said, 'Not a bad day for us oldies, eh?'

A month later, though, whilst Rominger had gone from strength to strength, the quest for the explanation as to why Indurain was suffering his first major collapse in the Tour continued. It was possible that he could have simply had a so-called 'bad day' – when the athlete's body, despite being in top condition, shuts down of its own volition and refuses to let itself be submitted to yet another session of overexertion that taking part in a stage race demands. There was also Riis' theory that he had tried to put Indurain 'into the red' for more than fifty minutes on the climb, because at any ascent lasting over forty minutes, Riis believed, Indurain would start to crack.

But a bad day would only have explained a short-term loss of power, followed by a bounce back, which would have been rare, particularly for Indurain, but not exceptional. On the next day's time trial, where Indurain lost 61 seconds and finished fifth behind Evgeni Berzin and then again when he lost a further 28 seconds to Bjarne Riis, the new race leader on the following stage to Sestriere, it became clear that this loss of power was not a one-day anomaly. Whilst not out of the frame completely, Indurain's four-and-a-half-minute deficit on Riis, and sitting in eighth place overall as the race left the Alps, meant the overwhelming favourite was in serious difficulties.

As to why this had happened, the unusually atrocious weather in the Tour's first week, with rainstorms, cold and even the cancellation of part of one Alpine stage because of blizzards 'didn't help', Unzué recalls. 'The cold wasn't exactly his weak point, it was more that he handled hot weather better than others.' Manu Arrieta says, 'I remember it rained so much that week, every day, he said to me, "Pff, this is going to be something we end up paying for." He would get colds easily and he did suffer from allergies. That was a weakness of his.'

The weather and Indurain's concern, expressed to Arrieta, could have been a warning sign, but that hardly explains that he would crack so dramatically. 'We had no idea that this was going to happen,' Unzué insists. As a case in point, Unzué says, 'I remember there had been a bad rainstorm the day before Les Arcs, on the stage to Aix-Les-Bains and the temperature dropped fast, but he got through the stage OK. He didn't have a fever, he wasn't sick and in fact on the next day, he was feeling so good he told his team-mates to toughen up the pace on the stage.' Fourteen riders had abandoned during the previous stage and there were three non-starters the following day, but Indurain, as Unzué says, got through. Furthermore, at Les Arcs, after the week of rain and cold lasted into the first three quarters of the stage, the sun finally came out.

What happened, Unzué says, was, 'Miguel miscalculated his strength, he felt empty, he hadn't eaten enough and he reached the top absolutely exhausted. Right the way from the bottom of the climb he told the team to go for it and then suddenly – boom! It was a clear sign that he was going well and then ran out of petrol, over-estimated his own strength.' After requesting a *bidon* on the stage – and getting fined and a time penalty for receiving one from a rival team director, Emanuele Bombini of Gewiss – Banesto team staff recollect Indurain devouring bars of chocolate and biscuits afterwards. 'It was the beginning of his end, the unravelling of his career, it all crumbled for him quite quickly after that,' observes Boardman. 'A monumental day.'

The chinks in Indurain's seemingly impenetrable armour were beginning to yawn open. 'Sestriere was very difficult, he suffered in the last kilometre,' continues Unzué. Speaking about mountain stages in general, he adds, 'You can't forget that he was ten or twelve kilos heavier than the rest and in stages with 4,000 metres of climbing then he was bound to pay a heavier price. That is why we had to be so cautious, and only use whatever energy there was in the tank. We had to play along the line of his limits, but there were no power meters back then to help you control your strength. When you don't have that kind of equipment, it's harder to see.'

Yet for such miscalculations to be made, Indurain had to be more confident of his possibilities than was realistic – and if so, that was a rare error. Nothing in the previous week's racing suggested that he was aware of any changes. His prologue performance had been slightly off par, finishing eighth. But in terms of time loss – twelve seconds to Alex Zülle – it hardly set the alarm bells ringing. On the next flat stage, theoretically one where the top favourites would hardly be prominent, Indurain had led the bunch under the last kilometre after it split apart in the final quarter of an hour of racing. Part of the reason for that would have been to avoid crashes but it was also a sign of his strength.

Jacinto Vidarte, the *MARCA* correspondent on the Dauphiné Libéré, believes Indurain's form was on the wane after he fought so hard to take the lead there. 'He lost time on the Ventoux stage but then buried himself on the Izoard and into Briançon and I think he paid a price for that later.' Could Indurain's late season finish in 1995 have had a knock-on effect? Again, it seems unlikely. 'He was in the best condition he'd ever been in, he killed them all in the Dauphiné and then in the rest of the Tour the weather got worse and worse, rain and cold from day one. But there wasn't really an explanation, he just wasn't going as well,' says Pruden Indurain, who was part of the Tour team that year. Indurain continued to be his usual phlegmatic self, Pruden says, saying to the team, 'I'm fine, *no pasa nada*.' Unlike Unzué, Pruden says, 'We certainly didn't think it was the start of a decline. There was never a specific moment when he cracked.' Twenty years on, he remains equally nonplussed. As did his brother after the stage: Indurain himself was baffled by what he later called 'loss of form so great that I was beaten by rivals I had the better of in the Dauphiné in June. Nothing out of the ordinary happened for me to lose that form, although I suffered more to get good form before.'

The most straightforward explanation could be the most logical; Unzué argues that Indurain was at 32 simply reaching a point where he was no longer as strong as he used to be: 'This is why I think Indurain, after the 1995 Tour, is conscious of "something" ... the weather didn't help, but he was definitely not at his best.' Indurain certainly, even before the 1995 Tour, seemed increasingly aware that there would be a point where he could not go on. 'I'm close to my limit now,' he said in an interview in 1995. 'I've been five years at the top and you start to notice the kilometres and the time you've been there ... It's not so hard if you have one good year and then disappear. It's this constant pressure which is more difficult. If I've got the form there's no problem, but I don't know how long I'll last.' Yet he remained defiant, saying, 'I may have to accept I can only win smaller races later in my life, but not yet.'

Fast forward twelve months and in a pre-Tour interview for *Cycle Sport*, even the headline '*Adiós Miguelón*' [Goodbye Big Mig] seemed to suggest the end of the road was that much closer. 'It's a question which is on my mind. I'm starting to feel saturated,' he warned. But there was still the same insistence on the priority the Tour would take for him, too. As he put it, 'right now, I would sign an agreement to win the Tour and spend the rest of the season coming second.' However, on leaving the Alps, the chances of Indurain doing so were at their lowest in six years.

Riis refused to rule Indurain out, saying, 'this guy was at four minutes, but he's won five Tours. You never cut him off.' Riis' nerves were understandable: he had never won a Grand Tour, and although in the lead on leaving the Alps, it was not clear he would be in yellow in Paris. There was also a brief attempt by Indurain to try and regain control of the race on the hilly second week stage to Superbesse by putting Banesto on the front on the final climb. This did no damage to Riis' position, but some other favourites lost time.

The knock-out punch came on Hautacam in the Pyrenees, the same climb where Indurain had effectively won the Tour in 1994. A lone attack by Riis, revving his motor three times with brief accelerations then blasting away from the other favourites in gears more commonly seen on flat stages – and this after he had ridden down the length of the leaders' group and back up to the front to assess each rider as he passed – proved to be the attack that was to win the Dane the Tour. For Indurain, it may well have made him think, however briefly, that he never would again. 'I wanted them to explode [crack], tease them first, and when I left them behind, they really exploded,' Riis said.

'Hautacam was where we all really got surprised. OK, so the opposition could take time on the shorter climbs. But we'd never seen Miguel crack as badly as he did on Hautacam. Psychologically it must have been very humiliating,' Olano argues. According to *El País*, after losing two and a half minutes to Riis, at the finish Indurain clambered into the back of the windowless team van that Banesto used to transport the riders in finishes the team bus couldn't reach, and told the first of his team-mates to arrive after him, José Luis Arrieta, that 'if we went home now, then the end result [of the Tour] would be the same.'

However, a final mammoth Pyrenean stage across the French frontier to Pamplona, designed by the Tour organisers as a homage to Indurain, awaited the next day. Indurain, knowing tens of thousands of Navarran fans and his family too, would be waiting, was aware that under the circumstances quitting was not an option. Instead, as Olano recounts, on a stage with five major Pyrenean climbs then 100 kilometres of constantly undulating roads to Pamplona, it was he and Rominger who went from being in a position to win to sporting self-destruction. Indurain, under the circumstances, was simply another victim of collateral damage in a battle that was no longer his own.

Still second overall, albeit at nearly three minutes, before the stage, Olano recounts that the racing that day was so tumultuous 'that even the stones on the roadsides got up and went on the attack. It was all because of orders from [Mapei owner Giorgio] Squinzi, who told me and Rominger we actually had to try to drop the field. He rang up Juan Fernández [Mapei director] on the car-phone and for the first and only time I've ever seen him do that, Juan put his foot down and told me and Tony directly that Mapei were going to go for it and then we had to attack. Squinzi said that second and third overall weren't good enough: me and Tony had to go for the win. We tried to say that we'd be better off waiting for the final time trial to do that, but that didn't matter.'

Acting on Fernández's orders, '[Mapei team-mates] Fede Echave, Arsenio [González] and [Jon] Unzaga actually came back and apologised to me and Tony for driving so hard at the front of the bunch. They began to kick hard on the Marie-Blanque [third climb of the day of five] to try and split the field apart even before it got really steep. And less than three kilometres up the climb, me and Tony had both been dropped.' With them, too, went Indurain.

'My team-mates had blown the race apart. And the riders who were ahead – Escartín, Virenque, Dufaux, and Riis, they were nearly all out-and-out climbers. So we were driving behind, Gines, Rominger, me and Miguel to try and catch up again. And after the Larrau [fifth and final climb] where things came back together briefly, we still had the break at barely half a minute. But then when we got to the roads towards Pamplona it was a very different story. The break went off and we were losing more and more ground behind.'

'The race broke apart and Miguel couldn't do anything,' Banesto rider José Luis Arrieta told Spanish magazine *Ciclismo a Fondo*, 'but we'd brought the break back by the foot of the Larrau. I asked Miguel if he wanted our team to collaborate with the rest, and he answered "What point is there in that? They're the ones that have accelerated away and dropped us before." And at that point they dropped us again.'

'We went up the Larrau and I remember it seemed like every cycling fan in Navarre was on the roadside, urging us on.

Chiappucci was even further back and caught us at the summit. He started yelling *¡Venga! ¡Vamos!* but I told him to calm down, there was still 100 kilometres to go, on roads with climbs which weren't marked in the route book but which you had to ride up, no matter what.'

Finally, after riding for another two long hours across roads he would have known like the back of his hand from training, Indurain and Olano sped through his village of Villava, eight minutes behind the leading group. He smiled and raised one hand in greeting to his family as he sped past. But this was no triumphal return home. After five years of conquests abroad, Indurain was forced to endure his greatest ever defeat on his own doorstep, on the roads he knew the best in the world, on the day that was supposed to be a celebration of his career. For the greatest Tour rider ever, this was the cruellest kind of reality check.

Even his rivals tried to give Indurain the recognition he so richly deserved in the Tour. Early on the stage, Riis, now far more confident of victory than he had been in the Alps, said he had tried to get Indurain to attack so that he could have the honour of winning on home soil. 'I stayed with him until the front group were over a minute ahead, and then I had to go,' Riis recalled later, although he then tried to soften the blow by insisting Indurain go up on the podium in Pamplona alongside him. But although Indurain agreed, and stood on the Tour podium for one last time as Riis raised his arm, it was a bleak kind of homage. As Unzué puts it, 'It was almost a funeral.'

Yet there was dignity in Indurain's defeat, too. 'If there was one day when Miguel was going to feel really upset, then that was in Pamplona. But he wasn't, not at all. And that to me forms part of his greatness, how he reacted and treated it as something normal. For me, it was another lesson in how to handle your rivals' superiority and probably, too, the confirmation of his own decline.' Other top riders suffering such tremendous defeats would, perhaps, have opted to go on a death-or-glory breakaway. But as Unzué says, 'there was never a question of vendetta, of turning things around like that, going out in a blaze of glory. That just isn't Miguel's style.'

In the public's eyes, Indurain's way of overcoming the destruction of his Tour de France dreams of a sixth victory – after he finally finished the 1996 race in eleventh place overall – was a return to a key part of his sporting roots: time trialling. In the 1996 Olympic Games, for the first time ever, professional cyclists were permitted to take part. For Indurain, more than sporting revenge for the Tour's defeat, the Atlanta Games represented a new challenge in itself, and an opportunity, too, to set the record straight after his disappointment at the 1984 Games in Los Angeles.

Yet following the Tour debacle, even as defending World Time Trial Champion, Indurain's selection for the time trial for Spain was no longer a mere formality. It was only following a bizarrely long meeting with the Banesto management after the last time trial, where Indurain placed second behind Ullrich, that it was confirmed he would ride.

The Atlanta course, as Boardman – who took the bronze – recollects, was not difficult in terms of terrain, although it was technical. Nor was it excessively long at 52 kilometres. The challenges were more weather-related than anything else. 'I had the form of my life which came out a couple of weeks later, but it was hot and very humid. It had poured down before the time trial and there was nearly 50 per cent humidity. I even threw my helmet away halfway through. I was up [and provisional best] on the first lap, up on the second lap' – even overtaking Bjarne Riis in the process – 'just then got whacked. On the last lap, I was on the edge of passing out.'

Indurain, on the other hand, was in his element. 'He works on solar energy,' José Miguel Echavarri once observed and although marginally slower than Boardman and Olano in the first third of the course, by the mid-way point, Indurain had overhauled his compatriot and closed the gap on the Briton to three seconds. By the finish, as Boardman suffered badly, Indurain forged on steadily to what turned out to be his last great triumph, and one that answered, for the moment, any questions about his motivation after the events of July. In Atlanta Indurain insisted in any case that 'this victory and not winning the Tour have nothing to do with one another ... I don't have to prove anything to anybody.' Rather than a debt to his public, he felt Atlanta resolved a debt to himself. 'It was the medal that was missing in my collection. I've won a lot of time trials and this confirms what I managed to achieve in Colombia last year.'

Indurain would later reveal he believed the Olympic Games victory would have represented the blaze of glory with which to sign off his career. Five days after his return from Atlanta when he was asked by Echavarri and Unzué at the Clásica San Sebastián about renewing for 1997, Indurain's answer was clear: 'I'm stopping.' Unzué says, 'After the Tour, we asked him to go on for another year and that's when he says no, I'm not going to do it. That's where he almost takes the decision not to race any more.'

The key word here in Unzué's recollections is 'almost'. The very success that had clarified the idea in Indurain's mind that it was the right time to pull down the curtain on his career intensified the speculation that he might continue. 'Atlanta showed us that Indurain was still alive and that he wasn't finished by any degree,' comments Jacinto Vidarte, at the time a cycling journalist with *MARCA* and the only reporter to be present at all the principal episodes of Indurain's final season. 'By that point, it was pretty clear that the relationship between Miguel and José Miguel and Eusebio had gone sour. There was the business with Sabino Padilla having to use his own car and sort himself out for the Tour.' There were later, unconfirmed accusations from Echavarri in *El País* that Padilla had become excessively influential over Indurain, saying, 'He took over Miguel during the Colorado training camp. He kidnapped him.'

'Indurain isn't a great communicator and the team were very hermetic, but by 1996 the relationship was beginning to deteriorate seriously,' says Vidarte. Delgado argues that, bizarrely enough, the very fact that the Spaniard's relationship with his directors had been so strong now began to play against him: 'It reminds me of something that Manolo Saiz used to say about how the best people he'd work with were blind, because they needed the support, the blind support as it were, of others. And Miguel was so trusting that it was easy that he should feel betrayed.' Once that trust had gone, though, it proved almost impossible to repair.

After the Olympics Echavarri began negotiating with Olano, widely tipped as Spain's most promising young rider and Indurain's successor, to break his contract for 1997 with Mapei and sign with Banesto. When Olano finally signed a preliminary contract with Banesto, just before the Vuelta, he still believed that he would be second-in-command and that Indurain would lead at the 1997 Tour. He saw Indurain's defeat in the 1996 Tour as more a glitch than a permanent setback. 'I didn't think Miguel was going badly [on Hautacam], it was just that his form wasn't so great. But I thought that he would be the same, normal Miguel when we went back to the Tour the next year. Anybody who rides a bike for a living knows that not every year is the same. Just ask Peter Sagan' – who had a near-disastrous first half of 2015, with numerous runners-up spots before coming back to win the World Championships. 'The differences can be minimal between winning and coming second. You can make a comeback.'

Vidarte believes that by the time that Olano's potential signing with Banesto came into play, 'the relationship with Indurain was already broken or on the point of doing so.' But it did nothing to alleviate the considerable confusion and speculation surrounding the issue, which intensified yet further when Indurain announced during the Vuelta a Burgos that August that he would be racing the Vuelta a España, which had moved to September in 1995 – and shortly afterwards, that he was doing so because he had been obliged to race it by the team.

Then, as now, it is not hard to find those who felt that after all the positive publicity Indurain had generated for his team, to force him to race the Vuelta was wrongheaded in the extreme. 'Indurain has always been a real gentleman and has never really wanted to talk about all of this,' argues Vidarte. 'But he felt – I think – exploited, used, and that once he'd decided to quit, the idea was to exploit him right the way through to the end.'

Olano cites a much-quoted phrase of Echavarri's: 'September is for those that fail in July', a reference to Spain's education system and its round of autumn re-sit exams. 'You go to the Tour, if you don't pass the exam in July, you have to go back [to the Vuelta] in September – just like in school. Miguel didn't want to go to the Vuelta, [but] if you were a little more coherent about everything that Miguel had given you, then if he says he's not up to going, then he's not up to going. And I think it was the fact it was imposed on him that forced him to quit [cycling].'

'It was an ignominious end for him, wasn't it?' argues Board-man. 'It wasn't controlled, and I sort of blame Banesto at the end, they forced him to ride the Vuelta, which was quite disrespectful.' Even now, Prudencio Indurain makes no bones of his feelings about Echavarri and Unzué. When asked what his opinion was of them as management figures, he states, 'I prefer not to give my opinion, we don't have any relationship now, nothing ... zero. It didn't end well, neither with me nor ... We live in Pamplona and we'll greet each other in the street, and that's it, we don't have much to say to each other. They went from being like parents to there being no relationship at all. But that's life.'

'It was a strategic error by the company. They wanted to save their not having won the Tour by having him do the Vuelta,' argues Saiz. 'That was the only mistake José Miguel made.' Rather than the rights or wrongs of Banesto's decision, Saiz points at the diffi-culties of the Vuelta itself as a logical reason not to send Indurain there: 'You don't sort out your season by racing it.'

Discussing their decision to take Indurain to the Vuelta, Unzué repeats a claim made by Echavarri after Indurain's retirement, that in fact they backtracked at the last minute and said they would be willing for him not to go. But by then, the damage in terms of broken trust was done. 'We said to him, "we don't have the moral right to ask you to do it, but it would be a nice thing to do for Banesto, who have never complained about you not racing the Vuelta since 1991."'

Unzué says the Vuelta could have been like a lap of honour for Indurain. 'I was convinced he wouldn't go on [into 1997], because Miguel, when he decides to do something ... I proposed that the Vuelta would be a good way to say goodbye to Banesto, to the country and the people.' Indurain's triumphs, Unzué points out, had mostly happened abroad and 'We told him to forget about the overall classification, and that this way the people of Spain could see him on the road.'

'Finally, maybe I got too insistent, and then Banesto told us, "Hey, if he doesn't want us to do it, then forget it."' But the idea of using the Vuelta as a three-week homage could well have fallen foul of the organisers, too, and by the time Banesto began to backtrack, Indurain had also told Unzué that if he did the Vuelta, it would be to go for the win. What Indurain thought of Unzué's initial insistence that he race the Vuelta was clear enough. 'It's the first time in my life that I've had something imposed on me,' he told Josu Garai, 'and I'm not taking it at all well.' As for Unzué, the regret at what he did is still palpable. 'Looking at what happened [in the Vuelta],' he says, 'we can't doubt that my insistence [about Indurain doing the Vuelta] was a huge mistake.'

There could be no doubt, either, that once Indurain started the 1996 Vuelta that September, he was not there to make up the numbers. When ONCE formed an echelon in a surprise attack on stage three to Albacete, both Fernando Escartín, the Kelme leader, and Rominger were caught out. But Indurain was on the right side of the split and collaborated with ONCE, pushing Escartín and Rominger to eight minutes. As the race continued for flat stage after flat stage across the south of Spain, Indurain, although losing nearly forty seconds when he was caught behind a crash near the finish in Murcia, remained very much in contention. Then in the stage ten time trial near Ávila, finishing third, merely twenty-five seconds down on Zülle and twenty-seven behind Rominger, elevated him into second overall. This was despite the rain, too, that teemed down most of the day in Ávila, and a rugged, highly technical course with no fewer than 186 different corners. There were few warning signs of what was to come, even then – apart from the way in which Indurain's comments after Ávila felt curiously non-committal. He described his time trial, which was a solid, if unspectacular performance, as 'one of the oddest I've ridden', and warned that ONCE, headed by Zülle and Jalabert, would be a force to be reckoned with. His prediction that the mountainous stages that followed almost immediately in Asturias 'would be very important for me' proved uncannily correct, if not his specific hope that his fortunes would change on the stage to the Lagos de Covadonga, 'a finish which traditionally has not been good for me.'

Even prior to Covadonga, the climb of El Naranco, the race's first summit finish and one of Spain's most emblematic ascents, began to show that the Ávila time trial was not a reliable form guide. Indurain had demonstrated that mentally he was still able to handle the idea of contending for the Vuelta until then, and en route to Naranco there was more evidence he was not thinking of abandoning when he and team-mate Orlando Rodrigues were the only two Banesto riders to make it into an echelon containing all nine ONCE riders. After that move was brought back, on the short and relatively benign ascent to the Naranco sanctuary, Indurain initially made it into a front group of eleven, which broke free thanks to a viciously hard acceleration by ONCE's Mikel Zarrabeitia. But when faced with a devastating attack by Alex Zülle two kilometres from the summit, Indurain was instantly left reeling. In two kilometres of fairly gentle uphill, he lost almost a minute – a serious setback for such a short distance.

After nearly two weeks of phoney war and some solid performances, Indurain's bid to win the Vuelta suddenly looked to be on the verge of total collapse. He was understandably pessimistic about his chances, whilst Spain's most veteran cycling journalist, Javier de Dalmases, wrote a blistering op-ed over the illogicality of Indurain's Vuelta participation in *El Mundo Deportivo*: 'Indurain deserves a resounding send-off to his career, but greed has caused the door through which he will presumably leave the sport at the end of the year to shrink ever smaller. We have to hit the red light and stop this sporting massacre as soon as possible. This is not the Indurain we know. It's a man overloaded with pressure who is pedalling to please the rest of the world whilst he thinks of his wife, his son, his home and his land. Let us leave him in peace for once.'

In the event, though, as he dismounted and walked through the door of Hotel El Capitán the next day, his Vuelta over with his first race abandon in six years, it was Indurain himself who pressed the red light.

Results from medical tests carried out on Indurain on the evening after Naranco later showed what had been increasingly obvious since July. More than able to handle a steady pace on flatter terrain – as could be seen in the time trials he had ridden in the third week of the Tour, the Olympics and again in the Vuelta echelons – Indurain's problem, Banesto team doctor Iñaki Arratibel explained, was a drop of aerobic capacity, or as he called it, 'a lack of punch'. Indurain, in other words, was riding on fumes: racing the Vuelta had been, as Unzué says, a colossal mistake.

For the historically inclined, there was, as Indurain had already pointed out two days earlier, a tradition for him to suffer misfortune in or near the Lagos de Covadonga. He had lost the Vuelta lead there in 1985 and in 1987 had abandoned a stage of the Vuelta that left from Cangas de Onís, the town at the foot of the climb. In 1989, meanwhile, he had broken his wrist on the descent from the Fito. Even when things were going relatively well like in 1991, when the Vuelta did the two 1996 Asturian stages in reverse order, it was always relative. That year, Indurain did not gain enough time on race leader Melchior Mauri either at Covadonga or Naranco to topple a rider whom nobody would have, prior to the Vuelta, considered capable of winning it – unlike Indurain.

Five years on, and just an hour or so after Zülle and Jalabert had continued ONCE's crushing domination of the Vuelta by taking a joint triumph at the summit of Covadonga, Indurain came down the stairs of El Capitán and analysed what proved to be the final, definitive defeat of his career to the press. Courteous as ever, he thanked fans for their continuing support on the roadside, and said he had started the stage wanting to fight back from the Naranco defeat. However, he also stated clearly that he was not motivated to go on fighting 'to finish fifth overall'. His laconic sense of humour had clearly not abandoned him, as he revealed when he was asked by the media what he had been thinking about as he pedalled towards El Capitán. 'I thought', he replied drily, 'that I was not having a good day.'

Indurain argued that his abandon of the Vuelta 'should not affect his future', but it was difficult to see how it could not. Rather than a victory in the Olympic Games as his curtain-call, the last images of Indurain as a professional – and watched in the Vuelta by an average viewing figure of four million Spaniards, a total that halved as soon as he quit – were anything but triumphant. Some of the Banesto team staff, Manu Arrieta says, were distraught at Indurain's exit from the Vuelta in such a spectacularly low-key fashion: 'He was cross because he wasn't in a good enough condition to go, and he was forced to go and then the day he abandoned, I was in tears. He never said he was going to stop, he just stopped and that was it.'

However, whilst Olympic success increased public speculation that he might continue, and had had the opposite effect on Indurain himself, his abandon of the Vuelta – as he was to reveal later – revived his own private interest in continuing his career. Bizarrely enough, to the broader public it felt like the end of an era, particularly as the Vuelta acted as yet another nail in the coffin, arguably the biggest, of Indurain's relationship with Banesto's management.

Key to it all was the seemingly unstoppable destruction of Indurain's trust in his bosses. Nor, at least as Delgado sees it, was that entirely Unzué and Echavarri's fault: 'From that moment onwards, everything that Eusebio and José Miguel say gets an answer of "no". [Indurain thinks] "The trust is gone, now I don't want to know anything." And I don't think life is like that, but at that precise moment and given Miguel's character, it was. Miguel had been obedient, they forced a yes to something out of him and then he said "OK, that's it. Game over."'

From Delgado's point of view, 'It's like a house of cards, many things fell apart incredibly fast. Miguel was respected, but he should have put his foot down, and said he wasn't up to racing the Vuelta, whatever Banesto said.' What had been the strongest element in Indurain's relationship with Echavarri and Unzué – the rock-solid trust between them – was now what was disappearing the fastest. Part of the reason, Delgado believes, is inherent in top-level sport. But once again Indurain's personality did him no favours: 'When you're a top-level sportsman your stress levels are at an absolute maximum. It's not just about riding a bike well. You have to put up with the people, the journalists, you've got no private life, it goes on for one year, for two years, for ages. So if your mental shelter is your team and your director and as Miguel is not communicative, you don't understand the few messages you're getting, then he's going to say, "These people aren't any good to me any more." And like the good Navarran he is, then it's over.'

Other teams, unsurprisingly, were not slow to pick up on the deterioration in Indurain's relationship with his lifelong squad and there was no doubt which was pushing the hardest, either, to be first in line should Indurain opt to continue into 1997.

'The first big moment of communication between us came on the road to Albacete [stage three], when I drove past Miguel when he and the ONCE riders were in the echelon,' recalls Manolo Saiz. 'And I say Miguel, it's time and he says "You're right" and he starts working with my boys. If there's a sporting moment of communication like that, then there can be a possible signing. You understand that there can be a chance.'

'For ONCE, having Indurain in their team would have buried the hatchet completely with the Spanish cycling fanbase,' argues Delgado. 'For them it was an ideal situation, for five or six years they were a Spanish national "product", but they had a Swiss rider [Zülle] and a French rider [Jalabert] attacking a Spanish rider [Indurain], so they were the "anti-Spanish" team. I can imagine that Manolo must have had a hard time of it sometimes.'

There was also another huge personal motivation for Saiz, as a director: the chance to work with cycling's greatest ever Tour de France racer. A few weeks after the Vuelta a España – 'during which our only aim had been to eliminate him from contention', Saiz says – Indurain, Sabino Padilla (as Indurain's friend), Saiz and ONCE manager Pablo Antón met in Vitoria with a very different subject to discuss. Although Indurain later said he had only attended out of courtesy, Saiz says that there was a definite meeting of minds in terms of the race programme and sporting criteria each side wanted to bring to a possible contract for 1997. The stumbling block was financial, with the difference in terms of hard economics, according to a comment Padilla reportedly made to a journalist at the time, considerable. 'He said, "ONCE wanted to buy a Ferrari at the price of a Seat 600,"' Vidarte recalls. 'The minute it went a bit wrong, it was all off,' Delgado observes.

Indurain was tracked down by one Pamplona reporter a few days after the Vitoria meeting to a local car dealer's where he reportedly had a business investment. Indurain was cautiously diplomatic: he told the reporter that he had noted similarities between ONCE and Banesto and said that he was sure there would be no difficulty in terms of how he and Jalabert could race together. However, he added that he had no idea how he and Alex Zülle could share out the calendar, given that they were so similar as racers. This was a problem that, in any case, Indurain would have had to face in Banesto after Olano's signing, although Olano appears confident it could have been easily overcome.

Saiz insists that there was 'more in common than there wasn't,' but points out that Indurain's contract was in a different league. 'When I went to sign Indurain, his contract alone was worth more than the whole of ONCE's budget for the following year. Our budget was at most five million euros [annually], just over half that of [top Italian squad] Fassa Bortolo. The fourth-ranked rider in Banesto was worth the same as the fourth rider in ONCE. But it was the top names who were worth so much more.' On the plus side, he says he encountered no opposition to signing Indurain 'when I discussed it with Alex [Zülle] and Laurent [Jalabert] on the plane over to race those last three Italian Classics [Giro di Lombardía, Milan–Turin and Piamonte].' Saiz even had a new sponsor theoretically on board for the team, a Spanish TV channel, to help pay for Indurain's salary, 'and that was the closest we've been to the teams actually having control of the TV rights to races.' (The question of TV rights is a longstanding bone of contention between race organisers and cycling's professional squads that continues to rumble through the sport to this day.)

But the ONCE deal failed to get off the ground, and subsequent alleged offers from Kelme and Lampre never gained any serious traction at all. The route of the 1997 Tour de France, with the novelty of the first time trial coming after the first major series of mountain stages in the Pyrenees, not before, was not ideal for Indurain, but it brought no comment either way from the Spaniard. With his last official race, the Vuelta, a fast-fading memory, by late autumn Indurain had made his last appearance in Banesto team kit at an exhibition race at Xàtiva, near Valencia. And whilst a prize-giving ceremony in Navarre for Indurain brought – possibly for the last time as a pros – Echavarri, Unzué and Indurain together, there was no last-minute reconciliation. Echavarri, using religious imagery to the last, said that he had lit a candle in a church – whether this was a metaphor or not was unclear – in the hope that it would act as inspiration to help resolve his differences with Indurain. 'By then it was ONCE or nobody,' Saiz claims and on 2 January 1997, coincidentally in the same Pamplona hotel where Reynolds had announced their sponsorship of a professional team seventeen years before, Indurain read a communiqué in which it became clear which choice he had taken.

Reading from a single sheet of paper Indurain acknowledged that the decision had been three months in the making but that – as the single year's contract in 1995 would seem to confirm – he had already been thinking of quitting since early in the year. Racing the Vuelta had almost made him change his mind, he confirmed, and he still felt that he could have won a sixth Tour de France at some point later in his career.

But as he put it in the communiqué, 'Being at the maximum level in this sport requires a great deal and every year that goes by it is harder to achieve. I think I have dedicated enough time to cycling, I want to enjoy this as a hobby. I think this is the best decision for me and my family. They are waiting for me, too.' And, after thanking his team, the media and, 'above all' the fans, Indurain's career was officially over.

Less than nine kilometres away, where Banesto were holding a team training camp in the outskirts of Pamplona, Echavarri watched the scenes on TV. Indurain, with his usual underestimation of how widely he was appreciated, had booked a hotel conference room that could only accommodate 80, far less than the number of journalists crammed in there to listen to the outcome of a dilemma that had gripped the country and taken 103 days to resolve. It finally took a police officer to beat a path for Indurain through the sea of microphones and up to the single table and chair behind which he sat, alone. There was no emotion in his voice as he read, no changes of tone, simply a summary of the news that he was quitting. It could almost have been about another person.

That was possibly the most shocking element of Indurain's exit: the lack of theatre, of anything special about it at all. It was almost to be expected that nobody from the team was with him, but Indurain's departure from a sport he had dominated was utterly low-key and strikingly solitary.

Unzué still regrets his part, as he sees it, in Indurain's leaving with so little fuss or recognition. 'When Miguel retired, if anybody deserved a homage it was Miguel, for everything he had done for cycling, for everything he had done for us,' Unzué argues. 'Unfortunately, the end was not the best we'd have liked and on top of that it was something which is open to many different interpretations. It became a farewell which he didn't deserve, and that is the biggest outstanding debt I have with my team's past. It's not something he needed, but something he should have had from cycling.'

Yet after all the drama and tumult of his final year in the sport, was it such a bad thing for Indurain to leave cycling with as little fanfare as possible? As might be expected with Indurain, the manner of his retirement underlined something, for one last time: that as a person, he remained as unchanged and as normal, in the very best sense of the word, as the streets of Villava where it had all begun, just a few kilometres away.

CHAPTER 11

Exceptionally Normal

High on the outskirts of a hillside village somewhere outside San Sebastián, Manu Arrieta, the former Reynolds *soigneur*, has a cabin opposite his house that feels like a cross between a bachelor's den, a Basque *pintxos* bar and a fan's shrine to a certain 1990s Spanish rider.

In the cabin's airy, brightly lit interior, three of the four walls surrounding the spotlessly clean rustic furniture are lined with posters of Indurain from his victorious Tours and Giros. The posters rub shoulders with framed team jerseys of Banesto and Reynolds from the Vuelta and Tour – several signed by Indurain, of course – and articles on Indurain. If you look hard enough above the cabin's wooden benches along the side of each wall, you can find a few small pictures of Arrieta when he himself was a rider. But there is no doubt who is the real star of the show.

As such places illustrate, there can be little doubt how much Indurain means and meant to Arrieta – capable of driving across half western Europe to see what kind of surprise his idol planned to unleash in the 1995 Tour – and to Indurain's other diehard cycling fans. But it was only once Indurain had himself driven away from the Pamplona hotel where he had announced his retirement that the broader, longer-term implications for Spanish sport of having had the Tour de France's most successful champion amongst its stars for over half a decade began to sink in.

Given the size of the vacuum Indurain was leaving behind and the six-month debate over whether he was retiring, when Indurain actually quit the sport the specualation as to who in Spain could be his successor was already in full swing. Much as Freddy Maertens was tipped to be Belgium's next Merckx from 1974 onwards, well before Merckx himself retired, in Spain the done deal was all about Abraham Olano. And it wasn't just inside Spain, either. As *The New York Times* put it in July 1997, when Olano won a stage in the Tour at Disneyland, Olano 'looks like Miguel Indurain, dresses like him in the Banesto team jersey and has finally started to ride like him.'

The way Olano's results were intertwined with Indurain's at the 1995 World Championships (as curiously enough, Maertens and Merckx had been in the 1973 Worlds, when Maertens left Merckx flailing in an equally controversial finale) proved hugely effective at helping the Spanish public to form a mental link between the two. In 1996 there was Olano's silver in the Atlanta Olympic Games behind Indurain to help maintain the association. For some, in any case, it was already set in stone: following the 1995 World time trial, Spanish national trainer Pepe Grande said categorically, 'Abraham is the Indurain of the future, in one or two years he'll be able to win any race he likes. He has the same kind of mentality as Indurain.' And that was well before anybody knew Indurain was retiring the year after.

Both riders also came from the north of Spain – Olano from Guipúzcoa, the Basque region closest to Navarre and a cycling heartland. Their characters – tenacious, quiet, unpretentious – seemed remarkably similar too, and so did their strongest suit: time trialling, at which Olano would go on to win the World Championships title in 1998. On top of that, Indurain left Banesto just as Olano was joining the team: from the outside, it looked like a seamless handover of the mantle of Spain's Grand Tour champion from one tall, dark-haired, tactiturn time triallist clad in blue and white to another.

But as Olano points out, the reality was was nothing like that at all. To start with, his racing background was totally unlike Indurain's, given Olano had turned professional as a sprinter-cum-all-rounder for the short-lived CHCS team. Secondly, after he slowly found his time trialling and – to a lesser extent – stage racing legs with Lotus (when CHCS folded), Clas-Cajastur, Mapei-Clas and Mapei-GB, Olano only signed with Banesto because his Mapei team owner, Giorgio Squinzi, gave him virtually no other choice if he wanted to break his contract with the Italo-Belgian squad for 1997.

There were other offers, but none of them satisfied Olano, who was keen to leave Mapei because 'it was going to focus almost exclusively on the Classics after 1996 ... Just before the start of the Clásica San Sebastian in 1996, somebody came up and gave me a piece of paper with the amount on it that Kelme were prepared to pay for me. It was a huge sum, but Kelme didn't have a reliable stage racing line-up. And when I told Squinzi I wanted to sign for ONCE, he said that I could go anywhere I liked but ONCE, because ... the last thing Squinzi wanted to do was make ONCE stronger. Finally there was an option with a new team Juan Fernández was trying to form for 1997, but we disagreed over his not wanting to sign Tony Rominger.'

Banesto might have been the best option, but they were thus the only option, too. But Olano is emphatic that he had no idea, when he signed his pre-contract, that Indurain was not going to be there in 1997. 'It certainly caught me out, Miguel had never said that he was going to leave and then all the pressure of being the lone leader was on me. My idea at the time was to go to Banesto to do the Giro and maybe the Vuelta, Miguel would still do the Tour where I would get a bit more experience under his wing.'

Olano, in fact, found himself expected by a sizeable proportion of the Spanish, to go on cranking out the Tour wins and 'if the Tour didn't work out for me, then I'd have to do the Vuelta.' Compared with what he signed up for, as he says with considerable understate- ment – something both he and Indurain do have in common as one of their favourite means of expression – 'It wasn't the same.'

Other options, despite Olano's evident ability at one-day racing and time trialling, not to mention the track, were not even taken into consideration. As Olano puts it, 'Even today, the Olympics aren't as valued as a Worlds or a Tour and in Spain there was no interest in the Classics. Time triallists weren't as appreciated as they should have been, that's why I never wanted to be a specialist in that. And if the team pays you to be a boss for the Tour de France, then that's what you prepare for.'

By 1997, Olano and Indurain had known each other for years – since they had met at a dinner after Indurain won his first Tour. Although they got on, Olano recollects with a grin what made the greatest first impression on him was 'the size of Indurain's hands when I shook one of them when we were introduced – they were scarily big.' Whilst he learned his racecraft from Rominger, with whom he spent four years in Clas-Cajastur and Mapei-Clas, Olano said he and Indurain never discussed the question of his 'succes- sion', in theory the strongest link between the two. 'Miguel's very reserved and so am I,' he points out, 'we've talked a lot but not about that.'

In Olano's opinion, the physical similarities between himself and Indurain were only superficial. 'My strongest point in a time trial was that I was more aerodynamic, and Miguel's was more about pure power output. For example, he always said his kidneys were too hard for him to bend over the bike at more than a certain angle, and he never went beyond that angle.' Olano, in fact, was something of a tech-head in the line of Chris Boardman, and, like the Briton, had a considerable amount of experience on the track. 'I had loved the track, ever since I was a junior and I worked with Guido Costa, an Italian track trainer' – who many decades before had overseen Italy's outstanding cycling success in the 1960 Olympics, garnering five golds, a silver and a bronze in seven events – 'during a period when I was training for the Military World Championships. I learned a heck of a lot from Guido.'

In Olano's opinion, there was not so much to be inherited in Banesto from Indurain, technologically. 'I liked his *Espada* time trial bike, but I didn't see any advances in it. He knew what was his best position, but aerodynamically, the numbers [efficiency] weren't so good. So you should have changed his position, which was the best for his strength, to improve his speed.'

In Olano's opinion, Indurain 'was basically thinking, "how many time trials do I do where the average speed is over 50 km/h" and [seeing there were not many] he did well in his calculations. But for the Hour Record say, that particular calculation didn't work.' In terms of trackcraft, too, Olano says there was little to learn from his predecessor and he gives an example to explain why: 'Indurain lost a little time in the curves because normally in an oval-shaped velodrome, if you come in to the curve too low' – as Indurain apparently would – 'then you overcompensate. But then if you go in to the corner slightly higher on the curve then you come out a little bit underneath' – but with a better overall line, and hence faster.

In terms of Banesto's racing philosophy, Olano says that during his time there was the same conservative approach to stage racing – 'keep the group together as much as possible and then go flat out in the time trial.' He also noticed that, in another possible hangover from the Indurain era, riders were trusted to turn up in top condition to race, rather than being constantly chivvied and kept tabs on. 'They think that if you've got as far as being a professional, you should know how your body works and what you should do. Everybody has their preassigned role and that's it.' Furthermore, there was also a clear pyramid structure for the Grand Tours. 'It's the same as Team Sky now, they have got such good *domestiques* that they could race for themselves in the Tour. Instead they were all focussed on one cause, working for the leader.' But how that leader would fare, after Indurain's exit and under the intense scrutiny and high expectations of the Spanish public, remained to be resolved.

If Olano avoided emulating Indurain on the track and an assault on the Hour Record with Banesto was never on the cards, on the road he followed a very similar programme. In 1997, Olano's fourth place overall in the Tour and a stage win, an overall win in the Euskal Bizicleta and second in the Dauphiné Libéré, despite a fair number of setbacks and injuries, would have been considered a relatively successful season – were it not for the constant Indurain comparisons. Fourth in the Tour, where Olano had only reached top form in the third week, felt light years away from Indurain's relentless run of success. Then the sight of Olano abandoning in the Vuelta in September 1996 as ONCE, once again, crushed the opposition brought back vivid echoes of Indurain's debacle in the same race the previous year.

Although there was a huge emotional debt with Indurain, according to Olano Banesto had few problems putting the Indurain era behind them in pratical terms: 'They brought through a lot of young riders, [José Luis] Arrieta, Txente [García Acosta] in 1997. People were motivated and the idea was that we would fight for the Tour.' But individually, Olano could not live up to the incredibly high standard set by Indurain before.

In 1998, Olano won several middle-ranking stage races in Spain including the Bizicleta Vasca and Vuelta a Burgos. Although he was injured and abandoned the Tour de France, he bounced back in the Vuelta with a vengeance, winning overall. He rounded off his season with victory in the World Time Trial Championships. But Olano and Banesto's management had fallen out, principally, he says, over their apparent failure to support him as leader when team-mate José María Jiménez began racing in his own interests in the Vuelta. A disgruntled Olano signed with ONCE for 1999, and spent the rest of his career with Banesto's key rival. 'I was very upset, because I felt the management weren't taking responsibility for their errors and at the same time I thought ONCE had more of a family feel to it. Also because Manolo [Saiz] might give his riders a bollocking, but he always defended them.'

As for the chances of him following in Indurain's wheel-tracks, Olano argues that it never felt like a reasonable proposition. 'I'm from northern Spain, we had very similar ways of racing, and I understood people labelling me as his successor. All I could do was do the best possible, and I'm very happy with my *palmares*, even if some people feel it didn't live up to Indurain's standards.'

History was not in his favour, though: 'Normally there's a new big name in cycling about once every ten years and that was Miguel in the 1990s and it would have been pretty weird that another, new rider, coming from the same area, impacted in the way that Miguel did. I never saw myself as a successor. I was labelled that way, above all in the period when I was with Banesto, but I never gave that label to myself. I was one of the best in Spain, but abroad there were riders who were better than me.'

'It was very unfair on Olano, he was a great rider, but first he had to handle all that stuff with the 1995 Worlds, even though it was simply a question of team tactics,' observes Delgado. 'If there had been a gap between him and Miguel, maybe it would have been much simpler. He could have finished fifth in the Tour three or four years later and people would have said, great. But instead he had to handle things immediately after Miguel had gone and that fourth or fifth place in the Tour – people weren't so impressed. In terms of time between one Tour and the next, there wasn't any space for them to lose interest and so Abraham had to go through everything he did.'

Ultimately what the Indurain legacy meant to Olano was not in terms of achievements, but rather its negative effect: 'I retired a lot earlier than I would have liked, because of the way Miguel had been treated by the media in the Vuelta and the criticism he had to handle there. I thought "If they are prepared to treat him like that, with all he's achieved, how are they going to treat me, a person who's achieved a heck of a lot less?" Something like that can scar you. A person [Indurain] who has done so much for cycling and for the sport, and then the day he cracks in the Vuelta which he didn't even want to do ... what are you going to do to the rest of us? Shoot us?'

Curiously, speculation in Spain about the next Indurain, though, all but stopped completely after Olano. There were murmurings about Ángel Luis Casero, also a tall, gifted time triallist, who won the Tour de l'Avenir in 1994 and Santi Blanco, about whom Echavarri famously said, in his umpteenth play on words, 'the 2000 Tour will be coloured "white" [Blanco]'. Both raced for Banesto but much as happened when Olano left Indurain's team, when Blanco and Casero quit for Mínguez's new squad, Vitalicio Seguros in 1998 (as did Prudencio Indurain), the comparisons dried up fast. And unlike in Belgium, where even Frank Vandenbroucke, twenty years on, was labelled as the next Eddy Merckx, or in France, where both Jean-François Bernard and Laurent Fignon were dubbed as potential Hinaults in the making, in Spain there seems to be no such need to fill the vast gap left behind by their greatest ever champion. Perhaps, though, that is due to the patchiness of Spain's 'cycling culture' outside the Basque Country and Navarre, and the massive emotional investment many Spaniards had made in Indurain.

'There was a legacy of interest in cycling as a whole, and within that the huge doubt, after one champion can there be another like him?' points out Manolo Saiz. 'In fact, we were lucky that after him, there were various stars, because we knew how to take care of the cycling base. But only Olano lived through the problem of "If Indurain won a Tour then so must you" because people, in general, wanted that to happen so much. But after him, there were no such issues for [later stars] Joseba Beloki or Alberto Contador or Alejandro Valverde.'

This lack of a hangover from the Indurain era was also partly due to a racing strategy that had no established links to Spanish cycling history. Traditionally its top Tour performers had been erratic climbers in the vein of Pedro Delgado and Federico Bahamontes or if they were gifted time triallists – like Luis Ocaña – were notably inconsistent or firebrand strategists. Barring Olano, the dearth of riders who produced consistently good results and who were also gifted against the clock – as well as the rapid emergence of a hugely talented and charismatic, if wayward, climber like José María Jiménez, all contributed to the idea that Indurain was indeed a unique cycling phenomenon.

'I don't think he's left a legacy in terms of how he raced, and to be honest I don't think that's a bad thing. It's not something the public particularly like,' argues Juan Carlos González Salvador. 'They prefer the Alberto Contador style of racing, attacking all over the place, testing the opposition just in case they crack at every point. Miguel never did that.'

'But he wasn't racing for his sponsor, for his public, for anything like that. He was racing to win, and simply because he had the most options of winning like that. And if there were people out there who didn't like it, well they don't have to watch.'

'I think more than the Tours per se, he's proud of how he did it. The self-sacrifices and the effort he had to put in to get them. The results – that's for other people to look at and consider.'

Not that Indurain had any intention, after his retirement, of capitalising on his popularity to forge a career. Rumours in the spring of 1997 that he would continue at Banesto after they offered him some kind of unspecified position within the company's organi-gram were quickly scotched. Equally, there was never any clear sign that Indurain would form part of another team's management or, although he has formed part of UCI committees, take up any other permanent role inside the cycling community. When he was linked, inaccurately, to Fernando Alonso's aborted cycling team project as a manager, Indurain denied it immediately.

Initially Indurain would very sporadically appear in commercials – mostly for food products, like yoghurts – and he still takes part in cyclo-tourist events, sometimes for top charities, and is sometimes a guest at races, or acts as a media consultant. But this was the profes-sional who once talked about how he would spend at least some of his retirement time with the senior citizens of Villava, playing cards – at which he is reportedly extremely good. Indurain's dedication to 'the quiet life' has been as consistent, then, as it was to his racing.

Still living in Pamplona, Indurain will make excursions to homages to his former team-mates, such as the one to Dominique Arnaud in France when a square was named after the Frenchman in the town of Les Mées in 2016, shortly before Arnaud's death. But it is never to play the star. 'I remember when he came to a showing of a cycling documentary,' says Pierre Carrey, a French journalist from near Pau, 'and he was really acting just like another normal person. After the documentary, he started stacking away the chairs in the hall – unasked. I can't see another big cycling name doing that.'

One element shines through all this: Indurain's dedication to his family, to his wife and three children. It was not just cycling: for the best part of one year Indurain used to drive from Pamplona to Barcelona with his son Miguel to watch Catalonia's top football team. Typically of Indurain, he insisted on doing so without publicity and paying his own way for the tickets.

'I do a bit of everything,' Indurain said in an interview with Catalan newspaper *La Vanguardia* in May 2016. 'Luckily I don't need to clock on for eight hours a day. There's a bit of advertising work, my business deals, a foundation [now run by the Navarran regional government with limited private backing and named after Indurain, who is its president] to help top athletes. I don't get bored. But what is true is that I don't travel as much. I started travelling at eighteen, now I'm fifty-two and it's getting harder and harder for me to leave home.' He has also, throughout the years, dedicated considerable amounts of time to fundraising events for charities. And every October, Indurain is the star of the show at the CC Villava dinner and team presentation, greeting and talking to parents about the same club that he attended – and as did his children, too.

'In Navarre, he's widely admired, socially speaking he's a positive reference point, but he's admired for being Miguel, and for being so accessible to, say, whoever wants to stop him in the street and have a photo taken,' comments Luis Guinea. 'That is what people like the most, there's no airs and graces, no showing off. I come across him training when I'm out on my bike and like everybody else, I can talk to him, the best ever Tour racer, about the most everyday things in the world. That's really amazing.' Nor is Guinea overly sure if Indurain, as a retiring, publicity-shy type, would be keen to have his legacy exploited more deeply.

As of 2016, Indurain told *La Vanguardia* he had 'no special project' in mind for the future but he spent a fair amount of time riding his bike, 'which is what I like doing. I like the open air, seeing how the countryside changes through the year with the changing seasons. I only go out now when the weather's good, though.' He is a keen walker and hunter. 'You can tell how much he likes the countryside,' says Manu Arrieta. 'And when you're following him in the mountains, he still goes walking along at one hell of a pace.'

Of his three children, the eldest, Miguel has been the most interested in cycling and until 2016, formed part of the Caja Rural amateur squad, one of Navarre's most important after the Banesto feeder team folded in 2001. 'I remember seeing Miguel [senior] at an amateur race in France, standing on the side of the road in a torrential rainstorm under his umbrella watching his son take part and nobody even realised it was him,' Saiz said. 'When I drove past him I stopped, he gave me a really big smile, we were pleased to see each other.' Indurain's comment was cheerfully dry when Saiz commented on the nasty weather the racers were enduring: 'Oh well, they shouldn't have chosen to be cyclists.'

The idea of Indurain as the image of modern Spain reverberated onwards after 1992 and the Euro-Tour victory. But by the time he quit, whilst still very much held up as a role model, his modern image was mentioned less than might have been expected in the mainstream media's analysis of his career. Spain had grown used to its new, more solid status in Europe, perhaps, and at least symbolically, Indurain – like the 1992 Barcelona Olympics, like the Expo '92 – represented a a breakthrough that was a thing of the past. But although Spanish cycling suffered from a major drop in interest when Indurain retired, as indicated by the halving of the TV viewing figures in the Vuelta when he quit, the stature of Spanish sport reached a new high tide mark both nationally and internationally thanks to him.

'Until [Rafa] Nadal appears he's rated as Spain's greatest athlete of all time,' argues Pedro Delgado. 'I didn't live through the Indurain era as an out-and-out fan,' adds Alberto Contador, whose *palmares* of two Tours, two Giro and three Vueltas has come the closest of any rider barring Chris Froome, in or ouside Spain, to Indurain's. 'I was only 15 when I started getting really interested in cycling, but I still remember how every July here in Spain in the early 1990s belonged to Indurain.'

'He made people feel he was part of their lives and after Indurain quit racing my big brother bought a series of five video tapes called "Indurain's Five Tours" and we wore them out, watching them again and again. He's somebody for whom I feel a huge amount of respect and admiration. He's never been in the limelight like other retired champions, but he's been a key example to follow.'

Yet the irony of any great champion is, of course, the greater he or she is, the bigger the gap left to be filled after they quit. Concerning Spanish cycling in the post-Indurain era, 'Well it dies a bit, doesn't it?' says Olano. 'But that's also because of other things. At WorldTour level we're still doing well, but there has not been one champion since that pulled the masses together like Indurain.'

'There had been an incredibly strong spotlight on cycling when Indurain was there, and when he went, people would say "but I just want to know about Indurain",' Delgado recognises. Yet Banesto remained as the team's sponsor until 2003, long after Indurain had quit. The first major drop of top-level Spanish teams did not occur until 2006 and the Operación Puerto anti-doping probe, which was followed by the worst economic recession since the 1950s. By 2014 Echavarri and Unzué's team was the only ProTour squad in Spain, and only one second-division squad, Caja Rural, remained in existence. Even Villava is no longer as strong a club as it was in Indurain's heyday. 'There was a time when there were 25 or 30 kids in each level and now there are only 80 altogether,' observes Pruden. Although the latest crop of champions – Carlos Sastre, Contador, Valverde, Joaquim Rodríguez – have carried the flame well, they are all nearing retirement or in Sastre and Rodríguez's cases, retired, and the lack of top teams makes finding substitutes an ever greater challenge.

'Long-term in Spain I'd say the only legacy left of Indurain is the Movistar team,' says Josu Garai. 'Echavarri and Unzué have always been labelled the discoverers of Indurain and I imagine this has opened a lot of doors for them.'

'But in Spain, in general, that golden age of Indurain and the boom of interest wasn't exploited at all. We've had some great riders – Contador, Sastre, Olano – but in terms of the base, building for the future, that didn't happen.'

As for the professional team Indurain left behind, if Olano could not fill the gap in terms of results, Unzué argues that Indurain's approach to racing endured for much longer. 'He left us with a sense of internal calm, wanting to take those three extra seconds before we said something. There's a saying in Spain *están las cosas mejor por decir que dichas* [things are better when they are still to be said] although maybe that doesn't make sense to a journalist. But then,' Unzué points out, 'Miguel was a master of the language of gestures.'

For all Indurain balanced his talent for non-verbal communication with a chronic inability to provide dramatic soundbites, he was still broadly liked, and appreciated, for his huge degree of empathy with the media. For those who argue that this could have been a way of currying favour, I would point to the degree of kindness Indurain showed towards everyone, not just the press. Javier García Sánchez, in his book *Induráin: una pasión templada*, illustrates this with an anecdote concerning Indurain heading for supper in the Banesto team hotel after his defeat at Les Arcs. Despite the physical exhaustion Indurain must have felt, as well as the massive disappointment and an urgent need to 'fuel up' with dinner, when he came through the hotel lobby he still took all the time in the world to sign autographs and pose with fans as he inched, step by step, to the dining room door. García Sánchez, who was witnessing the scene, says that it took Indurain a good fifteen minutes to cross a twenty-metre-wide lobby, during which time he was stopped no fewer than fifteen times by fans.

In terms of the media, I can remember, too, one Spanish cycling journalist telling me how he was on the point of being fired by his editor after his requests for Indurain to give him some exclusive thoughts on the Tour had been stonewalled, time and again, by the Banesto media department. However, a chance encounter in the team hotel with Indurain when the journalist was on the point of throwing his computer at the lobby wall in despair saw Indurain insist the two sit down and do the interview. Internationally, William Fotheringham recollects the courtesy Indurain always showed when he was interviewed. In 1991 he wrote that Indurain was the only rider he had known who was polite enough to come down to the hotel lobby to take him up to his room for the interview, rather than letting him find his own way there.

To say these are not typical kinds of behaviour on the part of a fair proportion of modern-day sports stars even when they only have a tenth of Indurain's fame and results would be an understatement. As for the better known names in cycling, attitudes vary, but – by way of example of the wrong kind of media handling – Saiz argues that the rider who (briefly) succeeded Indurain as a five-times Tour winner paid a high price for his arrogant attitude to the press. 'What brought Lance Armstrong down, ultimately, was his relationship with the media. Indurain never had that problem. He only ever saw the media for what it was, something that was there to tell people about what he did. He wasn't looking out for "good" journalists or "bad" ones. He understood your role.'

'People would ask him for photographs and they still do,' observes Pruden, who knows this from personal experience – in public he was often mistaken for Miguel, and still is, when looked at from behind. 'But we were never too bothered about the press, there was no Internet' – and hence less stress for the journalists to file their stories, too – 'so when they came to the house, we'd show them around a bit, give them a bit of wine. We'd get bus-loads of fans stopping outside the house and wanting to look, photographers ... the fans still look out for him, but it doesn't bother him very much.'

On the plus side for Unzué, Indurain's departure meant there was – in the mid to long term after it was realised what Olano's true limits were – a considerable drop in the level of expectation about what Banesto could achieve. This, in turn, allowed racing and directing to regain one pleasurable aspect. 'Afterwards there were great riders, but when you raced with them, you no longer felt so obliged to win,' he reflects. 'Winning the Vuelta with Abraham in 1998, say, was really something very beautiful, it was so difficult to do. We did the Vuelta knowing that there were a lot of days we could lose it. But [as with Indurain] you never had that obligation to win, which is the really tough part.'

Even the head of the strongest opposition in Spain (or else-where) to Indurain recognises that what struck him, as much as if not more than the victories, was the attitude of the man that captured them. 'What I most admired about him was his tran-quillity, his ability to treat things as normal,' says Saiz. 'I'd go to the Tour de France and get angry because they took half an hour to serve me my pasta in the hotel restaurant. He was always calm enough to say, "It doesn't matter, I'll eat it when it comes."'

'I remember one year we went to get the TGV to go to Paris and I was pissed off because it didn't arrive on time,' adds Saiz, 'and I said, "God, they're always late in this country," and he simply answered, "and who cares about that, if we have to do it anyway?"'

Unzué, too, is unstinting in his praise of Indurain's human qual-ities, saying 'When it turns out that you've got a world class figure living on your doorstep, somebody as straightforward and normal as Miguel, those qualities are what we still remember. It's very easy for me to say he's a legend, but it's true. There are other people who've won five Tours or who have a more splendid *palmares*, but the way he won them – that is what puts him on a special level.' As Olano confirms, 'Miguel as an athlete was brilliant but as a person, even more so.'

Indurain's ability to put a broader perspective on things never failed him, even in his worst defeats, confirms his brother Pruden. 'In 1996 in the Tour he was the one who calmed us down, everybody was upset except him. And the same thing happened with the Hour Record and when he retired from the Vuelta, it would be "hey, I'm fine, no problem, *no pasa nada*",'

Indurain himself, in a 1995 interview for the magazine *Cycle Sport*, was typically low-key about how he would like to be remembered: 'as a normal person who had a certain vocation and who did it the best he could.' He did not, he said, care what was written on his gravestone: 'Once you're gone,' he pointed out with a dose of his most laconic style, 'you're gone.'

Yet for all Indurain's calculating racing style was seen as a harbinger of modern Spain, in terms of cycling's fight against banned drugs and doping there was something *fin-de-siècle* about Indurain's succession of Tour wins, too. It is true that doping offences, or suspicions of them, have regularly stained one or another champion's copybook since bike racing began. But it's equally undeniable that from the late 1980s onwards, the background noise from stories involving banned drugs and professional cycling slowly but surely grew louder across the board. Olano himself was named by a French Senate report in 2013, 15 years later, as one of 18 riders in the 1998 Tour de France who had traces of EPO discovered in retro-active testing, a charge Spanish media later said he had rejected. What few direct accusations there have been concerning Indurain, though, as opposed to the steadily darkening cloud of suspicion that surrounds that period of time, have never been substantiated.

Regardless of the developments in cycling in the last 20 years, some for better and others for worse, Indurain's massive grass-roots popularity in Spain endures. Abroad, however, Indurain was – and sometimes still is – criticised as being excessively dull as a racer. As William Fotheringham once wrote in the *Guardian*, 'Indurain was the first Spanish stealth champion, and each July the most dramatic event was the annual ritual of watching him receive his birthday cake.'

Outside Spain, Indurain has also been attacked for failing to show the same degree of driving, all-out ambition as Hinault, Merckx or even Anquetil, the five-times Tour winner most similar to Indurain in racing style. The figures appear to back this up: in the Tour de France, in total Indurain spent 61 days in yellow and won 12 stages, four more days in the lead than Anquetil, but with four fewer stage wins. Merckx's Tour total of 96 days in yellow and 32 stages, and Hinault's 78 days and 21 stages, are far higher. Indurain's approach path to the summit, a steady, year-on-year improvement in the Tour de France – abandon in 1985 and 1986, 97th in 1987, 47th in 1988, 17th in 1989, 10th in 1990, 1st from 1991–5 – suggests little of an impulsive racer, either: rather someone who gradually but relentlesssly refined his strategies and performances.

Indurain's career, like Hinault's, was one of the shorter of the top champions – 12 years in comparison to Merckx's 14 at the summit and Anquetil's 15. Even José Miguel Echavarri recognised this up to a point when he once said, 'Of the four – Hinault, Merckx, Anquetil, Indurain's the best all-rounder ... for the Tour.'

It sometimes feels futile to compare different historical eras in cycling, given the way events were raced in different eras and their relative difficulty makes for an automatically distorted contrast. But what cannot be denied is that of the five-times Tour winners, Indurain has the leanest *palmares* outside it. And as Eddy Merckx has never been slow to point out when asked about Indurain, other races count, too.

To take the five-times winner most similar to Indurain, Anquetil lacked the voracity of Merckx or Hinault. But apart from nettting five Tours, two Giros and an Hour Record, like Indurain, he won five editions of Paris–Nice – two more than Indurain, as well as three events Indurain never did: a Monument – Liège–Bastogne–Liège – and two more of the most prestigious lesser Classics, Bordeaux–Paris and Gent–Wevelgem. Only in the World Championships – where there was no Time Trial event at the time – does Indurain have an edge on the Frenchman, with a TT gold, two road-race silvers and a bronze compared to one silver. There is one achievement, though, which is Indurain's alone: he is the first, and to date only, rider to have taken the Giro and Tour double in two successive years, 1992 and 1993. That particular feat even proved impossible for Merckx. What is fair to conclude, then, is that Indurain's victories in the Tour built up so quickly, they tended to overshadow, wrongly, the rest of his triumphs.

'When they attack people for having one objective [like Indurain in the Tour] then I say look at Chris Froome,' argues Olano in Indurain's defence. His point is that Froome has also given overwhelming priority to the Tour. But as Olano sees it, there is logic behind Froome's doing so – and by extension, Indurain's. 'It's clear that if you've got a peak of form for one objective in the year, then it's always going to be better than when you try to go for two objectives. And that first peak of form is always better than the second.'

As Olano sees it, Indurain's character is what gives his Tour wins their greatest value, and not just amongst his allies or inside Spain. He cites as an example when Laurant Jalabert gifted a win to a breakaway Bert Dietz in a stage of the Vuelta at Sierra Nevada in 1995, after closing down the former German amateur national champion's 200 kilometre breakaway just metres from the line – but that Jalabert had only done so because he was obeying Saiz's team orders. 'I think that's a winner's mentality, and that's normal when you are ambitious. I'm not going to say Miguel was generous, but he was respectful with his rivals. He always valued their hard work and if he beat them, he'd beaten a good rider – which indirectly made him an even better one. It wasn't like the Spanish media's attitude, which is when there's a football match they start saying how bad the opposition are and then when we lose the match, suddenly the opposition are very good.'

Furthermore, it was not only inside Spain that it was recognised that Indurain's human qualities gave his victories a special edge. 'He's always had his feet on the ground, he's an old-school champion,' points out current Tour boss Christian Prudhomme. 'He reminds me a lot of Poulidor' – 1960s star Raymond Poulidor, who also had a strongly rural background – 'even if Poulidor never wore yellow and Miguel won the Tour five times. There's that deep wisdom of the countryman, the patience and the sense of taking time to work things through. That story about Indurain treating the Tours like harvests, I think it sums him up perfectly.'

Prudhomme knew Indurain personally as a rider: he interviewed Indurain many times when working as a TV reporter in the 1990s and says that 'he was always very discreet, he didn't talk in French and that was a bit of a protective mechanism, he'd say something in fifteen seconds and Francis [Lafargue] would turn it into a minute long. But he was never somebody to try to stand out from the crowd on purpose ... We've seen him a few times afterwards, in retirement, it took a heck of a long time to persuade him to come to the Tour's 100th anniversary celebrations but finally, he came.'

Speaking from a personal point of view, Jean Marie Leblanc, a former team-mate of Anquetil's and the Tour's director throughout the Indurain years, argues that he was 'exemplary as a grand champion, physically graceful, and morally, too – no scandals. His performances in time trials were magnificent. As a racer he was one of the most graceful I've seen.' From the media's point of view, though, Indurain was, 'Less good, too discreet in the interviews. I'm no fan of over-talkative types, but he didn't talk enough.'

There are those, particularly outside Spain, who have argued that Indurain's Tour victories were favoured by an excess of time trialling. Certainly in comparison to the Tour under Christian Prudhomme's management, the total number of kilometres of time trialling in the 1990s Tours was way higher. But whilst Leblanc is a passionate defender of time trialling – unlike Prudhomme – he also points out that he 'cut down on the amount of time trialling from the years of [former Tour de France boss Félix] Levitan, so the routes were never "made" for Indurain.' Only in 1992, when the Pyrenees were all but eliminated from the Tour, could it really be said there was a lack of mountain stages.

Furthermore, Leblanc believes, time trialling has become sorely underexploited in the Tour. 'There's something very moving, eloquent, about them, as an absolute value in the sport, just as they were in the era of Anquetil. They can be magnificent events as performances, as they were with Indurain and even, albeit over a shorter distance, with Chris Boardman. And we have to show that.' Indurain's legacy in time trialling, he believes, should not be so quickly consigned to history – and it is hard to disagree.

Arnaud makes what is possibly the most valid criticism of Indurain: that is, not of the rider – whom he admired greatly – but rather that the Grand Tours are given far more importance than they deserve. 'In my opinion, what Eddy Merckx did in Milano–Sanremo, winning it seven times, has more value than Indurain, Merckx and Hinault winning the Tour five times. You have a bad day in the Tour, you can recover. They say that Milano–Sanremo is a lottery of a race, so many chances of misfortunes, crashes and so on. How many people do you know that have won the lottery seven times?'

As for *L'Équipe*, the semi-official newspaper for the Tour, 'Jean Marie Leblanc called him THE champion of the Tour. To say that is too much of a reduction because of what else he achieved, but at the same time, the phrase has a real ring of truth to it because the rest was never anything but a way of reaching his big objective: the Tour,' once wrote Philippe Bouvet, formerly *L'Équipe's* most experienced cycling journalist. 'He was never a born winner like Eddy Merckx because he never had the slightest taste for pointless victories but his absolute superiority in time trials put him at his ease in defensive racing, where he was unbeatable. So more than the memory of spectacular racing like the other icons of the sport, he leaves behind a *palmares* [which places Indurain] just behind the four greatest: Coppi, Hinault, Merckx and Anquetil.'

Yet no-one could deny that managing to remain on top of the Tour de France for five years, without once falling apart and with a limited series of skills, puts Indurain in a class of his own. 'The merit was not getting there, the merit was to stay there,' as Unzué puts it. 'He wouldn't engage in the race, because he didn't need to, he had a defensive style that was very effective, not flamboyant or particularly interesting, but very effective. A bit like [pre-2016 Tour de France] Sky,' observes Boardman. Indeed, Sir Bradley Wiggins, who took Sky's first Tour in 2012, is a self-confessed huge Indurain fan.

And where Indurain surely trumps almost everybody is how positive a legacy he leaves behind as a person, his acting as the living proof that the unpleasant, ruthless aspects that some claim are necessary for a top athlete to succeed can, in fact, be superfluous. 'The peloton can't make you win a race, but it can make you lose one,' observes Boardman. 'But people didn't think "I'm not letting that bastard do that" because he and his team treated you with respect, they were nice, they did a good job and that makes a big difference. Did people feel intimidated? I think I'd call it frustration because his team was almost impossible to combat, as well as feeling a deep fondness for him.'

'As a person, he's the greatest Tour champion,' comments Pedro Delgado. 'Everybody would agree cycling's greatest is Eddy Merckx and I myself have got a soft spot for Bernard Hinault for the way he raced. But as that son that every mother would like to have, or that sportsman showing a kind of dignity at all times who lets others have their moment of triumph ... that sense of fair play, I think Indurain is the example to follow. Totally.

'He wasn't just a champion inside his sport, but he was a champion off the bike as well. That, more than the Olympic gold, the five Tours, the World Championships, was the best legacy he left. People felt proud he was Spanish. His modesty is very much appreciated, because it's not normal that a top sportsman is so normal.'

Prudencio is careful to precede his remarks with 'he's my brother' but still calls Miguel Indurain 'the sportsman who's held in most esteem in Spain; him, Nadal and [basketball star Pau] Gasol.'

The question of whether Indurain, 'the most perfect human machine' as *El Mundo Deportivo* once called him, left cycling too early is perhaps the greatest unanswerable question hanging over his career. But if Manolo Saiz would have loved to have had Indurain in his team for at least a year, and if seeing Indurain race in a different squad would have been intriguing, Indurain himself never seems to have looked back too hard in regret. 'Am I sad? No,' *El País* reported him as saying in the only question he appears to have answered after his 1997 retirement press conference. 'No. I knew this was a day that was coming, and it's finally here.'

'I was pleased when he said he was quitting,' says his friend and *soigneur* for many years Manu Arrieta. 'A sixth Tour was possible, but five was enough. Because I've seen lots of champions dragging themselves along at the end of their career and he didn't. The day he said he was retiring, I went round to his house afterwards. I was the first one to go there, and I told him, "Even if you think you've made a bad choice one of these days, it was the best thing you could do. You didn't want to be dragging yourself along."' Arrieta concludes, 'I'm very grateful for what he did, but the thing is, he's irrepeatable.'

Perhaps the person, though, who feels he has gained the most from Indurain's career is not a fan or a Banesto staff member or a journalist: it is his brother Prudencio. 'I was lucky enough to race in the best team in the world with the best cyclist in the world and on top of that he's my brother,' he comments, and then pats his chest. 'Being together, eating, travelling, racing together, all of that – it's all in here.'

Afterword: A Face in the Crowd

High above the small town of Estella in western Navarre, the basilica dedicated to the Virgin Mary of Puy does not get too many religious visitors. Masses are only held twice a week, on Saturdays at 7.25 a.m. and Sundays at 1 p.m. Sales of recordings of the basilica choir seem scant, too, to judge from the poster on the church door advertising 'LP records at 1000 pesetas, CDs and cassettes at 2000 pesetas'. Even for those faithful few still playing music in those semi-defunct formats, the peseta went out of circulation over a decade ago.

Amongst any congregation, though, there will likely be a fair scattering of pilgrims walking the Santiago Way, the trail that crosses northern Spain, and through Estella, en route to the shrine of St. James in Santiago de Compostela, 800 kilometres further on. The historically minded might wish to see the plaque on the church's outside wall, dedicated to a number of generals who were executed against it during Spain's nineteenth-century Civil Wars. It's a safe bet, too, that pupils from next door's religious school are familiar with the basilica, formerly a medieval hermitage constructed when shepherds guided by a star – Estella in Latin, like the town's name – discovered an image of the Virgin in a cave on the hilltop.

And other visitors? Twice a year, in May and August, the local great and good of Estella will climb up the winding road from the town below to the basilica for local festivals in honour of the Virgin of Puy and Saint Andrew. But otherwise, the church is relatively quiet, with one notable exception: late each spring, when the basilica and the large stone-flagged courtyard immediately below it play host to a very different kind of spectacle.

On a warm Saturday afternoon, on the far side of the courtyard, Fermin Aramendi, the longstanding cycling commentator for the Basque ETB television channel, is sitting in a lone mobile TV broadcasting unit. Aramendi, a grizzled, whippet-thin fifty-something-year-old kitted out in shorts, sandals and T-shirt, is commentating on Navarre's top race, the Gran Premio Miguel Indurain. As Aramendi talks, the bunch are powering across the rolling, verdant farmland, en route towards the uphill finish in Estella – where Indurain, now approaching his third decade of retirement and still living near his home town in Pamplona, Navarre's capital, is set to give the prizes.

To judge by the finish line 'atmosphere' at 3 p.m., two hours before the riders are due, it doesn't seem as if there will be a warm welcome for the crowds. The large courtyard itself, lined with centuries-old oak and beech trees, is all but empty. Besides Aramendi's mobile TV unit, the only visible race-related structures are a finish line banner that looks as if it was built entirely out of white cardboard boxes (and is about as safe): a small field hospital tent that will be used for anti-doping tests; and next to it a mobile winners' podium and canopy, incorporated onto the back of a flatbed trailer.

A quick walk down some steps, past some backyards and onto a broad side road on the rear side of the basilica reveals why the courtyard is so deserted. The 191-kilometre-long GP Miguel Indurain consists of no fewer than four loops through Estella, each circuit completed when the peloton dashes along the Paseo de la Inmaculada avenue. This is Estella's main arterial road, which runs from one bridge to another in a straight line over a gigantic, U-shaped meander in the city's biggest river, the Ega.

To reach Estella, though, the riders have to tackle one of the steeper suburban roads on the line of hills on its northern side. It's here, on the unclassified Ibarra climb, that the bulk of the local fans are waiting. Standing in clumps of twos and threes and stretched along the roads, they are noticeably not wearing any of the usual diehard cycling paraphernalia – replica team jerseys or *musettes* being the most obvious giveaways. Instead the crowd is mainly parents with pushchairs, young couples with folding chairs and boxes of sandwiches, schoolkids on their way home after the 3 p.m. end-of-class siren has wailed out, or elderly folk easing back in the sunshine on some of the few benches. Perhaps as can be expected from a race ranked 1.1 – two categories lower than cycling's top league, the World Tour – this is very much a local crowd and a local event.

The 2016 line-up, though, does more than justice to a race named after Spain's greatest ever rider. Amongst the seventeen teams taking part are exotic 'minnows' like the Kuwaiti team (albeit without a single Kuwaiti rider): the Dominican Ineja-MMR squad; the Russian national amateur team; and a tonguetwister of a low-profile Latvian development squad, Rietemu-Delfin, which once boasted former World Time Trial Champion and longstanding Pamplona resident Vasil Kiryienka in their ranks. But at the head of affairs – and firm favourites – are Navarran-based Movistar, the latest incarnation of Indurain's lifelong squad and Spain's only

WorldTour team. Then there are the top American, Russian and Australian teams in the shape of Cannondale, Katusha and Orica-GreenEdge and, in a late coup for the race organiser, the Tour de France defending champion's squad, Sky.

The list of former winners of the GP Miguel Indurain is a strong one, too. Known prior to 1999 by the rather unwieldy name of Trofeo Comunidad Foral de Navarra (The Trophy of the Chartered Community of Navarre), it is the region's only professional one-day race, and most of Spain's current top names have triumphed there. They include Olympic champion Samuel Sánchez, Movistar's Alejandro Valverde, repeatedly ranked the world's number one racer, and all-rounder Joaquim Rodríguez, whose team-mate Ángel Vicioso, a Giro d'Italia stage winner, is the joint record-holder with 1940s and 50s Spanish racer Hortensio Vidaurreta and Juan Fernández, the triple bronze medallist in the World Championships for victories: three.

Also present in the roll of honour are numerous other riders who featured in Miguel Indurain's career. Apart from Pedro Delgado, there's Fernández, of course, a room-mate with Indurain in the Spanish national squad in the 1980s, and Julián Gorospe (not to be confused with his brother Rubén, also a racer) was a winner in 1992, whilst Marino Alonso clinched the race two years later. In 1996, Zülle, the runner-up in the Tour de France the previous year, won the Trofeo de Navarra in a spectacular long-distance break, triumphing with nearly two minutes' advantage over Laurent Jalabert. It almost goes without saying that Indurain, too, won the event in 1987, as he slowly but steadily clambered towards the realms of cycling stardom.

José Miguel Echavarri who hails from the nearby village of Abarzuza – the home town, as it happens, of those shepherds who stumbled on the Virgin's image a thousand years before – is back too. But Echavarri, rather than having any religious visions, has spent the eve of the GP Indurain in a cafeteria in Estella rubbing shoulders with various members of the Movistar team management, past and present. 'The Basilica is not a hard climb,' Movistar *directeur sportif* José Luis Arrieta observed during the informal gathering, 'but after 200 kilometres, it can make a real difference.'

As the lowest ranked event in which World Tour teams can take part, category 1.1 races are very much the borderline between squads from cycling's top league and the much more threadbare world of Continental squads. Whilst Sky's presence is easy to see thanks to their huge, black team bus, complete with their bikes neatly lined up and outside arm's reach behind the usual line of tape, the €30 million squad's deployment of vehicles line up next to a white transit rental van, home to the Kuwaiti team for the day.

No matter what their status, all the 136 riders taking part then thread their way down a narrow stone-flagged alleyway, past a gaudily painted van doing a roaring trade in *churros* – lengths of oil-fried dough that are a Spanish breakfast favourite – and into the Plaza de los Fueros square, the centre of old and new Estella, for the signing-on ceremony. Particularly for the locally born riders like Xavi Zandio, the Sky veteran, or Josu Zabala, racing with a Spanish Federation amateur team, this is not a straightforward or rapid operation. Bikes propped against the barricades, they lean over to greet huddles of family and friends in the crowds that pack the market square. In the ensuing tangle of athletes and machines, for riders like Australian all-rounder Michael Matthews, keen to do a pre-race recon of the Basilica climb, the quickest way out of the human traffic jam is to heave his bike over the barriers and pedal away.

The signing-on podium – which looks suspiciously like the same vehicle used for the winner's ceremony a few hours later – barely has space for a miniature easel for the papers where the riders sign. So it's perhaps not surprising that the man after whom it is all named, together with his brother Prudencio and his family, prefers to stand outside, chatting quietly to club staff as the riders slowly inch their way onto the podium and Juan Mari Guajardo, speaker for races across Spain but locally born, rattles off endless statistics about the more famous participants through the PA system. Indurain is not directly involved in organising the race – that is the CC Estella's responsibility – but from the cheers with which he is greeted as he strides in, it's clear he is the star act of the show, albeit a very under-stated one. 'His mere presence is a source of inspiration for all the riders who start today,' claims the GP Indurain race programme, 'and at the same time, it makes us recall those unique moments of his career that we all have in our memory.'

The locally based teams, given that this is far and away Navarre's biggest cycling event, are more likely to be thinking about how much they can achieve in the race itself. 'You don't notice the pressure, but there are a heck of a lot more fans here round the bus at the start,' says Hugh Carthy, a Preston-born second-year climber riding in 2016 for Caja Rural-Seguros RGA – like Movistar, a squad based in Pamplona. Speaking as Caribbean conga music, of all things, blares out on the PA system, Carthy says, 'This is a real hotbed of cycling round here and as part of Caja Rural you get that extra bit of support from the side of the road. You know the roads, it's a nice race for the team to do. I'm not sure why you don't get more top names here, to be honest: it's a great race to build up for the Vuelta al País Vasco [the Basque Country's biggest stage race, which starts the following Monday].'

Just after midday, the race's publicity 'caravan' – three vehicles at most – pulls away. Then whistles blare as officials wave the riders forward to the start line on the Paseo de la Inmaculada. In the first vehicle behind the pack, Indurain – as chief guest of honour – is seated next to the race president. After the riders and the endless lines of team cars and ambulances move off, bringing up the rear is the so-called broom wagon – a transit van that 'sweeps up' the riders who have abandoned and are too far behind their team cars to have their own transport. This is complete, in what is now a throwback, with a set of brooms stuck on each corner. Then as the barriers are cleared and the volunteers finally stop blasting on their whistles and redirecting traffic, the only relics of the race in the centre of town are route maps and a rather grungy-looking van with loudspeakers and Italian number plates, selling – or rather attempting to sell – packs of socks with the Giro d'Italia logo at five euros apiece.

Meanwhile, having headed out of town on a lengthy neutralised stretch past Estella's magnificent collection of Renaissance buildings, ahead of the peloton are 191 kilometres across the plains and moors of western Navarre. These contain four classified climbs, three second and one first category, the high points of roads constantly rising and falling between 400 and 800 metres above sea level. In what could be a nod to Echavarri's role as the father figure of Navarran cycling – and Movistar – the race route passes through Abarzuza twice. There's also a brief incursion round the local Navarre motor racing circuit: 'Maybe that's why they were going so fast,' Indurain jokes later. However, on such a perpetually undulating course and with a tough uphill finish, it's clear that rather than for the tougher sprinters – as the race used to be when it finished in Estella city centre – this is a day for the peloton's all-rounders.

It's perhaps no surprise that the two riders who reach the foot of the basilica ascent ahead of the rest of the pack at around 5 p.m. are two lightly built racers, Movistar's Ion Izagirre and Sky's Sergio Henao. Izagirre leads as they swing left past the bullring, past a large piece of graffiti warning against the effects of global warming and onto the initial 200-metre grind up to the basilica. He remains ahead as they take the first of two steep little hairpins leading to the top.

Theoretically at a disadvantage by being in front, Izagirre, a locally born rider who finished on the podium the year before, shows that his knowledge of the run-in to the finish is actually what counts. A feint left by Henao as the road steepens briefly to a painful maximum of fifteen per cent and twists into a U-turn fails to work out for the Colombian. On the next flatter hairpin, which leads into a narrow lane to the top, Izagirre accelerates hard as he comes off the apex, leaving Henao no option but to fall in behind. There the Colombian remains, boxed in by the narrow walls of barriers, outpaced by Izagirre, now out of the saddle on the final right-hand turn leading to the finish. Watched by a lone radio commentator on a race motorbike a few metres behind Henao as he turns his final pedal strokes, Izagirre yells in delight as he crosses the line well ahead of the Sky rider.

By now the crowds that were on the climb have flocked over to the finish outside the basilica in their hundreds. With no giant screen and only the speaker's information to keep them abreast of events, they cheer on the remainder of the finishers as they approach the line in ones and twos. Moreno Moser, the nephew of Italian cycling star Francesco Moser – to whom, coincidentally, Indurain was regularly compared in his youth – places third, Izagirre's team-mate Giovanni Visconti, who has proved instrumental in closing down counter-attacks behind, is in fourth. Carthy's lanky form, head nodding in near-exhaustion as he takes in the final corner, crosses the line in a more than respectable eighth, the second of his team home.

The ceremony, as ever in cycling events, takes a painfully long time to organise. Izagirre has about a dozen relatives and friends in the crowd, who cheer loudly as the 27-year-old – later to take an Alpine stage in the Tour de France that summer – walks onto the podium to claim his first win of the 2016 season. Movistar are not just present on the podium – Adriano Malori, an Italian team-mate of Izagirre's in convalescence after an appalling accident earlier that year, has been brought to the race by Movistar to help with his re-adaptation to racing and watches Izagirre get his trophies.

Indurain hands over the bulk of the prizes and then stands happily talking to all and sundry at the foot of the stage. It almost goes without saying that there is not so much as a security guard in sight. In an old-school, longstanding event like this, the crowd, organisation and riders mix and common sense and politeness means that nobody attempts to gatecrash the podium. Zandio, the Sky veteran, gets the award for being the first Navarran to finish in the race, which, considering there are only two Navarrans taking part, is possibly the easiest prize he has ever managed to net. The speaker, meanwhile, having reeled off the long list of thanks to the sponsors of the race, keeps the crowd entertained with one last piece of information – the numbers from the race's raffle.

The size and enthusiasm of the crowd, the small-scale yet efficient organisation, the solid line-up and a hotly disputed contest all seem to indicate that Indurain's race is in good shape. However, for all Aramendi has been commentating on races since time immemorial, 2016 marks the first occasion that Basque television ETB (and with them Eurosport) have broadcast the GP Indurain in nearly a decade. 'For years,' local newspaper *Noticias de Navarra* had observed in its preview, 'things have been very complicated for the GP Indurain.' As the newspaper puts it in rather melodramatic terms, it has been 'on the edge of the abyss'. ETB's return then is a sign that behind the scenes, a corner has been turned in the right direction.

As for the man whom this race honours, as the clusters of friends and relatives of many of the riders gather ever more thickly around the front end of the podium, it is only thanks to Indurain's height that you can still identify where exactly he is standing. As is so utterly characteristic of Indurain – and arguably what makes him, a five-times Tour de France winner, Olympic and World Champion, so special a sports star – he demands no special VIP treatment, does not need to be given constant pats on the back, metaphorically or otherwise, and has none of the self-conscious theatricality of many modern sporting celebrities.

A small but relatively solidly constructed event like the GP Indurain, just sixty kilometres away from his home town of Villava and in his home region of Navarre, is probably about as big a homage as he could want. Safe in the knowledge, presumably, that Indurain will be back again next year, nobody appears to make an exceptional fuss about the man often described as Spain's greatest ever athlete.

Here in Navarre, amongst his own people then, Indurain remains just another face in the crowd. And that, bizarrely enough, is precisely what makes him so unusual, and, ultimately, his legacy so enduring.

Palmares

Miguel Indurain
Place of birth: Navarre, Spain.
Date of birth: 16 July 1964
Turned professional: September 1984
Retired: 2 January 1997

1984: TEAM: REYNOLDS
Wins
Tour de l'Avenir (Tour de la CEE) stage 10 (TT)

Selected Placings
Tour de l'Avenir (Tour de la CEE): stage 11, 2nd

1985: TEAM: REYNOLDS
Wins
Tour de l'Avenir (Tour de la CEE): stages 6 first sector and
   10 (TT)

Selected Placings

Ruta del Sol: 2nd overall; prologue, 2nd and stage five (TT), 2nd
Midi Pyrénées: prologue, 2nd
Vuelta a España: 84th overall; prologue, 2nd
Vuelta a Burgos: prologue, 2nd

Other achievements:

Vuelta a Burgos: intermediate sprints classification winner
Leader of the Vuelta a España stage 2 to stage 5

Grand Tour abandons: Tour de France

1986: TEAM: REYNOLDS

Wins

Vuelta a Murcia: prologue and overall
Tour de l'Avenir (Tour de la CEE): prologue, stage 10 (TT) and
    overall

Selected Placings

Ruta del Sol: prologue, 2nd
Vuelta a Murcia: stage 5, 3rd
Vuelta al País Vasco: stage 5, second sector, 3rd
Midi Libre: stage one, 2nd and stage three, 3rd
Vuelta a Burgos: prologue, 2nd; stage 5 second sector, 2nd and hot
    spots sprints winner
Vuelta a España: prologue, 3rd and 92nd overall
Tour de L'Oise: prologue, 3rd
Tour de France: stage 7, 3rd and stage 5, 4th
Midi Libre: 6th overall
Spanish National Championships: 6th
Tour de l'Avenir (Tour de la CEE): stage 5, 2nd and stage 7, 2nd

Grand Tour abandons: Tour de France

1987: TEAM: REYNOLDS-SEUR

Wins

Vuelta a Murcia: prologue

Setmana Catalana: stage 4 second sector (TT) and stage 5

Vuelta a los Valles Mineros: stage 2, stage 3, stage 4 first sector, points classification and overall

GP Navarra

Volta a Galicia: stage 1

Selected Placings

Vuelta a los Valles Mineros: prologue, 2nd

Volta a Catalunya: stage 5, 2nd and stage eight, first sector (TT), 2nd

Vuelta a la Rioja: stage 1, 2nd overall

Setmana Catalana: 3rd overall plus points classification

Vuelta a Galicia: prologue, 3rd

World Championships: 64th

Tour de France: 97th

Grand Tour abandons: Vuelta a España

1988: TEAM: REYNOLDS

Wins

Volta a Catalunya: overall and stage 6, first sector (TT)

Vuelta a Cantabria: stage 4, first sector

Selected Placings

Vuelta a Andalucia: prologue, 2nd

Setmana Catalana: stage 2, second sector, 2nd and stage three, second sector, 3rd

Vuelta a Burgos: stage 2, 2nd

Vuelta a Galicia: stage 1, 2nd

Volta a Catalunya: stage four, 2nd

Clásica San Sebastián: 6th
Flèche Wallonne: 40th
Tour de France: 47th overall

Grand Tour abandons: Vuelta a España

1989: TEAM: REYNOLDS-REYNOLDS/BANESTO
Wins
Paris–Nice: overall
Critérium International: stage 3 (TT) and overall
Tour de France: stage 9

Selected Placings
Paris–Nice: prologue, 2nd; stage 4, 2nd; stage 5, 2nd; stage 7, second sector (TT), 2nd
Tour de Suisse: stage 6, 2nd
Tour de France: stage 15 (TT), 3rd and 17th overall
Flèche Wallonne: 7th
Liège–Bastogne–Liège: 10th
Tour de Suisse: 10th overall
Milano–Sanremo: 42nd
Grand Tour abandons: Vuelta a España

1990: TEAM: BANESTO
Wins
Vuelta a Valencia: stage 5
Paris–Nice: overall and stage 6
Vuelta al País Vasco: stage 5, first sector
Tour de France: stage 16
Vuelta a Burgos: stage 6 (TT)
Clásica San Sebastián

Selected Placings

Paris–Nice: stage 1, 2nd

Critérium International: stage 3 (TT), 3rd

Tour de France: stage 2 (TT), 2nd; stage 14, 2nd; stage 12 (TT), 3rd; stage 20 (TT), 4th

Vuelta al País Vasco: 3rd overall and stage 3, 3rd and stage 5 second sector (TT), 3rd

Vuelta a Asturias: 3rd overall

Vuelta a Burgos: 3rd overall plus points classification

Spanish National Championships (RR): 3rd

Flèche Wallonne: 4th

Vuelta a España: 7th overall

Tour de France: 10th overall

Liège–Bastogne–Liège: 12th

Amstel Gold Race: 19th

1991: TEAM: BANESTO

Wins

Tour de Vauclause: stage 1, second sector (TT) and overall

Euskal Bizikleta: stage 2 and stage 5

Tour de France: stage 8 (TT), stage 21 (TT) and overall

Volta a Catalunya: stage 5 (TT), points classification and overall

Selected Placings

Tirreno–Adriatico: stage 5, 2nd

Tour de Vauclause: stage 4, 3rd

Vuelta a España: 2nd overall and stage 19, 2nd

Tour de France: stage 13, 2nd and stage 17, 2nd

Euskal Bizikleta: 3rd overall

World Championships (RR): 3rd

Liège–Bastogne–Liège: 4th

Milano–Sanremo: 124th

1992: TEAM: BANESTO

Wins

Tour de Romandie: stage 4, second sector (TT)

Giro d'Italia: stage 4 (TT), stage 22 (TT), Intergiro classification and overall

Spanish National Championships (RR)

Tour de France: prologue, stage 9 (TT), stage 20 (TT) and overall

Trofeo Castilla y León: stage 1, first sector (TT)

Volta a Catalunya: overall

Selected Placings

Paris–Nice: stage 1 (TT), 2nd, and 3rd overall

Tour de Romandie: 2nd overall

Giro d'Italia: stage 1 (TT), 2nd; stage 13, 2nd; stage 18, 3rd

Volta a Catalunya: stage 4, 2nd

Tour de l'Oise: 3rd overall

Tour de France: stage 13, 3rd

World Championships (RR): 6th

Milano–Sanremo: 167th

1993: TEAM: BANESTO

Wins

Vuelta a Murcia: stage six (TT)

Giro d'Italia: stage 10 (TT), stage 19 (TT) and overall

Vuelta a los Valles Mineros: stage 2 and stage 4

Tour de France: prologue, stage 9 and overall

Trofeo Castilla y León: stage 1 (TT) and overall

Vuelta a los Puertos

Selected Placings

Vuelta a Valencia: stage 2, 2nd and 3rd overall

Tour de Romandie: prologue, 2nd

Giro d'Italia: stage 1 first sector, 2nd; stage 14, 2nd

Vuelta a los Valles Mineros: stage 1, 2nd

Spanish National Championships (RR): 2nd

Tour de France: stage 11, 2nd; stage 19, 2nd; stage 10, 3rd; stage 16, 3rd; stage 15, 5th

World Championships: 2nd

Volta a Catalunya: stage 1 (TT), 2nd and 4th overall

GP Gippingen: 8th

Liège–Bastogne–Liège: 51st.

Vuelta al País Vasco: 54th overall

Milano–Sanremo: 123rd

1994: TEAM: BANESTO

Wins

Vuelta a Valencia: stage six (TT)

Tour de l'Oise: stage three, second sector (TT) and overall

Tour de France: stage 9 (TT) and overall

Trofeo Castilla y León: stage 3 (TT)

Selected Placings

Vuelta a Valencia: 2nd overall

Giro d'Italia: 3rd overall; stage 18 (TT), 2nd; stage 1, second sector, 3rd

Tour de France: prologue, 2nd; stage 11, 2nd; stage 18, 2nd; stage 19, 3rd; stage 17, 5th

Tour de Romandie: prologue, 3rd

Milano–Sanremo: 31st

Other achievements:

Hour Record: 53.040 kms

1995: TEAM: BANESTO
Wins
Vuelta a Aragón: stage 4, second sector (TT)

Vuelta a los Valles Mineros: stage 4

Vuelta a la Rioja: stage 1, first sector, points classification and overall

Vuelta a Asturias: stage 1 (TT) and stage 5

Midi Libre: overall

Dauphiné Libéré: stage 3 (TT) and overall

Tour de France: stage 8 (TT), stage 19 (TT) and overall

Vuelta a Galicia: stage 1 and overall

World Time Trial Championships

Selected Placings
Vuelta a la Rioja: stage 2, 2nd

Midi Libre: stage 6 (TT), 2nd; stage 1, 3rd; stage 3, 3rd

Dauphiné Libéré: stage 1, 2nd; prologue, 3rd; stage 4, 3rd; stage 6, 3rd

Tour de France: stage 7, 2nd; stage 9, 2nd; stage 10, 2nd; stage 13, 3rd

World Championships (RR): 2nd

Vuelta a los Valles Mineros: stage 1, 3rd and 3rd overall

Vuelta a Asturias: 3rd overall

Classique des Alpes: 6th

Spanish National Championships (RR): 6th

Clásica San Sebastián: 9th

Milano–Sanremo: 132nd

1996: TEAM: BANESTO
Wins
Volta ao Alentejo: stage 1 (TT), stage 5 and overall

Vuelta a Asturias: stage 1 (TT) and overall

Euskal Bizikleta: stage 5, points classification and overall

Dauphiné Libéré: stage 5 (TT), stage 6, points classification and overall

Olympic Games Time Trial

Selected Placings

Vuelta a Aragón: stage 2, 2nd

Euskal Bizikleta: stage 3, 2nd; stage 4 second sector, 2nd

Tour de France: stage 20 (TT), 2nd; stage 8 (TT), 5th; stage 9, 5th

Vuelta a los Puertos: 2nd

Vuelta a Burgos: 2nd overall and stage 4 (TT), 2nd

Vuelta a Asturias: stage 5, 3rd

Dauphiné Libéré: stage 2, 3rd

Vuelta a España: stage 10 (TT), 3rd

Classique des Alpes: 8th

Tour de France: 11th overall

Clásica San Sebastián, 12th

Olympic Road Race: 26th

Milano–Sanremo: 115th

Grand Tour abandons: Vuelta a España

Acknowledgements

Many thanks to William Fotheringham, my brother, for analysis, recollections of the Indurain era and advice; to Stephen Farrand, for the encouragement; to Barry Ryan for phone numbers, advice, interest and recollections; to Jacinto Vidarte for taking the time to scratch through his memories of the 1990s and to Karlis Medrano of karlistudioa.com for advice, phone numbers and general good-hearted help.

A very big thank you to Pepe Barruso, for his hospitality and recollections, both way back in 1992 when I first turned up in the CC Villavés club house on a freezing autumn night and much more recently when I began re-digging along some long-cold trails concerning Indurain's life.

A big thanks to Dan Benson, editor of *Cyclingnews*, and Edward Pickering, editor of *ProCycling*, for their assistance in Ed's case, access to his fine 1990s cycling magazine collection, and in Dan's case, access to his interviews and podcasts about the 1996 Tour and Olympics. Also (in alphabetical order) Sam Abt, José Luis Benito Urraburu, Tom Bromley, Pierre Carrey, Sam Dansie, Josu Garai, David García,

Eduardo González Salvador, Luis Guinea, John Herety, Liz Marvin, Dave Prichard and Metro Books, Granada, and Graham Watson.

Thanks as ever to my agent, Mark Stanton of Jenny Brown Associates, for all the necessary help in putting this all together – appreciated.

This book also contains one of the last full-scale interviews with Reynolds, Puch, Wolber, La Vie Claire and Banesto rider Dominique Arnaud before he died in July 2016. From the moment he opened the front door of his home to me, it was clear that Dominique was somebody who had dedicated a huge part of his life to cycling as a trainer, team director, rider and fan, and who was a warm-hearted, generous person, too. If this book can act, in some way, as a tribute to one of the unsung greats of the sport, I would be proud.

And last, but very much not least, my thanks to my mother, the author Alison Harding, and to Mar, for the suggestions, the support and not forgetting the jokes – good, bad and rubbish – either.

Bibliography

Interviews:

My thanks to all those interviewed for their time and their insights. In alphabetical order:

Dominique Arnaud, 7 April 2016

Manu Arrieta, 6 April 2016

José Luis Benito Urraburu, 10 July 2015

Pepe Barruso, 14 November 2015

Chris Boardman, 19 December 2015

Alberto Contador, 11 January 2017

Pedro Delgado, 18 December 2015

Josu Garai, 13 January 2017

Eduardo González Salvador, 15 January 2016

Juan Carlos González Salvador, 6 April 2016

Luis Guinea, 16 January 2017

José Luis Jaimerena, 15 December 2015

Prudencio Indurain, 16 December 2015

Jean-Marie Leblanc, 17 April 2015

Abraham Olano, 14 October 2015

Christian Prudhomme, 22 April 2015

Manolo Saiz, 6 April 2016

Eusebio Unzué, 14 December 2015

Jacinto Vidarte, 1 November 2016

Books

(Published in English)

Sam Abt, *Champion: Bicycle Racing in the Age of Indurain* (Bicycle Books, 1993)

Lucy Fallon and Adrian Bell, *Viva La Vuelta!* (Mousehold, 2005)

Alasdair Fotheringham, *The End of the Road* (Bloomsbury, 2016)

William Fotheringham, *Bernard Hinault and the Fall and Rise of French Cycling* (Yellow Jersey Press, 2015)

William Fotheringham, *Racing Hard* (Faber & Faber, 2013)

Sean Kelly, *Hunger* (Peloton Publishing, 2013)

Richard Moore, *Etape: 20 Great Stages from the Modern Tour de France* (HarperSport, 2014)

Matt Rendell, *The Death of Marco Pantani* (Hachette, 2006)

Bjarne Riis, *Riis: Stages of Light and Dark* (Vision Sports, 2012)

(Published in Spanish)

Javier Bodegas y Juan Dorronsoro, *Con Ficha de la Española* (Urizar, 2003)

Dani Cabrero y Sergio Fuente, *El Clas. El Equipo de Asturias. El Sueño de su Afición* (Camelot, 2015)

Pedro Delgado, *A Golpe de Pedal* (El País, 1995)

Juan Dorronsoro, *Historia de la Volta a Catalunya* (Urizar, 2007)

David García, *Nuestro Ciclismo, por un Equipo* (Libro de Ruta Ediciones, 2014)

Javier García Sánchez, *Induráin una Pasión Templada* (Plaza & Janes, 1997)

Diario De Navarra, *Miguel Indurain, Veinte Años de Ciclismo en Navarra* (Diario de Navarra, 1996)

Josu Garai, *Miguel Indurain, El Señor del Tour* (Recoletos, 2002)

Josu Garai, *Ciclismo del Norte* (Recoletos, 1994)

Christian Laborde, *El Rey Miguel* (Juventud, 1996)

Juan Carlos Molero, *Historias del Arco Iris* (Unipublic, 2005)

Pablo Muñoz, *Miguel Indurain y el Mito se hizo Hombre* (Editorial Prensa Ibérica, 1996)

Benito Urraburu, *Indurain Corazón de Ciclista* (Dorleta, 1993)

Various authors, *Club Ciclista Villavés* (Club Ciclista Villavés, 2000)

(Published in French)

Various authors, *Tour de France 100 Ans* (L'Équipe, 2002)

Newspapers, Magazines, News Agencies and Websites

(Published in English)

Cycle Sport, ProCycling, Velonews, www.cyclingnews.com, *Guardian, The New York Times,* AFP, AP, *Observer.*

(Published in French)

www.memoire-du-cyclisme.eu, *L'Équipe,* AFP, *Le Dauphiné Libéré, Le Figaro*

(Published in Spanish)

MARCA, As, El País, El Diario de Navarra, El Mundo, El Mundo Deportivo, El Periódico, ABC, *El Diario Vasco, El Correo, Deia, La Vanguardia*

(Published in Italian)

La Gazzetta dello Sport

INDEX

Abdoujaparov, Djamolidin 116–17
Alcalá, Raúl 100, 112, 147
Almárcegui, Antonio 8, 12
Alonso, Marino 3, 29, 135, 137, 206, 288
Amaya, Serguros 32, 189, 191
Andueza, José Ignacio 8
Anquetil, Jacques 35, 152, 159, 163, 167, 168,
    198, 199, 220, 221, 278–9, 280, 281, 282
Antequera, Paco 46
Antón, Pablo 255
Aparicio, Vincente 204, 206
Aramendi, Fermin 286, 293
Ardennes Classics 53, 73, 76, 201 *see also under*
    individual race name
Ares, Javier 80
Argentin, Moreno 116, 188
Ariostea 116, 189
Arizcuren, Juancho 8, 9
Armstrong, Lance 123, 202, 212, 227, 275
Arnaud, Dominique 23, 37, 49, 62–3, 74, 78,
    82–3, 84, 88, 96, 98, 99, 100, 105–6, 115,
    120, 121, 125, 129, 131, 132–3, 135,
    136–8, 148–9, 210–11, 270, 281
Arratibel, Iñaki, 252
Arribas, Carlos 205–6
Arrieta, José Luis 242, 243–4, 266, 289
Arrieta, Manu 53, 55, 127, 203, 238, 253, 260,
    271, 283–4
Arrieta, Ramón González 206, 215
Arrizkoreta, Manolo 26, 27, 29
Arroyo, Ángel 31, 50, 51, 52, 54, 55, 73, 74, 81,
    82, 83, 94, 99, 107, 151

Bahamontes, Federico Martin 15, 44, 81, 107,
    122, 144, 146, 268
Banco Santander 190–1
Banesto 3, 6, 11, 27, 33, 76, 94–100, 101, 102–3,
    104, 105, 110, 112–15, 116, 117, 118, 119,
    120, 122, 125, 127, 128, 129, 130, 132,
    134–5, 136, 138, 141, 143, 148–9, 152, 153,
    155, 156–9, 162, 165, 168, 171, 175, 181,
    182, 183, 184, 186, 187, 189–91, 192, 201,
    206, 208–9, 210–15, 216, 217, 218, 221,

223–4, 225, 229, 231, 232–3, 235, 239, 241,
    242, 243, 245, 247, 248, 249–50, 251, 252,
    253, 254–5, 256, 257, 258, 260, 261, 262–3,
    264, 265–8, 269, 271, 273, 274, 275–6, 284,
    298, 299, 300, 301, 302
Baqué 39, 40
Barberena, Juan García 35, 36, 94, 95
Barruso, Pepe 7–9, 10, 11, 12, 14, 15, 16,
    18–19, 20, 21, 22, 23–5, 43, 44
Barteau, Vincent 217–18
Bauer, Steve 82, 100, 101
Belda, Vicente 57–8
Beloki, Joseba 33, 268
Berlusconi, Silvio 189
Bernard, Jean-François 57, 61, 86, 113, 117,
    120, 121, 125, 134–5, 137, 138, 149, 161,
    169, 196, 206, 268
Berzin, Evgeni 143–4, 192, 193, 194, 195, 199, 238
BIC squad 35, 152
Bizicleta Vasca 134, 237, 266
Blanco, Santi 85, 224, 267, 268
Boardman, Chris 177–9, 184, 185–6, 196, 199,
    205, 207, 216, 233, 239, 245–6, 249, 264,
    281, 282–3
Bombini, Emanuele 239
Bontempi, Guido 150
Bottaro, Dario 212, 217
Bouwmans, Eddy 164
Boyer, Éric 202
Breukink, Erik 82, 86, 95, 101, 102, 112, 117,
    122, 147, 203
Bruyneel, Johan 202, 203, 209, 212, 213, 214
Bugno, Gianni 101, 120, 121, 122, 134, 147,
    162, 163, 164, 165, 170, 171, 189, 192, 226

Cabestany, Pello Ruiz 63, 87, 104
Cadena Ser 51, 80
Caja Rural 271, 273, 290
CajaMadrid 40
Carrera 164, 171, 188, 193, 215
Carrera, Enrique 66
Casartelli, Fabio 219
Casero, Ángel Luis 267, 268

Cerrón, José Luis López 190
CHCS 262
Chiappucci, Claudio 100, 101, 106, 110, 111, 119–20, 121, 122, 123, 127, 146, 150–1, 162, 163, 164, 165, 168–9, 170, 171, 172, 188, 189, 193, 195, 206, 209, 220, 226, 230, 244
Chioccioli, Franco 150
Chozas, Eduardo 62
Clarke, Danny 73
Clas-Cajastur 13, 171, 209, 262, 263
Clásica San Sebastián: (1990) 108, 170, 225; (1995) 223–4; (1996) 246, 262
Club Ciclista (CC) Villavés 6–13, 17, 18, 19, 24, 270
Conconi, Professor Francesco 73, 75, 154, 184
Conde, Mario 95, 190, 191
Contador, Alberto 33, 268, 269, 272, 273
Coppi, Fausto 168, 282
Cornillet, Bruno 90
Costa, Guido 264
Costa, Rui 231
Critérium du Dauphiné 205
Critérium International: (1989) 93; (1992) 149
Cubino, Laudelino 67, 86, 87
Cuevas, Armand de las 121, 138, 150, 158, 163, 189, 192, 196, 197

Dauphiné Libéré: (1995) 205–6; (1996) 237, 240; (1997) 265
Davy, Thomas 184
Dejonckheere, Noël 13
Delgado, Pedro 31, 33, 35, 37–8, 49, 50, 51, 52–4, 55, 73–4, 75–6, 78–85, 86, 87, 88, 90–1, 92, 93–9, 100, 101, 102–3, 104, 105–8, 109, 110, 112–13, 116, 117, 120–1, 122, 125–6, 128, 129, 130, 131, 135, 137, 141, 142, 144, 146, 148, 151, 152, 158, 161, 162, 163, 168, 182, 185, 190, 191, 192, 204, 206, 216, 218, 225, 226, 227, 229, 230, 234, 247, 254, 255, 267, 268, 272, 273, 283, 288, 307
Delors, Jacques 66
Dietz, Bert 279
Donati, Sandro 184

Echarte, María Luisa 26–7, 28, 56, 243
Echavarri, José Miguel 24–5, 31–2, 33, 35, 36, 37, 38, 40, 49, 51, 52–5, 56, 57, 59, 61, 65, 66, 71, 73, 74, 75, 76, 77, 78, 83, 92, 93–4, 95, 97, 98, 100, 102, 103, 105, 107, 109, 110, 113, 117, 118, 119, 123–4, 135, 137, 151–2, 153, 154, 155, 157, 158, 159, 160, 165, 166, 170, 175, 180, 182–3, 184, 185, 186, 188, 189, 190, 193, 196, 200, 208, 213, 216, 223, 224, 225, 229, 233, 243, 246, 247, 248, 249, 254, 257, 258, 267, 273, 278, 288–9, 291
Echave, Fede 97, 225, 243
EPO 183–4, 277
Errandonea, Paco 165
Escartín, Fernando 243, 250

Fernández, Alvaro 45
Fernández, Juan 13, 225, 242–3, 262, 288
Festina 189
Fignon, Laurent 48, 49, 58, 90, 96, 123, 164–5, 201–2, 268
Flèche Wallonne 149; (1987) 76; (1989) 93; (1990) 108
Fondriest, Maurizio 188, 228
Fotheringham, William 123, 274–5, 277–8
Française des Jeux 62

Froome, Chris 123, 272, 279
Fuerte, Anselmo 104

Galdós, Francisco 149
Garai, Josu 54, 154, 180, 191, 229, 250, 273
García, José María 80–1, 107
García, Marcelino 237
Gastón, Iñaki 28, 29, 77, 171
Gatorade 165, 171
Gaul, Charly 168
Géminiani, Raphaël 171
Gewiss 212, 215, 239
Giesbers, Jan 189
Gil, Koldo 7
Gimondi, Felice 48, 172
Giovanetti, Marco 104
Giro d'Italia 13, 28, 39, 92, 100, 101, 104, 127, 156, 208, 263, 272, 278, 288, 291; Baby Giro 39; (1987) 170, 227; (1988) 79, 81, 113, 159; (1989) 93, 96; (1990) 100; (1991) 79, 113, 115; (1992) 79, 141, 147–51, 164, 167, 170, 171, 174, 187, 191, 227, 279; (1993) 79, 174, 187–9, 191, 196, 279; (1994) 79, 143, 187, 191–5, 196, 199; (1995) 79, 205; (1996) 187; (1998) 152
Goicoechea, Marisa López de 174–5
Golz, Rolf 58
Gomez, Marc 62, 64, 65
González, Arsenio 243
Gorospe, Julián 31, 40, 49–50, 55, 58, 59, 61, 72, 73, 74, 75, 81, 99, 104, 139, 151, 152, 173, 206, 288
Gran Premio (GP) Miguel Indurain 286–94
Grande, Pepe 261
Guay, Stéphane 62
Guimard, Cyrille 92, 152
Guzman, Alfonso 64

Hampsten, Andy 159, 206, 224
Hernández, Carlos 57
Herrera, Lucho 82
Heulot, Stephane 189, 236
Hinault, Bernard 30, 38, 42, 50, 63, 65, 66, 91, 122, 136, 159, 182, 198, 199, 216, 220, 221, 268, 278, 281, 282, 283
Hoban, Barry 153
Hostal Manolo, Zegama 26–9
Hotel El Capitán, Asturias 222–3, 252, 253
Hour Record 73, 166, 179–80, 265; (1993) 178, 179; (1994) 177–86, 231, 232, 278; (1995) 224–5, 228–9, 231–5, 264, 277; (2015) 232

Indurain, Daniel (cousin) 17, 30
Indurain, Javier (cousin) 10, 17
Indurain, Luis (cousin) 10, 17
Indurain, Miguel: amateur cycling career 23–5, 26–46; background/childhood 5–25; doping and 182–4, 277; early years as a cyclist with Club Ciclista (CC) Villavés 6–25, 270; legacy and achievement 260–84; life after retirement 269–71, 285–94; marriage 160, 174–5; Palmares 295–303; pro cycling career see under individual race name; retirement 1–4, 222–59; Spain, as representative/symbol of 140–76, 176, 191, 220, 221, 271–7
Indurain (Senior), Miguel (father) 7, 8, 10, 14, 15, 17, 21, 24, 31, 55–6, 99, 158, 185
Indurain, Prudencio (brother) 6, 10, 11, 14, 15, 17, 19, 20, 26, 30, 42–3, 45, 143–4, 172,

173, 195, 237, 240, 249, 268, 273, 275, 276–7, 283, 284, 290
Indurain, Toribio (grandfather) 15, 16, 42, 160
IOC (International Olympic Committee) 83, 182

Jaimerena, José Luis 10, 11–12, 27, 29, 38, 39
Jalabert, Laurent 202, 203, 208, 211–13, 214, 215, 216–18, 219–20, 226, 251, 253, 255, 256, 279, 288
Jaskula, Zenon 172, 173, 189
Jiménez, José María 224, 266, 268

Kelly, Sean 13, 14, 22, 28, 59, 86
Kelme 27, 57–8, 73, 250, 257, 262
Knickman, Roy 66, 67, 68, 69, 70

La Vie Claire 62, 63, 66, 67
Lafargue, Francis 52–3, 169, 175, 280
Laguía, José Luis 52, 54–6, 59, 72, 79
Leali, Bruno 188
Leblanc, Jean Marie 280–1, 282
Leblanc, Luc 110, 111, 117, 179, 197, 199, 236
Leclerc, Roland 64
Legarra, Jesús 33, 34, 37
Legarra, José 33, 34, 39
Lejarreta, Marino 13, 87, 114–15, 116, 225
LeMond, Greg 48, 86, 96, 98, 100, 101, 102, 106, 110–12, 117, 119, 120, 121, 122, 123, 163, 164, 165, 197
Lezaun, Robert 138–9
Liège-Bastogne-Liège 147, 149, 203, 225, 279; (1987) 76; (1991) 116
Lino, Pascal 166, 169
López, Pedro 11
Lotus 178, 262
Louy, Xavier 83
Ludwig, Olaf 227
Luquin, Javier 10–11, 43, 137

Maassen, Frans 100, 101
Madiot, Marc 90, 91–2, 93
Maertens, Freddy 261
Magro, Jesús Rodríguez 82, 121, 137
Mapei 242–3, 247, 262, 263
Marcos, Joaquín 18, 20, 30
Marie, Thierry 150
Martín, Antonio 190
Mauri, Melcior 113–15, 116, 189, 209, 212, 216–17, 252–3
Mejía, Álvaro 172, 173, 206, 226
Memorial Valenciaga 40
Merckx, Eddy 30, 33, 91, 122, 140, 153, 159, 167, 168, 172, 174, 184, 198, 199, 201, 216, 220, 221, 225, 228, 261, 268, 278, 279, 281, 282, 283
Midi Libre (1995) 205
Milano-Sanremo 37, 76, 147, 149, 208, 281; (1985) 62; (1986) 56; (1988) 154; (1989) 92
Millar, Robert 81
Mínguez, Javier 32, 35, 54, 78, 190, 268
Montalbán, Manuel Vázquez 144–5
Monument Classic 56, 92, 116, 279 *see also under individual race name*
Moore, Richard 146, 168
Moser, Francesco 22, 73, 92, 94, 107, 166, 185, 292
Mottet, Charly 57, 117, 120
Movistar 31–2, 155, 273, 287–8, 289, 290, 291, 293
Múgica, Jokin 44
Museeuw, Johan 227

Navarran amateur championship: (1983) 43
Navarro, Javier Gómez 84, 118

Obree, Graeme 179–80, 181, 184, 185
Ocaña, Luis 13, 15, 33, 34, 49, 91, 103, 107, 122, 146, 147, 192, 198, 206, 226, 268
Olano, Abraham 133–4, 228, 229, 230, 231, 234–5, 236, 242, 244, 246, 247–8, 256, 261–8, 272, 273, 275, 276, 277, 279–80
Olympic Games 263, 288; (1960) 264; (1984) 29, 45–6, 245; (1992) 142, 174, 178, 272; (1996) 245–7, 252, 253, 261, 283, 294
ONCE 3, 4, 13, 21, 33, 114, 115, 116, 138, 139, 198, 207–10, 211, 212, 213–14, 215, 216, 217, 218–19, 221, 231, 235, 237, 250, 251, 253, 255–7, 262, 265, 266
Oosterbosch, Bert 58, 59
Operación Puerto 273
Orbea 40, 44, 64, 151

Padilla, Sabino 125, 173, 180, 185, 192, 233, 234–5, 247, 255
Pantani, Marco 152–3, 193–4, 196, 197, 203, 206, 215
Paris-Nice 121, 278–9; (1981) 90; (1989) 89–92, 94, 98, 136; (1990) 108; (1992) 149
Paris-Roubaix 76, 149, 225; (1987) 73
PDM 52, 62, 78, 112, 117, 122, 190
Peace Race 45, 48
Peeters, Ludo 65
Pensec, Ronan 100, 101
Perini, Giancarlo 164
Peron, Andrea 212, 217
Peschel, Uwe 228
Philipot, Fabrice 189
Pinarello 36, 177, 180, 181
Pineau, Franck 62
Piqueras, José Luis Pascua 37
Planckaert, Eddy 65
Poblet, Miguel 76
Podenzana, Massimo 212
Pollentier, Michel 13
Poulidor, Raymond 165, 280
Prudhomme, Christian 280, 281
Puig, Luis 83–4

Recio, Pepe 80–1
Reynolds 3, 10, 16, 22, 24–5, 26–9, 31–46, 47, 48, 49–63, 67, 68, 69, 72–6, 78–80, 81, 82, 83, 84, 86, 88, 92, 94–5, 96–8, 107, 108, 114, 120, 127, 132, 135, 143, 151, 257, 260, 295, 296, 297, 298
Reynolds-Banesto team 95–9, 114 *see also* Banesto *and* Reynolds
Ridaura, Vicente 28, 29
Riis, Bjarne 203, 204, 215, 219, 236, 237, 238, 241–2, 243, 244, 245–6
Roche, Stephen 82, 89–90, 92, 108, 121, 123, 162, 163, 170, 188, 202, 211, 214, 227
Rodrigues, Orlando 251
Rodríguez, Joaquim 230–1, 273, 288
Romani, Arturo 95, 97, 190
Rominger, Tony 1, 3, 134, 143–4, 171, 172, 173, 174, 185–6, 191, 192, 195, 196, 197, 199, 203, 205, 209, 220, 224, 226, 231, 232, 236, 237, 242, 243, 250, 262, 263
Rondán, Hector 35–6
Rondón, Abelardo 69
Rooks, Steven 226

Rubiera, José Luis 27
Rue, Gerard 90, 91–2, 111, 133, 138, 195, 204, 215
Ruiz, Bernard 168
Ruta del Sol 58, 208, 210

Saenz, Alfredo 191
Saiz, Manolo 3, 21, 114–15, 135, 138–9, 144, 152, 153, 198, 207–14, 216, 218–19, 247, 249, 255, 256, 257, 266, 268, 271, 275, 276, 279–80, 283
Saligari, Marco 127
Salvador, Eduardo González 22, 32, 38, 39, 40, 43, 44, 45, 52–3, 57–8
Salvador, Juan Carlos González 22–3, 24, 28, 70, 71, 105, 124, 128, 129–30, 134, 135, 142, 151, 152, 153, 203, 225–6, 269
Sanz, Luis 181
Sastre, Carlos 27, 33, 273
Seur 74, 94
Six Days of Madrid (1986) 73
Skibby, Jesper 161
Sorensen, Rolf 116
Spanish Cycling Federation 190
Spanish National Road Racing Championship 28; (1981) 21–2, 43–4, 133; (1992) 171, 196, 225
Squinzi, Giorgio 242, 243, 262
Stephens, Neil 212, 213, 216, 217
Super Prestige Pernod International 108
SuperSer 13, 33–4, 36, 37, 155
Système U 90, 92

Team Sky 179, 265, 282, 288, 289, 291, 292, 293
Theunisse, Gert-Jan 108
Tinchella, Daniele 13–14
Tirreno-Adriatico 37, 56, 57–8
Tour de France 3, 17, 28, 33, 43, 44, 58, 69, 70, 79, 152–3; (1961) 163; (1962) 163; (1971) 198; (1973) 91, 103, 192; (1977) 13; (1978) 123; (1983) 37, 49–53, 107; (1985) 60–1, 65, 107, 158, 278; (1986) 65–6, 72, 107, 158, 278; (1987) 77, 78, 88, 163, 170, 227, 278; (1988) 78, 82–5, 87, 88, 94, 99, 101, 102, 105, 107, 182, 278; (1989) 94, 95–9, 100, 102, 105–6, 108, 111, 117, 118, 162, 163, 278; (1990) 19, 56, 98, 99–104, 105, 106, 108, 109, 111–12, 117, 118, 122, 163, 170, 220, 278; (1991) 17, 110–12, 116–24, 125–6, 131, 134, 136, 147, 149, 161, 188, 196–7, 230, 278; (1992) 123, 141, 161–70, 171, 173–4, 187, 193, 271, 278, 279, 281; (1993) 145, 171–4, 179, 278, 279; (1994) 178, 179, 180, 182, 195–200, 202, 205, 241, 278; (1995) 161, 201–5, 206–21, 223, 224, 233, 235, 240, 260, 278; (1996) 3, 11, 235–45, 247, 276–7; (1997) 123, 247, 257, 265; (1998) 152, 266, 277; (2000) 267; (2005) 6; (2008) 33; (2012) 122, 282; (2016) 123, 293
Tour de l'Avenir (Tour de la CEE, 1986–91) 41, 47–9, 197; (1968) 48; (1984) 46, 47, 48, 49, 57; (1985) 48, 61, 67; (1986) 47, 48, 66–71, 72, 90; (1988) 48; (1994) 267
Tour de L'Oise 182
Tour de Romandie 167
Tour du Midi-Pyrénées 58, 63
Tour of the Alentejo 237
Trofeo Navarro 77, 288

UCI 83–4, 86, 166, 171, 182, 183, 186, 227, 269; Individual World Ranking 171
Ugrumov, Piotr 188–9, 196, 199

Unipublic 62, 80, 191
Unzaga, Jon 243
Unzué, Eusebio 29, 31–2, 33–5, 36, 38, 39, 40, 41–2, 43, 44, 49, 55, 57, 61, 67, 69, 71, 73, 74, 78, 94, 100, 102, 103, 105, 108–9, 119, 128, 137, 138, 144, 145, 148, 153, 154–5, 156–62, 164, 166, 175–6, 178, 180, 181–2, 184, 185, 190, 194–5, 196, 197–9, 200, 201, 203, 214–15, 216, 221, 223–4, 230, 231, 233, 234, 238–9, 240–1, 243, 244–5, 246–7, 249–50, 252, 254, 257, 258, 273–4, 275–6, 282, 308
Urdaníz, José Ignacio 8, 12
Uriarte, José Ramón 135
Urraburu, Benito 150

Valverde, Alejandro 109, 230–1, 268, 273, 288
Van der Velde, Johan 65
Vandenbroucke, Frank 268
Vidarte, Jacinto 240, 246–7, 248, 255
Villar, Jesús Blanco 49
Villava, Navarre, Spain 5–25, 30, 42, 112, 123, 141, 174, 244, 259, 269, 273, 294
Virenque, Richard 205, 206, 243
Vitalicio Seguros 268
Volta a Catalunya 85–7, 133, 146, 149, 171
Vuelta a Andalucía 62, 138–9
Vuelta a Aragón 28, 73, 171, 205
Vuelta a Asturias 237
Vuelta a Burgos 248, 266
Vuelta a España 1, 36, 38, 46, 52, 70, 80–1, 86, 87, 147, 222; (1979) 13–14; (1982) 52, 83, 94; (1983) 49–50, 107; (1984) 53; (1985) 57–60, 61, 65, 72, 77, 80, 81, 252; (1986) 62, 64–5, 72; (1987) 73, 74, 76–7, 81, 252; (1988) 79, 80, 81; (1989) 92, 93–4, 107, 133, 252; (1990) 100, 104–5, 106, 108, 114; (1991) 113–16, 123, 155, 189, 208, 212, 252–3; (1992) 147, 148, 180, 189; (1993) 148; (1994) 191, 192, 195; (1995) 191, 208, 248, 279–80; (1996) 1–4, 11, 208, 222–3, 248, 249–54, 257, 265; (1997) 208, 247, 257; (1998) 276; (2001) 27; (2012) 155
Vuelta a Galicia 73
Vuelta a los Valles Mineros 77
Vuelta a Murcia 56, 63–4
Vuelta a Navarra 31, 43, 45
Vuelta a Salamanca 44
Vuelta a Toledo 41, 44, 45
Vuelta a Valencia 37, 108, 134, 139, 175
Vuelta a Valladolid 35
Vuelta a Vizcaya 45
Vuelta al País Vasco 52, 70, 108, 192, 290

Wiggins, Sir Bradley 122, 232, 282
World Championships, Road 22, 140, 147, 279, 283, 288, 294; (1973) 226, 261; (1983) 44; (1987) 225, 227; (1989) 225; (1990) 225; (1991) 225–6; (1992) 226–7; (1993) 227; (1994) 180; (1995) 224–5, 227–31, 233, 234, 246, 261, 267; (1998) 262; (2013) 230–1; (2015) 248
World Time Trial Championships: (1995) 227–8, 229–30, 261; (1998) 266

Zabala, Herminio Díaz 3, 212
Zandio, Xavier 6, 289, 293
Zarrabeitia, Mikel 189–90, 192, 251
Zegama, Spain 26–9, 46
Zubiri, Father Jesús María 16, 19, 24
Zülle, Alex 171, 203–4, 206, 209–10, 212, 217, 219, 237, 239, 250, 251, 253, 255, 256, 288